Managing Today and Tomorrow with On-Line Information

Managing Today and Tomorrow with On-Line Information

Linda Gail Christie

DOW JONES-IRWIN
Homewood, IL 60430

HD30,2
C485
1986

This publication is designed to provide accurate and
authoritative information in regard to the subject matter
covered. It is sold with the understanding that the
publisher is not engaged in rendering legal, accounting, or
other professional service. If legal advice or other expert
assistance is required, the services of a competent
professional person should be sought.

*From a Declaration of Principles jointly adopted by a Committee
of the American Bar Association and a Committee of Publishers.*

ISBN 0-87094-666-8

Library of Congress Catalog Card No. 85–72257

Printed in the United States of America

1 2 3 4 5 6 7 8 9 0 K 3 2 1 0 9 8 7 6

ACKNOWLEDGMENTS

I would like to thank the people and organizations that helped in the making of this book. The featured product manufacturers and their public relations firms graciously supplied press kits, pictures, software, manuals, free on-line time, and answers to numerous questions. The software and manuals they loaned to me for review provided excellent hands-on information. I couldn't have maintained the quality of this book without their support.

A special thanks goes to Mead Data Central and to Dow Jones News/Retrieval, who invited me to their facilities for a first-hand look behind the scenes.

The following Tulsa, Oklahoma businesses provided advice, personnel time, demonstrations, and technical information. These people played a key role in making this book factually correct and relevant:

Amoco Production Company—John C. Westervelt

Cities Service Oil and Gas Corporation—Linda L. Hill

Dowell Schumberger Technical Center—C. S. Britt

Oklahoma University Tulsa Medical College—Janette Minnerath

Phillips Petroleum Company—Ruth Bond, Annabeth Robin, Dr. H. "Ram" Jayaraman, Lou Payne, Joan O'Brien, Ruth Munsch, and J. G. N. Rushbrook, Ph.D.

Public Service Company of Oklahoma—Carol Hayhurst and Barbara Henke

Tulsa City–County Library—Info II—Martha Gregory

University of Tulsa—Dr. George P. Schell

Many friends contributed time, energy, expertise, and computer systems to help me review products. A special thanks goes to Gary Bullard, Don Singleton, Mark Perloe, Larry Hill, and John Christie.

I wish to thank my literary agents Bill Gladstone and Barbara Lowenstein for all they did to advance my writing career. And, I'd like to thank my first editor John Hunger who had the faith to give me my first break.

A special thanks goes to my writing coach Peggy Fielding who has done more to inspire and guide my writing career than anyone will ever know.

Linda Gail Christie

CONTENTS

List of Figures

APPENDIX C

INTRODUCTION

Are your customers profitable?

What are your competitors planning?

What are unions demanding?

Is your market and industry growing?

Are your suppliers in a solid position?

What coming government regulations will affect your industry?

Every day managers and specialists are assembling intelligence on a wide spectrum of corporate considerations: marketing, sales, finance, R&D, product development, manufacturing, legal, personnel, community relations, planning, safety, and purchasing.

Traditionally, these specialists have gleaned data from a variety of sources, including:

- Newspapers, business magazines, and trade journals.
- Special reports, newsletters, and surveys.
- Conferences, workshops, seminars, and associations.

Collecting the data and combining it into recommendations for policies, strategies and plans is both tedious and time-consuming. Since management's decisions and actions are formulated using this information, it's critical that they receive the "best" information available. With the information explosion of the past decade, finding the best information is becoming increasingly difficult.

Over the past 10 years the volume of information has grown at mind-boggling rates. Just in the field of personal computers, which didn't even exist 10 years ago, we've seen some 200 publications sprout up. Not only can my budget not keep up with this information explosion, but I don't have time to read it all. Necessity has forced me to narrow my focus even though I know I'm missing important articles, news releases, and product announcements in my area of concentration.

Multiply this phenomenon by the complexities of running a corporation, and you may gain some insight into the information overload managers face. Management must stay abreast of industry trends, of stockholder actions, of the economy, of the competition, of supply lines, of environmental requirements, of government regulations, of market growth, of customer profitability, of pricing controls, of energy costs, of import duties, of patent expirations, of OSHA rulings, of sociopolitical changes, of population demographics, of labor union settlements, of legal decisions, of competitor performance, of promotion and advertising trends, and of industry news.

Like the personal computer industry, each of these fields has spawned enormous quantities of information. A great deal of care must be taken when limiting information sources because narrowing focus will skew the information used for decision making. Today, fortunately, companies need not limit their information resources as much as you might expect.

By putting management information on computers, database producers have given you the power to search for and retrieve intelligence as never before possible. On-line database services have been recording, cataloging, abstracting, and coding libraries of information. Currently more than 362 companies in the electronic publishing business provide over 2,453 different databases. And the industry is growing at approximately 35 percent per year.

You can gain access to these repositories by using your personal computer and telephone to call their computer. With these simple tools you can search the database as though you had a direct terminal into the system.

I won't be so bold as to suggest that you can find any information you want from on-line databases; but the technology and service is expanding so rapidly that it won't be long until you will be able to do just that. Look at what's already available.

D&B–Dun's Market Identifiers from Dun & Bradstreet Corporation provides information on 2 million U.S. public and private companies with 10 or more employees. Information includes location, executive names, trends data, sales and size, and corporate family linkage. If that's not adequate, the Electronic Yellow Pages contains over nine million company listings with location, telephone number, and line of business. In addition, Disclosure II's financial records summarize 9,000 publicly held company reports filed with the U.S. Securities and Exchange Commission. These three resources provide demographic data, credit information, and potential customer profiles. In addition, you can research potential suppliers, competitors, and financial trends.

If you need business news and trends, you can search ABI/INFORM, Trade and Industry ASAP, and PTS F & S Indexes/PTS Promt. These on-line databases contain the full texts (complete articles) from hundreds of business and management newsletters, magazines, newspapers, journals, and specialized trade journals, including *Fortune, Forbes, Harvard Business Review, Business Week, Inc., Newsweek, United States Banker, U.S. News & World Report,* the *New York Times, The Wall Street Journal, The Washington Quarterly,* and *Wharton Economic News Perspectives.*

A number of database providers also offer research reports from major accounting firms and business analysts. They also allow you to use powerful computer software packages for analyzing data and creating reports. You benefit not only from their data but also from their professional advice and analytical tools.

So, in short, on-line databases put the answers you need to run your business at your fingertips.

MANAGING TODAY AND TOMORROW WITH ON-LINE INFORMATION will tell you how to secure and take advantage of strategic business information available from on-line database providers. You'll learn the following:

- How on-line information will improve the quality of information you use to make corporate decisions.
- How to match your company information needs to on-line information sources.
- How to design and implement a system for utilizing on-line database services.

Part I of this book will tell you how to identify your information needs, how to select database services, how to access on-line database services, how to select and purchase telecommunications hardware, how to select and purchase computer software, and how to protect and control information purchased through on-line services. Numerous examples illustrate how companies are already benefiting from on-line information. This book will help you decide if on-line database services would enhance your business's performance.

Part I also discusses the advantages of telecommunications and electronic mail. You'll find out how you can improve communications while reducing overhead for labor, stationery supplies, postage, and interoffice mail services.

Part II of this book reviews the features and benefits of the major on-line services including Dialog and Knowledge Index, BRS/BRKTHRU, SDC Orbit, Mead Data Central's LEXIS and NEXIS, The Source, CompuServe, MCI Mail, I. P. Sharp, Dow Jones News/Retrieval and Delphi. These detailed descriptions and reviews will help you decide which on-line services you should investigate further.

Two appendixes highlight the features of modems and telecommunications software available from major manufacturers. The glossary gives you quick reference to telecommunication terms.

MANAGING TODAY AND TOMORROW WITH ON-LINE INFORMATION will prepare you to enter the modern age of instant information.

PART ONE

Getting Started

1

The Information Edge

Before leaving for the airport, Glen Majors leafed through the proposal one last time. "We forgot to include the demographic data for Seattle," he said. He showed the figures to his marketing analyst, Jean Farr. "I need to know which part of the city has the highest concentration of well-educated homeowners, making over $35,000."

"Have it in a minute," Jean said as she turned to her personal computer and typed a few words. The computer dialed the on-line database service and she entered the search parameters. Soon the printer tapped out the missing report and she handed the data to Glen.

"Thanks," he said, glancing at the figures. "Looks great. Be back tomorrow with the contract."

* * * * *

In today's fast-moving business climate, success depends not so much on what you know, but on how fast you can find it out.

Recently a major oil company tried to fight off a takeover bid. To quote one of their top managers,

> We increased our competitive advantage by retrieving information from *on-line database services*. Hourly throughout the crisis, our public affairs research department provided us with up-to-date financial information and news releases. This quick access to current information was vital to our timely and effective decision making—which ultimately lead to our company's survival.

3

According to on-line research specialists, most search requests come from technical staff seeking scientific and engineering bibliographical data and patent information. "Before beginning a new project, our scientists and engineers used to spend a week or more searching through the literature in the library," said the special librarian for an international chemical company. "Now with the availability of on-line databases, they just give me a description of the project and the type of information they need. Within hours I give them a more comprehensive summary than they could have collected themselves."

Special librarians report that few departments take advantage of on-line search services.

Unfortunately, most specialists and managers don't understand how on-line database searches can improve their performance and enhance the company's position in the marketplace. This may be due in part to a number of commonly held beliefs about printed media. Comparing the benefits of on-line, electronic search with printed media will shed some light on these attitudes.

Forget that printed information sources are current.

Typically, books are in production for a year or more after the writer completes the manuscript. Therefore, when it's first released, the data in the book will be 12 to 24 months old. Magazines require two to six months for typesetting and distribution, making data four to eight months old. Monthly or weekly newsletters do somewhat better since they tend to print information only a few weeks old.

In contrast, on-line data (e.g., stock market quotes, and UPI and AP news releases) may become available within seconds of its creation. Databases are updated daily, weekly, monthly, and even quarterly. Depending on your information needs, your choice of a database may be influenced by updating practices.

Forget that printed information sources are complete.

Newspapers usually skim over information, titillating you with salient points but never achieving the depth needed to justify proposing policy changes. Companies with facilities in different communities and different countries find it even more difficult to keep up with local trends and company image. It's impossible for most people to spend the time required to read a dozen or so newspapers and magazines each day.

In contrast, researching the topic in numerous on-line sources will provide a fuller picture in far less time. With full-text databases such as Dow Jones News/Retrieval and NEXIS, you'll have instant access to the information you need. Although a number of on-line databases contain only bibliographic data, with a bibliographic search, an experienced researcher can locate most salient information. Since bibliographical databases often provide abstracts, you'll be able to identify the articles you wish to read. When the full text isn't available on-line, database vendors usually provide document ordering services that can mail you article copies within a couple of days. These services tend to be expensive though, charging from $4 to $12 per article. Where time isn't critical, interlibrary loans provide a fairly inexpensive source for document copies.

Databases containing abstracts (summaries) and full text (the entire document) offer more precise searching methods. A key word search of the abstract and/or text will often reveal sources not apparent from article titles. The ability to download (electronically retrieve) detailed material brings a new dimension to instant information gathering. Fortunately, with the decrease in magnetic storage costs, the number of full-text databases is growing rapidly.

Forget that printed information is convenient to review.

Scanning through hundreds of pages a week is time-consuming and inefficient. Even well focused journals and newsletters contain superfluous information. Not only may important items be overlooked, but irrelevant stories and advertising may consume too much attention. In contrast, reviewing on-line generated bibliographies and abstracts allows you to narrow your focus and then retrieve the exact text needed for in-depth analysis.

Forget that printed information sources are inexpensive.

Magazine subscription rates range from $9.95 to $80.00 per year, and specialized newsletters may cost hundreds of dollars per year. If a number of people in a company subscribe to the same journals, the company pays even more for duplicate information. If, to save costs, the same magazine is routed to 10 or 15 people, it may take weeks for it to cross everyone's desk.

On-line information isn't cheap. However, you don't pay for extraneous information as you do with most subscriptions. In addition, *gateway* services provide on-line information without subscription fees for each magazine database, newsletter database, newspaper database, and so forth. For example, a Business Communications Network (BCN) account provides a *gateway* to a number of database providers including the *Washington Post,* The Wall Street Transcript, Dissertation Abstracts On-Line, and Standard & Poor's Corporate Descriptions.

Forget that printed information is easy to retrieve later.

How many times have you said to yourself, "I know I read that *somewhere*"? Retrieving information from printed media is difficult. And individually maintained cataloging and indexing systems are expensive since the company is paying for duplicate efforts. Important news items and articles may be overlooked or discarded because it's difficult to anticipate what information may be valuable months from now.

In contrast, on-line information may be easily found and retrieved. For example, if you're trying to find out something about the *Zenith personal computer,* you might enter < FIND ZENITH AND COMPUTER >. If the database finds ZENITH adjacent to TELEVISION it won't report a match. Only articles, abstracts, or bibliographic data containing both ZENITH and COMPUTER are flagged for your attention. Search techniques and strategies, far more sophisticated than this illustration, offer amazing power and flexibility. And as your needs change, the nature of your search can change.

Forget that printed information sources are not biased.

The company can only afford a limited amount of printed information. If the books, journals, and news media chosen are the only sources consulted for decision making, important information may be overlooked. Decisions will not only be made without regard to the total, available body of information but also will be biased by the limited information sample.

Using on-line services doesn't guarantee you'll find everything, either. If you limit your on-line search to a narrow selection of database providers, similar biases may occur. In addition, searching the "wrong" database will also distort the information base. The report of "no information found" does not necessarily mean that no information exists. Experienced searchers know where to find the most information for the optimum cost. They know the correct procedures and search strategies for identifying the appropriate data. Tapping a broad spectrum of data sources reduces the odds of using biased data.

Forget that printed information is delivered like clockwork.

Sometimes subscriptions don't arrive on time. In fact, some issues never arrive. Also, if a publisher goes out of business, you can lose the balance of your subscription fee. When your address changes, you'll have to notify everyone, and it may be months before past issues arrive.

On-line database services are always at your fingertips. Some may not be as current as you'd like; but as a rule, you'll never find yourself at a total loss.

Forget that printed information is inexpensive to store.

Back issues of magazines and newspapers occupy expensive space and shelving. And in time, important issues may be lost, stolen, or damaged. Replacing a copy is tedious, expensive, and sometimes impossible. Often a trained staff is needed to properly administer archival storage, cataloging, and organization.

You pay no storage and maintenance overhead for on-line data. Your only expense will be a personal computer, communications software, printer, and modem (a modem is an electronic device that translates computer data into signals that can travel over telephone lines and then reconverts incoming telephone signals into computer language)—well under $2,000. Unless the database is regularly purged of archival information, the text is there for you indefinitely. Services that erase themselves every few days will have to be searched regularly.

Forget that printed information can be easily incorporated into documents.

If printed data, charts, tables, and other information are incorporated into correspondence or proposals, someone must recreate them—the information must be copied, redrawn, retyped, and so on. Not only does this cost money, but it also adds an unnecessary time delay to distribution.

In contrast, downloaded (electronically telecommunicated and magnetically stored) on-line information may be manipulated by personal computer word processors, database managers, and spreadsheets without time-consuming manual data entry. In addition, downloaded cataloging and indexing information may be used to create a customized reference. Downloaded information may be searched and utilized repeatedly without incurring additional on-line charges. It can also be transmitted over local area networks and electronic mail services. [NOTE: The database services, copyright lawyers, and courts haven't yet agreed on who "owns" downloaded data. More about these issues will be discussed later in this book.]

Forget that printed mail is the most efficient and reliable method for communicating outside the company.

The cost for writing, typing, retyping, printing, and mailing a letter ranges from $6 to $10 each. Think of what the company spends annually for typewriters, ribbons, paper, letterhead, envelopes, labels, maintenance agreements, and postage. And each year consumable supplies must be purchased.

Electronic mail offers an economic and viable alternative. With MCI Mail you can send a 1,000-word letter overnight to any major city—printed on your letterhead and signed with your signature—for approximately $2. Not only that, but you can store mailing lists on the electronic mail service's computer at *no charge.* Just enter your letter using their word processor and tell them where you want it sent. You only pay for each piece of mail sent and a small long-distance telephone charge.

If you need faster delivery, for $1 you can send 1,000 words instantly to another MCI Mail subscriber. The addressee can download your information and print as many copies as needed.

SUMMARY

A number of advantages are available to companies using on-line services:

1. More immediate, up-to-date facts.
2. A more complete sample of available information.
3. Convenient electronic searching.
4. Elimination of numerous and sometimes duplicate subscription fees.
5. Effective referencing for future retrieval needs.
6. Elimination of information biases.
7. Reliable information delivery.
8. Inexpensive information storage.

9. Electronic retrieval that eliminates the need for entering the data into personal computer word processors, spreadsheets, and/or database managers.
10. Fast and economical mail services.

Today a smart manager can't afford to say "I don't know." With on-line information at your fingertips, you will never be in this position. Even if only a few of these advantages appeal to you, you'll benefit from on-line information, the data resource of the future.

2

What's an On-Line Database?

Today you can find out almost anything using on-line database services such as CompuServe, The Source, NewsNet, Dialog, SDC Orbit, and Dow Jones News/Retrieval (DJN/R). Applications of DJN/R are illustrated in Figure 2–1. A smart businessperson can evaluate a territory with demographics, can stay on top of the latest business news, can create targeted direct mail lists, can check the background of employment candidates, and can search for the latest published information on almost any topic. In addition to database services, several electronic mail services offer relatively inexpensive, rapid transmission of data.

Becoming an on-line database or electronic mail subscriber sounds rather easy on the surface. You can probably find out how to do it from an ad in any computer magazine. Despite this, selecting the right service for your needs is as complex as buying the right computer and software.

This chapter won't discuss the pros and cons of each service, but it will attempt to describe the various types of business services available. After you've read this book, you may wish to order updated information from specific services; this field changes so fast that once you've taken the time to describe it, your description has almost become obsolete.

The on-line database technology has a unique vocabulary. The following will acquaint you with a few of the new buzzwords you'll need to know.

FIGURE 2-1   Dow Jones News/Retrieval Applications

DOW JONES NEWS/RETRIEVAL APPLICATIONS

CHAIRMAN/TOP EXECUTIVES

Daily briefings
  Industry
  Government: legislation and
    regulatory agencies
  Foreign
  Economic
  Monetary
  Stock/Bond markets
Track competition
  Compare performance of competitors to the industry
Executive changes
Dividend announcements
Analysts meetings

TREASURER/FINANCIAL

Investments/Portfolio management
Taxes
Bond Markets
Stock Markets
Foreign Exchange
Competition
Interest rates
Block trades
Stock repurchases
Economic indicators and forecasts
Securities and Exchange Commission
  Policies
  Filings
Government
  Legislation
  Regulatory agencies

CORPORATE PLANNING

Merger, acquisition and tender offer activity
  Compare performance of companies to
    their industries
  Monitor industries and companies
  Evaluate acquisition candidates
  Monitor stock trading: price, volume,
    repurchases, block trades
Examine new directions and trends in industries
Monitor competition in U.S., Canada and overseas
Competitive analysis
Track political developments in Congress, Executive Branch and
Agencies, as well as foreign events
  Common Market Policy
Capital investment
  Internal or in industry
Increase/decrease in plant capacity in industry
  Plant closings
Economic and monetary analysis and forecasts
Foreign exchange
Trade
Keep abreast of major events
Securities and Exchange Commission
  Regulatory matters
  Companies 10-K, 10-Q, 8-K reports
  Policy statements
  Dates of filings during last 2 years

PUBLIC RELATIONS

Monitor press releases of competitors
Gather information for press releases
Track industry developments, shareholder and public opinion
Keep abreast of social and political events which influence particular
industries
  Congress
  Executive
  Departments and Agencies
Daily briefings
Speech writing
Labor relations and issues
Shareholder/investor relations
International events
Encyclopedia for facts and figures
Government and Regulatory Agencies
Proxy statements
Dividend announcements
Earnings reports
Analysts meetings

LAW/LEGAL DEPARTMENTS

Justice Department: Fast-breaking news
Supreme Court: Tomorrow's news today
Antitrust actions
Product liability/Recalls of products
Mergers, acquisitions and divestitures
Joint ventures
Securities and Exchange actions
Labor issues
Earnings reports
10-K, 10-Q and other SEC filings
Class action suits
Corporate histories
Stock repurchases
Estates and wills
Stock prices

SALES/MARKETING

Examine prospective customers
  Know customer's products
  Know customer's industry
  Know customer's financial position
Monitor economic statistics
  Forecasts
  Analysis
  Indicators
Evaluate markets and competitors
Credit markets
Defense contracts and other contracts
Industry profiles
International trade
Examine competition
  New products
  Pricing
  Capital investment
  Acquisition
  Plant closings

Dow Jones & Company, Inc. • PO Box 300 •Princeton, New Jersey 08540 • 1-800-257-5114 • in New Jersey 609-452-1511

On-line database (data bank). This is a comprehensive, computerized collection of data such as an on-line encyclopedia. The database is stored on a mainframe computer and may be accessed over common telephone lines by personal computers with telecommunications software. By entering commands, the end-user can download (retrieve) bibliographies, article abstracts, complete articles, stock market information, statistical data, legal information, airline rates and schedules, weather information, yellow-page listings, and data on a myriad of other subjects.

The database provider actually enters the information into the mainframe computer. That is, they type bibliographies, write abstracts, optically read text and so forth. Some database providers have expanded their utility by offering other on-line services; for example, MCI Mail offers both electronic mail and access to Dow Jones News/Retrieval. In the role of offering the Dow Jones database, MCI Mail also is a database vendor. As the database providers offer additional services and data banks, the water gets muddier. See Smorgasbord Database below.

Smorgasbord database. A smorgasbord database is a large collection of professional and business computerized data banks. Such a service provides access to 50 to 300 different data banks. The smorgasbord services do not actually catalog and enter the data onto the mainframe computer; instead, they are vendors for data banks created elsewhere. A smorgasbord database service may satisfy all of your needs. However, major companies usually find they need to subscribe to several.

The three most popularly used smorgasbord services are Dialog, SDC Orbit, and BRS. Dialog emphasizes business, SDC emphasizes science and technology, and BRS emphasizes education and medicine. Since the techniques for accessing information on these services are somewhat complex, new users probably should attend one of the training courses offered by the services. In just minutes, the novice, through casual browsing on these professional quality services, could spend hundreds of dollars. An experienced searcher, however, can locate salient information for minimal costs.

Consumer-oriented database. This is a collection of a wide variety of computerized data banks that appeal to both the general public and the business community. Consumer-oriented databases are easier to use than smorgasbords, but they tend not to be as comprehensive. Consumer services may also provide recreational and personal activities such as teleconferencing, bulletin boards, electronic shopping, electronic mail and electronic banking. CompuServe and The Source are excellent examples of consumer-oriented databases.

Full-text database. A *full-text* database is a data bank that contains the full text of articles; for example, NewsNet, LEXIS, and Newsearch. *Cover-to-cover* or complete full-text databases include all articles in listed journals. *Selective* databases include only a select number of articles. You could miss important information if the selective database does not enter a particular article related to your area of interest.

Videotex (view data). The electronic exchange of data between a personal computer and a central mainframe computer that is continually "broadcasting" text is called videotex. Videotex may be transmitted over telephone lines or cable television. A customized keyboard may be used to interact with the system to retrieve specific pages of information. The biggest stumbling block to date has been the relatively high cost of the customized terminals; however, the personal computer promises to open up the field both to company and home users. Videotex brings color and graphics to the bland world of monochrome alphanumerics provided by on-line database services. The transmission of charts, photographs and diagrams greatly enhances the quality of information. The only prominent videotex provider is a subsidiary of Knight-Ridder Newspapers. Viewdata operates Viewtron out of south Florida. TRINTEX, a combined effort of Sears, IBM, and CBS, promises to be the first large-scale, commercially successful videotex operation. However, until this service goes on-line in 1987, we won't know what services it will offer or how it will offer them.

Reference/bibliographic database. This is a data bank that holds bibliographic information and possibly article abstracts. For example, an on-line encyclopedia or magazine index might be considered a reference database. The database provider usually offers a document retrieval service that will send printed copies of articles for a fee—$4 to $12 per article.

Numeric/fact database. This is a data bank consisting of numeric and/or statistical information; for example, the Instant Yellow Page Service and the Producer Price Index from the Bureau of Labor Statistics.

Command-driven. A database service that may be searched by entering a series of commands according to established procedures is command driven. Though faster than menu-driven databases, the user must be thoroughly familiar with the procedures and the command syntax (vocabulary and grammar) to avoid costly delays and mistakes. Dow Jones News/Retrieval and Dialog are examples of command-driven databases.

Menu-driven. A menu-driven database service offers rather user-friendly menus (options/choices) that lead the novice user through the search process. BRS After Dark, CompuServe, and The Source are examples of menu-driven databases. These database services provide an excellent training ground for new users.

Electronic mail. You can send electronic or electronically generated hard-copy mail throughout the country and even overseas on this computer service. The subscriber calls the service with a personal computer and electronically uploads messages for (1) personal computer users who also subscribe to the service, (2) personal computer users who subscribe to other electronic mail services, and/or (3) anyone who can receive hard-copy U.S. mail.

When the computerized addressee calls the service, his or her messages are downloaded for reading. Some electronic mail services merely provide a mechanism for leaving messages for personal computer users. However, full-service electronic mail vendors like MCI Mail will send a hard copy (laser printout) to a noncomputerized addressee. The advantages of electronic mail include faster delivery, lower costs, and the ability to electronically generate and manipulate the data on both ends.

Gateway. A gateway is a computer service that mediates connections between the subscriber and the database service (including smorgasbord services). By calling the gateway the user can access a number of services without paying individual database service membership fees. The gateway only bills the end-user for connect time (defined below) and downloading charges. Gateways help standardize accessing procedures; for example, the user has only one log-on (sign-on) procedure for all the services the gateway provides. Eventually gateways may also help standardize searching techniques. Along with database access, the gateway may provide telecommunications software; for example, SuperScout from Business Communications Network (BCN).

Telecommunications service. This is a data communications service that provides toll-free, long-distance telephone lines to the database services. Their services are paid by the database provider to offer local dialing capabilities. Telenet, Tymnet, and Uninet are three popularly used telecommunication services. The quality of these lines varies from city to city. Some companies use them interchangeably; for example, they will automatically dial another service when there is a busy signal on the first. Some services provide their own long-distance dialing systems to bring you directly into the service with minimal log-on procedures; for example, Mead Data's MeadNet. You'll learn more about automatic dialing and log-on procedures in the communications software chapter.

Information broker. An on-line database search requires personal computer equipment, a modem, a printer, communications software, and access to one or more database providers. The searcher must have training and experience to be effective and efficient. To avoid all this expense, some companies prefer to use professional information brokers, who perform the search for a fee. Information brokers may be found in most major cities. Also, public libraries often offer fee-based on-line search services.

Document retrieval service. A company that supplies copies of documents ordered from on-line database services offers document retrieval service. Usually you can purchase the copies by leaving orders with the on-line service while you're connected with it. Getting material through the interlibrary loan system is less expensive, but tends to take more time.

Selective dissemination of information (SDI). Many on-line services allow you to store a search strategy (series of search commands) on their computer. You can either reuse these commands yourself or direct the on-line service to perform the search each time the database is updated. If the service automatically runs the search (SDI) and mails you a printout, you don't have to log on or spend any more money for connect-time. You will only be charged for the search, printout and royalties.

Connect time. The actual time that your computer and modem are communicating with the database system's computer is called connect time. The rates you're charged for this time vary according to the time of day and the specific database service. In addition, the charge may be based on the speed of your transmission (300 bits per second is usually less expensive to use per minute than 1200 bits per second, but 300 bits per second is one fourth as fast as 1200—more about that later).

Offline print. Rather than having the citations printed on your computer screen or your printer, you may prefer to disconnect and have the database provider print them on their printer. You'll usually receive the citations by mail in a few days. This procedure will not only save you on-line charges, but will also provide you with a letter-quality printout. Offline printing is usually cost-effective if you order 75 or more citations.

CPU–based charges. A CPU–based charge is sometimes levied for the time your search demands of the database provider's computer processor (CPU). This charge is associated more often with time-sharing operations that allow you to manipulate data with their software and mainframe computer resources.

BUSINESS DATABASES

Databases have different personalities. Some databases resemble *business magazines*, which cover such subjects as advertising, marketing, social sciences, aerospace, automobiles, government, economics, electronics, science, and energy. Other databases resemble sections found in *newspapers*; they may include financial information, stock market reports, general news, or hot-breaking news stories. Still other databases resemble *reference books and directories:* for example, yellow-page listings, demographic data, standards and specifications, and patent listings. Below you'll find a discussion of these major categories and suggested resources for each type of data.

Magazine-Styled Database Services

Some of the business and technical magazine-styled databases are full-text, while others contain only bibliographic listings and abstracts. They cover a broad range of information, including business and performance information about companies. They may also list technical information about, for example, electronics, computers, energy, chemistry, medicine, the environment, engineering, advertising, and marketing research.

A number of business/technical database providers supply text from the major trade magazines of one particular field. The Computer Database from Management Contents contains over 70,000 citations with abstracts from 650 computer journals, books, tabloids, newsletters, research reports, and course materials.

Other databases offer broader industry focus—in everything from the entertainment industry to oil and gas. The Trade and Industry Index from Information Access Company provides comprehensive, broad-based, bibliographic information from 300 trade journals and the full text of articles from over 80 journals, as well as selected information from 1,200 additional newspapers, magazines, and serial publications.

Newspaper/Newsletter-Styled Databases

By subscribing to newspaper/newsletter-styled database services, you can cut down on the cost of subscription fees for hundreds of printed news sources and reduce archival storage costs. Subject-focused searches allow you to scan quickly through hundreds of news publications to find exactly the information you need.

Newspaper-styled databases contain full-text articles from newspapers and specialized newsletters. For example, NEXIS contains the full text from over 100 newspapers, journals, and newsletters including *American Banker, Financial*

Times, Legal Times, the *New York Times,* and the *Washington Post.* The specialized newsletters include *Ad Day, ChemWeek Newswire, International Petrochem Report, Latin America Commodities,* the *Morgan Guaranty Survey,* and the *Wharton Economic News Perspectives.*

Dow Jones News/Retrieval contains the full text of *The Wall Street Journal, Barron's* and the Dow Jones News Service (newswire).

If you need to monitor the news as it happens, United Press International (UPI), Associated Press (AP), Dow Jones News Service, and PR Newswire will send you the news as fast as it does to your local newspaper. These news services are available on a number of different database services.

Reference/Directory-Styled Databases

The reference/directory-styled databases provide demographics, census figures, sales-potential studies, and profiles. CACI, Inc., Donnelley Marketing Information Services, and Urban Decision Systems, Inc., sell *demographic information* reports from the U.S. Census Bureau and many other federal government agency reports.

You can retrieve company *financial records* from Standard & Poor's Online, Dun's Principal International Businesses, PTS Annual Reports Abstracts, and TRW Business Credit Profile. PTS provides 4,500 annual report narratives, including information on product lines, new products and technologies, acquisition activities, corporate goals, and the stories behind the statistics. In contrast, Standard & Poor's Online covers information in the SEC filings (10-K) as well as information from reports filed with other government regulatory bodies, newspaper articles, and public legal documents meeting the needs of the investor.

Stock market databases include services such as Dow Jones Quotes, Media General Data Base, and Quotdial. These services provide raw data as well as a variety of statistics, including key performance ratios and historical data. Many of these services also sell software or on-line computer services, which you can use to analyze and catalog the data: for example, Dow Jones' Market Analyzer, Market Manager, and Market Microscope. These software packages are discussed in more detail in the software chapter.

The *patent and trademark* databases, such as PAT-

SEARCH, CLAIMS, World Patent Index, and PATDATA, are used extensively by research scientists and engineers to search the literature for supportive information and to avoid duplicate research. Searching patent data will help you determine what projects your competitors are working on or what companies may need to buy your services or products. Mead Data's LEXPAT provides the full written text of every patent. At present they cannot offer illustrations on-line. CLAIMS contains patents for chemical formulas, mechanical designs, electrical equipment, botanical plants, and fabric designs. TRADEMARKSCAN helps you search trademark and product names from over 1.4 million marks, collected since 1920. Graphic trademarks are provided on request (not on-line).

The *Electronic Yellow Pages* database allows you to download names and addresses by geographical (zip code) area. With this information, you can create a client list as well as analyze market potential. For example, you can determine how many retail lawn and garden equipment companies serve a particular city and find out how to contact them. Specific directories are available for such subjects as construction, financial services, manufacturers, retailers, and wholesalers.

The *OCLC* service provides an on-line bibliography of over 11,000,000 books and periodicals. Maintained by the public and special librarians around the country, this database service can locate any book by title or author and will tell you which libraries have it in their inventory. This is especially useful for arranging interlibrary loans.

SUMMARY

What's an on-line database? Answering this question is as difficult as answering the question, "What's a library?" On-line databases satisfy many different information needs of businesspeople and home-based personal computer users. On-line databases serve many of the same needs as printed media; they also provide powerful search capabilities.

The remaining chapters will tell you how other organizations take advantage of on-line database services. You'll find out how both centralized and decentralized search organizations operate, how managers and specialists utilize the services, and how organizations incorporate on-line database information retrieval into everyday operations.

3

A Survey of Database Providers, Services and Carriers

According to an article in *Business Week,* the average manager now spends 25 percent of his or her time in such unproductive activities as making phone calls that aren't answered or searching for people and information. The article goes on to say that "managerial productivity can be significantly improved by electronic mail, information retrieval systems, and other tools of the automated office." Using on-line database and electronic mail services, you can potentially slash this overhead and increase your managers' productivity.

Cuadra Associates, Inc., publishers of the *Directory of On-line Databases,* reports that the number of on-line databases has grown more than 500 percent in the past five years. Today, a total of 2,453 databases are offered on 362 on-line services. Choosing which database and which database service to use can be a monumental undertaking. As a result, many companies just subscribe to one or two large vendors and use what information they can. Dialog Information Services, SDC Orbit, BRS, Mead Data Central, Dow Jones News/Retrieval, CompuServe, and The Source offer a full range of subjects. However, if you limit yourself to these resources, you may be missing unique information. And buying information from these services may not be price-competitive.

This chapter will give you an overview of the major database services. The information in this chapter is designed to introduce you to the many types of database services and is not intended to recommend one service over another. The database vendor you choose must meet the unique information requirements of your company. What's good for one company or department may not be good for another. Chapter 5 presents factors to consider when choosing a database service. Part II of this book is comprised of detailed descriptions of the most popular database services.

THE BIG PLAYERS

Dialog continues to lead the on-line industry as the largest database supermarket. BRS seems to be specializing in education and biomedicine while SDC Orbit is especially suited to searching complex scientific databases. LEXIS, from Mead Data Central, dominates the legal information slot. NEXIS, Dow Jones News/Retrieval, and NewsNet provide full text for many of the most popular business magazines, newspapers and newsletters. The Source and CompuServe offer a broad spectrum of both consumer- and business-oriented information.

The following is a synopsis of the major players in the on-line information game. Part II of this book discusses many of these sources in greater detail.

Financial Information

The five most popular sources for financial information are Automatic Data Processing (ADP), Interactive Data Corporation (IDC), I. P. Sharp, Wharton Economic Forecasting Associates and Huttonline.

AUTOMATIC DATA PROCESSING (ADP) offers a wide variety of databases to meet such diverse needs as forecasting sales, studying competitors, analyzing potential investments, and assessing economic conditions. The service provides the Townsend-Greenspan & Company's long- and short-term economic forecast information as well as the Bancall Database Scan 200 which offers SEC 10-K-type information on bank holding companies, commercial banks, and savings and loan associations. In addition, ADP has a collection of the most used business indicators of the U.S. economy. ADP's target market is major financial institutions, large brokerage firms, investment banks, and commercial banks.

INTERACTIVE DATA CORPORATION (IDC) provides financial information on more than 10,000 foreign and domestic companies, 14,000 banks, and 250 utilities. It contains data on more than 60,000 North American securities and 26,000 securities traded outside the continent. Commodities, financial futures, foreign exchange data, economic history, and forecasting can all be found on the Chase Econometrics databases. This collection contains over 2.5 million weekly, quarterly, and annual time series that detail consumer, demographic, industry, and general economic activities in more than 175 countries.

I. P. SHARP maintains over 100 different public, numeric databases including information on economics, securities, banking, finance, energy, aviation, and insurance. As a time-sharing computer service, they also offer the ability to access public database data and combine it either with information from other I. P. Sharp databases or with your company's private data. Other on-line software packages are available for performing sophisticated econometric analysis and forecasting.

WHARTON ECONOMIC FORECASTING ASSOCIATES specializes in national and international economic data. Wharton is a leader in offering a wide variety of data delivery methods, including timesharing, magnetic tapes, downloading to personal computers, mailing data disks to micro users, and real-time delivery. Wharton offers exclusive data on Europe and the Middle East.

HUTTONLINE from E. F. Hutton & Company allows Hutton's clients access to Hutton's computer files. These files contain Hutton's Research and Investment Briefs as well as the client's own accounting records. The system also allows the client to send messages to his or her Hutton account executive and receive investment reports and messages. Also, Huttonline customers can access quotes for all listed securities and options, and NASDAQ stocks.

General Information Databases

DIALOG INFORMATION SERVICES provides access to over 200 databases containing more than 90 million items of information extracted from technical reports, journals, magazines, newspapers, books, conference papers, patents, trademarks, and statistical records. Subjects covered include chemistry, medicine, business technology, law, current affairs, social sciences, humanities, and education. Dialog offers access to such databases as BLS Consumer Price Index, Commerce Business Daily, D&B–Dun's Market Identifiers, D&B–Million Dollar Directory, DISCLOSURE II, Donnelley Demographics, Electronic Yellow Pages, *Harvard Business Review*, Management Contents, Moody's Corporate Profiles, PTS Annual Reports Abstracts, PTS F&S Indexes, PTS PROMT, Standard & Poor's Corporate Descriptions, Standard & Poor's News, CA SEARCH, MEDLINE, CHEMLAW, CLAIMS, Derwent World Patents Index, COMPENDEX (synopses of worldwide engineering journals), Magazine Index, Newsearch, UPI News, *Washington Post* Index, DOE Energy, Electric Power Industry Abstracts, Academic American Encyclopedia, Books In Print, GRANTS, Information Science Abstract, SCISEARCH, and World Affairs Report. Most companies cannot afford to be without Dialog.

SDC INFORMATION SERVICE'S ORBIT offers 55 million citations on 70 databases covering business and economics, chemistry, engineering and electronics, energy and the environment, patents, life science, government and legislation, science and technology, social sciences, and more. Specific databases include BANKER, ACCOUNTANTS, INFORM, POWER, TULSA, PAPERCHEM, ENVIROLINE, GRANTS, ERIC, BIOTECHNOLOGY, and ENERGYLINE. SDC has a definite technical slant.

BRS and BRS/AFTER DARK offer in-depth coverage of such subjects as business and finance (ABI/INFORM, *Harvard Business Review*/ONLINE), education (ERIC), energy, the environment, news, patent information (PATDATA), medicine (MEDLARS), psychology, science and technology (CHEMICAL ABSTRACTS, ROBOTICS), social sciences and the humanities (Sociological Abstracts). In a user-friendly format, the searcher can access and retrieve information from nearly 50 million records. The late-hour BRS/After Dark service offers substantially reduced rates.

KNOWLEDGE INDEX, also available after dark, is a subsidiary of Dialog. This database provides low-cost access to over 17 million summaries of articles, reports, and books from over 10,000 sources covering these major subject areas:

Agriculture.

Books (Books In Print).

Business information (ABI/INFORM).

Computers and electronics.

Corporate news (Standard & Poor's News).

Education (ERIC).

Engineering.

Government publications.

Legal information.

Over 450 popular magazines (Magazine Index).

Mathematics.

Medicine (MEDLINE).

News (Newsearch, *New York Times, Washington Post, The Wall Street Journal,* etc.).

Psychology.

DELPHI offers not only a number of databases, but also financial services and electronic conferencing services, including a bulletin board (a public message system) and a private mail system. The conference facility provides real time communication with one person or with a group. Delphi's financial services include banking, bill paying, financial calculations, stock prices, brokerage, and advisory services.

Delphi's answer to the newspaper classified service, ONLINE MARKETS, gives a marketplace for buying and selling. In addition to travel information and travel services, DELPHI serves as a gateway to Dialog, a bibliographic service offering such databases as the following: ABI/INFORM (covers all phases of business management and administration), American Men and Women of Science, BLS Consumer Price Index, BLS Labor Force, Books In Print, CA SEARCH (chemical abstracts), CHEMSEARCH, CLAIMS (patents), Disclosure II (extracts of reports filed with SEC), DOE Energy, Dun's Market Identifiers, Electronic Yellow Pages, ERIC (education), MEDLINE, Newsearch, PATLAW, PTS Promt (Predicasts Overview of Markets and Technology), SCISEARCH, Standard & Poor's News, and many, many more.

One of the largest general interest information services, COMPUSERVE, provides more than 200 databases on home services, on business and finance, on personal computing, and services for professionals. In addition, CompuServe offers an electronic mail system (EMAIL), aviation and weather information, and electronic forums for special interest groups. Some of the databases offered are The Executive News Service (Associated Press), the *Washington Post*, SUPERSITE (U.S. demographics and ACORN—A Classification of Residential Neighborhoods), On-Line Travel Services, Standard & Poor's, Disclosure II, and Value Line Data Base II. In addition, CompuServe professional services include stock market reports, commodity market analysis, portfolio valuation, and banking and brokerage services. CompuServe's menu-driven system makes access easy for most personal computer users.

THE SOURCE offers many consumer databases similar to CompuServe's. However, The Source is directed more toward the daytime business user than the computer hobbyist. You can access more than 800 databases in categories such as communications; business news and services; education and careers; government and politics; home and leisure; news and sports; science and technology; travel; dining and entertainment; and user publishing (PUBLIC). The Source also offers electronic mail and computer conferencing. A popular service called PUBLIC allows users to read newsletters, magazines, and other files created by Source subscribers and to submit their own files for electronic self-publishing. On The Source you can get stock and bond price quotes, check your own portfolio, perform a historical stock analysis, and review up-to-date business news via UPI Business Wire. Management Contents abstracts articles from journals such as *The Banker, Business Week, Dun's Review, Forbes, Fortune, Harvard Business Review, INC., Venture,* and *Wharton Magazine.*

The News and More

DOW JONES NEWS/RETRIEVAL offers information on over 80 news categories, 7,000 U.S. and Canadian companies, and 60 industries. DJN/R also provides news extracted from *The Wall Street Journal, Barron's* and the Dow Jones News Service as well as current and historical information from four major stock exchanges. With DJN/R you'll be able to retrieve information on corporate earnings, dividends, price-earnings ratios, and stock performance. Some of the databases offered are Academic American Encyclopedia, Cineman Movie Reviews, UPI World Report, Corporate Earnings Estimator, Japan Economic Daily, Merrill Lynch Research Service, *The Wall Street Journal* Highlights Online, Dow Jones News, and *Weekly Economic Update*. Through DJN/R you can also access the MCI Mail network. (*Note:* Due to restrictive downloading policies, Encyclopedia is not available to personal computer users.)

MEAD DATA CENTRAL'S NEXIS contains the full text of scores of leading newspapers, magazines, wire services, and other information resources. For example, you can access the *Washington Post,* the *New York Times, Newsweek, Dun's Business Month (Dun's Review), Business Week,* and *U.S. News and World Report.* Also included is the Associated Press and UPI news wires as well as reference works like the Encyclopaedia Britannica and The Federal Register. NEXIS also offers specialized trade journals such as *Electronics, Coal Age, ABA Banking Journal, Synfuels Week, Offshore, Oil & Gas Journal, Aviation Week,* and *Space Technology.*

NEWSNET, a subsidiary of Independent Publications, Inc., provides access to publications dedicated to specific fields of interest. As such, NewsNet provides the full text for over 200 newsletters, which, if subscribed to individually, would add up to over $50,000 per year. To be listed with NewsNet the newsletter must be published at least once a month and cost over $100 per year. With NewsNet you can find up-to-date information on many subjects:

Advertising and marketing.

Aerospace.

Automotive.

Building and construction.

Chemical.

Corporate communications.

Education.

Electronics and computers.

Energy.

Entertainment and leisure.

Environment.

Farming and food.

Finance and accounting

General business.

Government and regulations.

Health and hospitals.

Insurance.

International.

Investment law.

Management.

Medicine.

Metals and mining.

Office.

Politics.

Publishing and broadcasting.

Real estate.

Research and development

Retailing.

Social sciences.

Taxation.

Telecommunications.

NewsNet provides all this plus the PR Wire, which features industry press releases, the Official Airline Guide, and UPI News.

The Law and Patent Information

MEAD DATA CENTRAL'S LEXIS is the world's leading computer-assisted legal research service. It contains major libraries of federal and state law, codes, and regulations. In addition, LEXIS offers special law libraries dealing with tax, securities, trade regulations, international trade, communications, bankruptcy, labor, energy, admiralty, military justice, law reviews, public contracts, patent, trademark, and copyright. Designed by lawyers for lawyers, LEXIS provides instant legal information for law firms, judges, federal and state agencies, corporate law departments, and most law schools. Mead's LEXPAT is a computerized patent search service that provides the full text of U.S. patents issued since 1975. Mead adds approximately 70,000 new patents to this database each year.

WESTLAW is West Publishing Company's computer-assisted legal research service containing case laws from all U.S. Federal District and Circuit Courts of Appeals, the U.S. Supreme Court and all 50 states. WESTLAW Libraries include federal statutory, regulatory, and administrative law as well as special federal libraries such as tax, securities, patents, trademarks, copyright, antitrust and business regulations, communications, and bankruptcy. WESTLAW also offers MCI Mail and EUROLEX, a full-text, computer-assisted legal research service offered by the European Law Centre, Ltd., London.

Electronic Mail

Many of the on-line database services offer their own electronic mail/communications networks; for example, The Source and CompuServe. Others offer access to the major independent electronic carriers such as ITT's Dialcom, Western Union's EasyLink and MCI Mail. Some of these telecommunications services require both parties to have personal computer communications systems and a subscription to the on-line service. Other services will send a printed copy of electronically generated mail to a noncomputerized addressee.

MCI MAIL offers a number of services. You can send instant mail to an addressee's electronic mailbox, you can get four-hour paper delivery by courier to 17 major metropolitan areas, overnight paper courier delivery by noon the next day in 20,000 continental U.S. cities, and an MCI Letter (paper) delivered locally by the U.S. Postal Service from any one of the 17 major metropolitan areas. If you want paper copies printed on your letterhead with your signature, you can arrange for that, too. In addition, Telex Dispatch enables MCI Mail users to transmit messages to more than 1.6 million Telex subscribers worldwide.

EASYLINK from Western Union also allows you to send a wide variety of electronic and written messages throughout the United States and around the world. You can send a full range of Western Union messages to electronic mailbox subscribers, to 200,000 Telex subscribers, and to 1.5 million

WorldWide Telex network subscribers in 154 countries. You can send mailgrams (overnight letters) anywhere in the United States, Puerto Rico, and Canada; telegrams to any location in the 50 states and Canada; cablegrams overnight to any country other than the United States and Canada; and computer (generated) letters that are usually delivered within three business days in the 50 United States and Canada. Overseas priority letters can usually be delivered within two days to any location in the United Kingdom. As an EasyLink customer you'll have an EasyLink Telex Number in addition to your EasyLink Mailbox Number. This number works just like a regular Western Union Telex Number. Many of these communication options carry message length restrictions that are spelled out in the manual.

DIALCOM from ITT is one of the largest providers of electronic mail. The typical customer is a large corporation with thousands of users. Half of the U.S. House of Representatives use Dialcom's electronic mail services. Dialcom offers letter-quality printing, personalization of correspondence and mass mailing capabilities. Also, Dialcom provides a gateway to a number of database services, including Dialog, BRS, Travelscan, UPI, *Los Angeles Times, Washington Post*, Bureau of National Affairs, and the Official Airline Guide.

THE LARGEST ON-LINE CARD CATALOG—OCLC

Perhaps you've wondered how public and special libraries know where to locate a document they don't have. Most librarians use the OCLC on-line database.

OCLC is the oldest and largest of the automated library networks and has more than 2,200 subscribers. The OCLC system contains 13.4 billion bytes (characters) of information about books and other library materials. OCLC's database contains more than 6 million bibliographic records for books, serials, audiovisual materials, maps, manuscripts, scores, sound recordings, and other library materials. The database is growing at about 25,000 records per week. Libraries use the OCLC system to catalog books, to order custom-printed catalog cards, to maintain location information about library materials, and to arrange for interlibrary loans. OCLC members also receive on-line access to the Library of Congress Name-Authority file of records.

OCLC, Inc. is a not-for-profit corporation chartered in the state of Ohio. It does not issue stock or distribute earnings and is self-supporting through fees charged to member libraries.

THE COTTAGE TELECOMMUNICATIONS INDUSTRY

Even though the 1984 on-line industry shakeout saw the demise of some 70 databases, more than 200 took their place. The industry is growing at a rate of about 35 percent per year. And many newcomers represent a new cottage electronic publishing industry. Individuals or small companies are using the database services to self-publish highly time-sensitive materials such as technical and professional directories. These companies have found that the data is obsolete by the time it's printed and bound if they use traditional print media. So they use instant electronic publication and inexpensive, rapid updating.

Other entrepreneurs are adding value to existing on-line information. Value-added services let the user manipulate data in a way not directly supported by the on-line database provider. One value-added service ties the data from the Electronic Yellow Pages to the power of an electronic mail service. With this, you can send personalized mail to a selected mailing list. Value-added vendors stand to make fortunes by filling in such gaps in existing services, much as the early personal computer software developers did.

Many of the cottage-industry database providers are snapped up by the larger services such as Dialog or CompuServe. Those who remain independent may face an uncertain future.

INFORMATION CARRIERS

An information carrier provides the end-user with a local access telephone number for dialing on-line services. There are three major telecommunications networks. Telenet is run by GTE. Tymnet is operated by Tymshare, Inc. And Uninet is a service of Uninet, Inc. (In Canada, Tymnet is known as Data-Pac.) These services are to data communications what MCI and Sprint are to telephone service, with one exception: They bill the database service instead of the end-user. The database service in turn bills the subscriber for the long-distance telephone service. Charges vary from $5 to $12 per hour depending on your location and the time of day.

Choosing a carrier is almost a flip of the coin. Often companies will use whichever service's line isn't busy. Or, if they get cut off from one service due to interference or computer failure, they'll dial back on another service. The quality of the carrier service seems to vary from one city to another. You may have to experiment with each one to decide which carrier to use first.

SUMMARY

On-line database services come in a number of sizes and specialties:

1. Generalized and large-sized (50 or more databases).
2. Generalized and modest-sized (under 50 databases).
3. Financial information.
4. Business news and allied information.
5. Legal and patent information.
6. Electronic mail and telecommunications.
7. Focused information.
8. Interlibrary loan and card catalog information (OCLC).

On-line services can be accessed locally from three major telecommunication carriers: Tymnet, Telenet, and Uninet. These long-distance services are paid by the on-line service, which in turn bills the subscriber for long-distance charges.

The next chapter will help you decide which of these services can best meet your company's information needs.

4

What On-Line Capabilities Does the Company Need?

What on-line capabilities does a company need? The answer to this question is different for every company. There is no standard prescription according to size or industry. Each company and each management team must determine what will best serve their specific strategic information needs.

WHO WILL CONDUCT THE STUDY AND MAKE RECOMMENDATIONS?

Some companies assign a staff department to conduct the needs analysis and make recommendations for an on-line search program: for example, management information services, special library, or public affairs departments that are already chartered to gather and process information.

Other companies form a special task force or team to perform the information needs analysis. If the task force consists of representatives from different areas of the company, management will view their recommendations as more valid and more valuable. One or more members should be intimately familiar with on-line search services and the task force should be aware of the pros and cons of using on-line services to supplement current information sources. If necessary, an outside consultant should be contracted to provide information about on-line database services. Using a task force is also beneficial because when the special task force members return to their regular jobs, they'll be able to promote the on-line information services operation to their colleagues.

The task force will face a number of decisions and recommendations. Not only must the team determine what information is needed, but also who will retrieve it. Will specialists and managers have personal computer data retrieval workstations on their desks? Will a new information resources department be created to conduct on-line searches? Or will the more traditional special library staff perform on-line information retrieval?

If a centralized search strategy is chosen, the team must determine who will assume the overhead of on-line search operations. If a decentralized search strategy is chosen, then the expense of workstations must be justified.

The task force will also need to decide if on-line retrieval services will be *offered* or *sold* to managers. Will on-line searches become *standard operating procedures* or will they only be used by the few who recognize their value? Will the on-line information services department be *reactive* to day-to-day requests, or *proactive*, anticipating information needs in response to corporate plans and goals?

Once these questions are answered, then the team will need to establish policies and propose a budget for purchasing equipment, software, and on-line information. Policies and procedures must be established for managing data security, copyright protection, staff development, and training.

This chapter highlights the methods for diagnosing company information needs. Later chapters discuss the installation and operation of in-house information retrieval services.

CONDUCTING THE NEEDS ANALYSIS

First of all, members of the task force should determine what information the company requires to conduct business, to develop short-term plans, and to formulate long-term goals. They should assess not only what information each department requires to perform daily activities but also what intelligence top management needs for strategic planning and decision making. The survey may be as informal as a series of personal meetings or as structured as a written questionnaire. Although many methods will produce the information, the preferred method will depend on timing requirements, political considerations, and accepted company practices. Whatever the approach, the information highlighted in the following questionnaire can serve as a guide.

Figure 4–1 contains a list of questions the task force might ask. This questionnaire is only a general guide and should be modified for the specific needs of a particular organization. The results of the needs analysis can then be used to determine such things as the following:

1. The best/most frequently used sources for information.
2. The costs for obtaining and maintaining information.
3. The relative benefits of on-line sources.

Following is a discussion of each area of interest.

FIGURE 4–1   Information Needs Analysis

DATE: _____
DEPARTMENT NAME: _____
TITLE: _____

1. List the outside sources you use to stay abreast of business trends and technology (journals, newspapers, newsletters, directories, reference books, magazines, on-line database services, etc.). Use a separate sheet if necessary.

2. Estimate the annual cost for your subscriptions and purchases:

   News media   _____
   Journals   _____
   Books   _____
   Directories/surveys   _____
   On-line database services   _____
   Other (specify) _____   _____
        Total   _____

3. Estimate the time you or your staff spend reading this material (please include time at home):

   News media   _____
   Journals   _____
   Books   _____
   Directories/surveys   _____
   On-line database services   _____
   Other (specify) _____   _____
        Total   _____

FIGURE 4-1 *(concluded)*

4. Estimate the time you or your staff spend extracting and/or cataloging information from PRINTED media:
   Extracting   _____
   Cataloging   _____
   Filing and storage   _____
   Other (specify) _____   _____
   Total   _____

5. What information would you like to get but have difficulty finding? Please explain why it's hard to find and how you'd use this information.

6. What information would you like to get but believe it's too expensive? Please explain why it's too expensive and how you'd use this information.

7. What information would you like to get sooner? Please explain the source of the delay (publication delays, routing delays, mail delays, other) and why faster delivery would be an advantage to you.

8. What information would you like to get but doesn't seem to be available? Please explain how you'd use this information.

9. What company services do you utilize to help you get information? Please indicate the number of times per year you use these services.

   _____ Special library resource services
   _____ On-line retrieval services
   _____ Public/community relations services
   _____ Information services
   _____ Other (specify) _____

10. Attach a list of your major goals and projects for this year. Indicate for each item the outside resource materials you'll require to research the project.

Compile a List of Currently Used Media

Many people don't realize how many journals, newspapers, newsletters, reference books, directories, and other printed materials they actually use. This question will alert them to the amount of material they wade through. The task force can also determine which publications are used elsewhere in the company, and management may institute cost-saving measures to avoid unnecessary duplication.

This list will also help determine the best on-line database providers to subscribe to. For example, the company might decide to eliminate certain printed subscriptions in favor of on-line searches. Or, they might decide to use on-line sources for purchasing additional resource material. In either case, knowing what employees are using now is a good base point.

If on-line database services are currently available, you should assess who is and is not using them and determine how adequate current search services and procedures are. This knowledge will provide valuable information for establishing or developing the company's on-line information services.

Estimate Annual Costs for Printed Media

This exercise may be an eye-opener for both the person filling out the survey as well as for management. A frequent objection to on-line database searching is its expense. Once you have a handle on your current expenditures for printed media, you'll be able to select the optimum methods for distributing both printed and on-line resources.

Estimate Amount of Time Required for Reading Printed Media

People are often unaware of how many hours they spend on and off the job reading newspapers, journals, newsletters, and so forth. On-line searching reduces this time so it may be spent more productively. Compared with traditional search methods, employees using on-line searches typically review more material and still have more time for analyzing and utilizing the information. Instead of having to browse through piles of old magazines and newspapers to find statistical data and business trends, on-line searchers review bibliographies and/or article abstracts addressing a selected subject. Only the most relevant articles are obtained for in-depth analysis.

Estimate Amount of Time Required for Extracting/Cataloging/Filing

To avoid time-consuming searching through stacks of newspapers, piles of magazines and shelves of books, many people develop indexing and filing systems that lead them directly to needed data. However, the indexer must anticipate future needs, or the appropriate articles and materials won't be cataloged. Selecting the "right" material is not necessarily easy. In fact, it is often quite tedious.

Maintaining individual cataloging and filing systems is an inefficient use of company time. And if an employee is transferred to another position or leaves the company, the information often goes with him or her. The department loses vital intelligence. Keeping track of information is best done by computers, only once—by an on-line database service.

Information Difficult to Find

On-line searching often enhances the employees' ability to locate "hidden" data. In these situations, on-line searching may actually improve productivity and enhance performance.

Information Expensive to Purchase

Many times a specialist or manager won't subscribe to a specialized newsletter or purchase a survey report because the cost seems prohibitive. However, the information reported in the newsletter or report may be ideal for a project or for effective decision making. Actually, the cost of the time spent searching for the information elsewhere may be greater than the price of the report.

Many on-line database services provide access to hundreds of specialized newsletters and statistical reports. Subscribing to the service takes the place of subscribing to each publication. In this way you only pay for the information you want. The first step in determining which on-line services to subscribe to is finding out what people need.

Information Needed Sooner

Some operations require access to information as soon as possible: for example, community affairs and finance. Waiting for a monthly journal, or even waiting for tomorrow's newspaper, may delay the company's responses to critical issues. In fact, these delays may cost the company money or create embarrassment.

The analysis will help identify who needs instant information and what they need to know.

Information not Available

People may say the information they require isn't available. What they may really mean is that it's too hard to find, too expensive to acquire, or simply not worth the effort. On-line information services may provide just what these people need, at cost-effective prices.

Utilization of Company Information Services

The company may already provide information retrieval services to employees: for example, special libraries, communications, and public affairs. The needs analysis will help determine how these services are being utilized and by whom. If people aren't using the current services, you need to find out why:

- Do employees not know about the service?
- Is the service too hard or inconvenient to use?
- Does the service fall short of their needs?
- Does the service cost too much?
- Does the service take too long to provide the information?

Answers to questions like these will tell you what you're already doing right and where you need to improve.

Compile a List of Projects and Goals

The on-line information service should help people accomplish their daily tasks and achieve department and company goals. To tailor the information service to these needs, you must know what these tasks and goals are. A proactive information service organization will use this list to anticipate the information people need to perform their jobs.

ANALYZING THE RESULTS OF THE NEEDS ANALYSIS

Once the task force identifies the company's information needs, data analysis begins. Each company will devise its own method for examining the results, but basically, the information should fall into one of the following categories. Each of these factors may be subdivided further by company function or department.

Information source versus frequency of use (by department).

Information source versus cost (by department).

Time spent reading versus department/function.

Time spent cataloging/filing versus department/function.

Sources used for information difficult to find/cost.

Sources too expensive to purchase/cost.

Information needed sooner/current source and cost.

Information not available.

Utilization of company information services:

Service versus usage (by department).

Costs (overhead or charge back/department).

Corporate goals and department projects with timetables.

Analyzing this data will give a realistic view of the potential gains from using on-line services. The task force can also analyze the benefits of instituting other cost-saving measures, such as substituting or consolidating information resources.

SUMMARY

In this chapter you've learned how to conduct an information needs and utilization analysis. A task force with members from different departments and with at least one member intimately familiar with on-line database services can effectively recommend where on-line services will enhance company performance. The team may choose to gather the information by conducting interviews or by circulating a written survey. Regardless of the methods, the objectives are to learn what information is being used, who is using it, who is having difficulty finding economically priced information, and what the information is costing the company. Armed with this data, the task force will be able to make recommendations for on-line database service usage.

The task force will not only have to examine the costs for accessing these services, but will also have to determine how the services are delivered to the users. The next chapters will discuss the features of database services that should be evaluated before signing a user contract. Chapter 6 will discuss how to implement your in-house operation.

5

Matching Company Needs to Database Vendor Specifications

Identifying your company's information needs and finding on-line services to supply that information are the first steps in deciding which databases to subscribe to. As you probably realized from the Chapter 3 overview, you often can access a particular database on a number of different on-line services. Since the quality, ease of use, and costs of these services vary considerably, you need to examine and compare them in much more detail before subscribing. You'll want to determine how often the database is updated and how easy it is to access the type of information you need. Also you'll want to assess what other services the vendor might offer. Although it's difficult to compare on-line charges, discounts, and other costs, you'll want to make sure that you're fully informed before signing on the dotted line.

The vendors you choose must support the method your company uses to access on-line services. For example, if you have a highly trained, experienced, and centralized search organization, you may buy more complex on-line systems, such as Dialog and SDC Orbit. If your users are decentralized and relatively inexperienced, you may wish to buy more user-friendly services, such as The Source and CompuServe. (Refer to Chapter 6, Designing the On-Line Search Operation, for more information about the methods companies use to establish in-house search operations.)

The first section of this chapter suggests a number of questions you may wish to ask about each database provider and on-line information vendor. The last part of this chapter discusses how vendors charge for long-distance telephone access, information, computer usage, and other services.

QUESTIONS TO ASK BEFORE BUYING

Before you begin reading volumes of vendor brochures, user manuals, and magazine reviews, decide what information you wish to collect and compare. If you prepare a standard form as a guide, you'll improve the consistency and quality of your analysis. Figure 5–1, Database Evaluation Form, suggests categories you may wish to include on your evaluation sheet. This chapter defines and discusses each item on this form. Not all factors will apply to every database and vendor you evaluate. You may wish to refer back to the form as you read this chapter.

Database name. The name of the database is generic to the database provider: that is, the company that actually abstracts the information and enters the data into the computer. For example, ERIC, MEDLINE, CHEMLAW, CLAIMS, Magazine Index, and Books In Print are databases. Some databases are offered on-line directly by the people who create them. Many databases may be accessed through one or more on-line vendors, such as The Source, Dialog, or Delphi. Much of the search power stems from the services offered by the on-line vendor; so you should find all ways to access it.

Vendor (access). The vendor is the on-line service providing computer services that let you utilize the information stored in the database. The database provider may be the vendor. Or, the database may be offered on one or more on-line services such as SDC Orbit, Dow Jones News/Retrieval, CompuServe, NEXIS, and BRS. The features, benefits, and charges of these vendors vary considerably. Selecting the "right" vendor can be a complex process.

Contact. As you gather information on each database provider and/or on-line service, keep a record of who you talked to, what their position is, and what they promise to send you. This way you'll know with whom to follow up for answering additional questions or finding missing materials. You will always receive more personal treatment if you give

FIGURE 5-1   Database Evaluation Form

Date:
Database name: Vendor/Provider name:
Contact: Contact:
Address: Address:
City, State, ZIP: City, State, ZIP:
Telephone: Telephone:

Carriers/Toll-free lines:

Transmission Speeds (circle each): 300/1200/2400/other _____

General description (subjects, journals, newspapers, numerical data):

Type (full-text/bibliographic/abstracts/numeric data/software/cover-to-cover/
   selective coverage):

Size/Time-span:

Frequency updated:

Geographic scope (local, national, international):

Languages:

Computer tapes/disks availability:

Search capabilities (free-text/numeric search/proximity logic/truncating/
   ability to display search steps/range limits/field specification, saving
   terms):

SDI Services (specify printing format/specify database):

Documentation (manuals, newsletters):

Customer service (training, training aids, telephone help line):

References:

Comments:

Charges:

Subscription/Minimums:

Bonuses/free time:

Connect hour: 300 baud _____   1200 bps _____   2400 bps _____

Long distance charge (if separate):

FIGURE 5–1 *(concluded)*

Per search charge:

Computer resource charge:

Database resource charge:

On-line printing charge:

Off-line printing charge:

Royalty charge:

Downloading charges/policies:

On-line storage charge:

Software usage charge:

Time of day discount:

SDI charges:

Training, manuals, newsletters:

---

someone's name. Usually you can get more complete information about the database contents from the database provider (source company). The on-line services may provide only a brief summary of each database they offer.

City/state/zip/telephone. You may need this contact information later, so you might as well record it initially and save having to look it up again. Record this data for both the database provider and the database vendor. Frequently they offer toll-free customer service telephone numbers. You can save a large long-distance phone bill by recording these numbers.

Carriers/toll-free lines. Record which carriers (Telenet, Tymnet, Uninet, etc.) offer access to the on-line vendor in your location(s). Some vendors provide their own toll-free system. If so, find out if they have a local access number in your city. If they don't, you'll need to consult with the long-distance phone service to determine how much this will cost. [Note: Even though the vendor may provide toll-free access, you'll eventually pay for the long distance charges. Long-distance services are either billed separately or folded into the hourly connect time. See sections on charges later in this chapter.]

Transmission speeds. The most common telecommunication speeds offered today for personal computer users are 300 and 1200 bits per second (bps) or 30 and 120 characters per second. Since the 1200 bps service is in *theory* four times faster than 300 baud, the on-line service may charge a premium for faster access. During the interactive keyboarding time, higher speed isn't necessarily more efficient, because the user can only think and type so fast. You'll find, however, that systems like NEXIS and LEXIS, which present a full screen of information at a time, will create these screens much faster at 1200 and 2400 bps. Also, during peak usage periods the on-line service's computers may react slowly and thus not take advantage of rapid transmission capabilities. Faster transmission rates are particularly beneficial for uploading (sending) or downloading (receiving) large files of data. Now that 2400 bps equipment (modems) is becoming less expensive (below $1,000), services are offering this option.

[*Note: Baud* is a measure of data transmission speed. One character of information (a letter, number, or punctuation mark) requires approximately 10 binary numbers (ones and zeroes) to represent it, much like the dots and dashes of Morse code represent the alphabet. Therefore, 300 baud equals 30 characters per second and 1200 bps equals 120 characters per second.]

General description. Compile a list of subjects and printed media covered in the database. Magazine Index includes information from over 400 different magazines published in the United States and Canada. You may only need to summarize the types of information (for example, business, chemical engineering, etc.) or you may wish to list specific journals, newspapers, and statistical reports. The results of your needs analysis in Chapter 4 will indicate the type of information to gather. You may wish to attach to the analysis lists or advertising brochures that highlight additional services, such as time-sharing, data storage, and electronic mail. At this point, you might also comment on the power of the system, its user-friendliness, and other relevant issues.

Type. The type of information available on database services varies from full-text to bibliographic only. You need to know whether you can download (print) the full text of articles, or whether you'll only receive a bibliography, or both. You also need to know if the database provides abstracts. If it's a numeric database, you may want to find out how the data is organized, and how you can search for and organize the information.

Another important consideration is whether the database provider includes printed media in a cover-to-cover fashion or only selectively. If the journal is entered *cover-to-cover*, no articles will be omitted. In fact, the database may include allied information such as editorials, news releases, and short subjects. If the database has *selective coverage*, only certain articles from their sources will be included, at the provider's discretion. Usually this is done to narrow the focus of the database; for example, an article on college starting salaries might be omitted from a chemical engineering database. Unfortunately, you may be quite interested in retrieving this information even though it's not on chemical engineering per se. Also, if the database has selective coverage, it can put together impressive advertising about how it includes information from hundreds of sources, when in fact it doesn't have cover-to-cover coverage. Instead, it may only include an occasional article from each source. And you may have to dig to find out exactly what the database offers.

Size/time span. Size may be expressed as number of citations (bibliographic references), number of bytes (characters) of data, and/or number of journals, newspapers, and newsletters included. The database will indicate how far back in time it extends, as well. For example, you may find a database that has full text for the past two years and abstracts for eight years prior to that. Or, you may find databases with cover-to-cover, full text for the past week—but records any older are erased. You probably shouldn't subscribe to a service based on size alone. The important thing is whether it contains the information you need.

Frequency updated. A news database such as NewsNet, NEXIS, and Dow Jones News/Retrieval is updated several times each day, almost like a newspaper with morning and evening editions. UPI and AP news wires provide news as it happens. Most databases, however, don't put information online quite that quickly. The sales literature will usually specify something like, "10,000 records added monthly." You'll want to find out if those are journals published this month, last month, or last quarter . . . a database may only be as useful as it is current. Heavy on-line users will tell you if there are discrepancies between advertised claims and actual updating practices.

Geographic scope. Some databases concentrate on state issues while others have national or international scope. Don't discount the value of a small, specialized database, because it might be a stronger source of state information, for example. A database originating from another country is likely to have better information on that country.

Languages. If you do need foreign information, make sure that the database includes foreign sources. If you don't, make sure you can exclude those citations from your search. There's no sense paying for information you cannot use.

Computer tapes/disks/microfilm. At times it may be more economical to purchase an entire database rather than to access it on-line. For example, the TULSA petroleum abstracts database is available on SDC Orbit and on computer tape. And the Magazine Index is available both on Dialog and microfilm, which are periodically updated. Purchasing the data "in bulk" will save you on-line charges as well as provide software manipulation capabilities; for example, you save money because you incorporate statistical information into trend analysis models *without* having to reenter the data into your computer.

Search capabilites. The search techniques vary considerably from vendor to vendor. If one database is available from more than one vendor, you may prefer to purchase it on the vendor with the most powerful and/or user-friendly search capabilities.

For example, if you search for < PRESIDENT REAGAN > and < MARGARET THATCHER > in article titles, you'll obviously miss an article titled, "British and U.S. Heads of State Meet in Washington." However, if the database allows you to link the two names together and to search through the abstracts and/or article text, you'll find the information in no time at all—without wasted effort. This is called performing a *free-text search using proximity logic.* You might say something like, < FIND REAGAN WITHIN 10 WORDS OF THATCHER >. The computer then searches millions of words of text to locate the words <REAGAN> and <THATCHER> appearing within 10 words of each other. The service will then present you with a listing of articles that meet your criteria.

Let's say hypothetically that you find 500 citations meeting this requirement. Downloading that many references may be too expensive. You may have to reconsider your search strategy and apply a *range limit:* for example, <SINCE 1983>. Now the computer reports only 146 citations. This type of system obviously has great power.

Rather than discuss all the types of search capabilities in this chapter, I'll refer you to Chapter 10, Planning and Designing Search Strategies.

You'll probably need a professional on-line searcher to advise you on the pros and cons of vendor search capabilities. And, when evaluating these features, you should always keep your end-user in mind.

SDI (selective dissemination of information). Sometimes you'll want to repeat a search each time a database is updated. For instance, you may wish to retrieve all new mousetrap patents or information on new legislation that affects the mousetrap industry. Once you've formulated your search strategy, you may not need to alter the procedures. If so you can store the search strategy on the on-line service's computer and request an automatic rerun of the search at each update. Some services allow you to specify the citation printout format. You'll receive updated computer printouts in the mail.

If you know you won't change your search strategy, SDIs are a convenient way of staying informed without incurring additional log-on charges or tying up personnel time. The service may not charge you for storing your search strategy, but you will be charged for the off-line printing and for each citation.

Some companies prefer to store their searches and manually repeat them as the database is updated. This allows the experienced searchers to modify the strategy if they detect changes. Thus, the search strategy can be updated to take best advantage of information available on the service. You may wish to repeat the search manually a few times before making it an "automatic" SDI.

Documentation. Most database vendors provide manuals, training aids, and newsletters to help users utilize their services. The quality of these publications varies considerably. Be sure to examine these materials with reference to the person(s) who will be using them. Remember that the needs of someone with only basic computer literacy are quite different than those of an experienced on-line searcher. The aids must be well organized and written clearly and accurately or they won't be of value to the user. The manuals should be well indexed and perhaps have tabs separating major sections. Illustrations and examples should show how to perform important steps. The vendor should also supply periodic updates to keep the manual current.

Newsletters are also quite helpful, especially if they give hints for improving search techniques and allow subscribers to share tips with other users.

Find out if the database offers on-line HELP. If you're confused about the exact use of a command—for example, the command < FIND >—you might be able to type < HELP FIND >. The vendor's computer would then display a definition of the FIND command and give some examples. Another form of on-line help is being able to use menus or choices instead of having to construct a search process by entering a series of commands. If the system offers both options (menu-driven and command-driven), it will probably suit the needs of both novice and experienced users.

Customer service. Find out if the vendor supplies classes, training tapes, and/or free or inexpensive on-line practice sessions. Examine the training aid descriptions to determine if they are well thought-out and complete. Talk to other on-line users about the quality of the training and subsequent customer support. Find out if the vendor provides a toll-free customer service line. Ask other users if it's easy to get through to customer service, and if the vendor is helpful and supportive of the user.

References. Talk with companies who use the service similarly to the way you plan to use it; for example, if your chemical research librarian plans to use SDC Orbit, talk to other chemical company libraries using this service as well as other services. You should also discuss the pros and cons of the services' features and get the inside story on such things as response speed, customer service, updating practices, and so forth. You really cannot over research this area.

THE PRICE OF INFORMATION

Comparing prices of database vendors is almost impossible. It's about as complicated as comparing employee benefit packages of different companies. For example, one company benefit plan may offer dental insurance and another a country club membership. Even though the contents of benefit packages vary, their overall costs may not be much different. However, the potential value employees perceive may differ considerably. That is, if you're anticipating orthodontic work for three children, one company's package might appear much more attractive.

The same reasoning applies to on-line services. Getting a cheaper connect hour may mean sacrificing powerful and efficient search techniques that would actually save you connect time. And, if you look at the big picture, whether you pay $18 or $24 for 30 citations appears insignificant when compared to spending half a day in the public library. I'm not encouraging carelessness. However, don't be a penny-pincher if saving money means sacrificing important services. It may not pay off in the long run.

Improvements in computer software and hardware are changing the way on-line vendors charge for services. In the past, the vendor charged for connect time (the time spent "talking" with the computer) and for specific information downloaded (each citation read). This pricing structure developed from the practice of time-sharing computer services. However, with the improvements in mainframe computer performance, the machines are capable of performing much more complex tasks in much less time. Thus, by upgrading their hardware and software systems, the vendors have cut into their profits.

In addition, the end-user is using more powerful systems to retrieve the data. Instead of 110 baud (11 characters per second) dumb terminals, they use 1200 and 2400 bps (120/240 characters per second) modems and intelligent personal computers. With this equipment they can retrieve the data nearly 10 times faster. Plus, with automatic log-on features and search techniques, the end-user can cut on-line time to a bare minimum. These developments have lead vendors to rethink their pricing structure.

The following is a discussion of vendor charges shown in

the second half of the Database Evaluation Form in Figure 5–1. Each database provider may not make all of these charges; still, you should investigate all charges as best you can. You don't want any hidden surprises when you get your first bill. Sometimes it's very difficult to estimate what a search will actually cost. What seems relatively simple and straightforward to you may require quite a bit of effort by the vendor's computer. If they charge for that effort (computer resource charge), you'll pay more for a search than you might expect. Find out if the service provides on-line help for computing the price of a search prior to running it.

Subscription/minimums. About one third of the database vendors require a basic subscription fee. This fee may cover costs for providing manuals and even some "free" on-line practice time. Or, it may just set you up an account. Some vendors charge a minimum usage fee and others operate on a pay-as-you-go system. If you seldom use the service, the pay-as-you-go method will be to your advantage. However, if you're a heavy user, you can negotiate some attractive volume discounts. If you're willing to guarantee a minimum usage (billing) each month, you can get discounts up to one third. Usually these discounts only apply to the connect time and not to such things as royalty charges or downloading charges. Be careful, though, because sometimes the discount is only calculated on the guaranteed minimum and not on use above that figure; for example, you may pay 60 percent of the first "guaranteed" $1,000 of service and 100 percent above $1,000. (See also the Time of Day Discounts section below.)

Be cautious about making large commitments to a new vendor. You may want to wait until you are satisfied with their service and have an idea of how much you'll be using them each month before taking an expensive plunge.

Bonuses/free time. Sometimes you'll get a couple of hours of free connect time with each new subscription. Some telecommunications software vendors supply coupons for free subscriptions and free on-line time. (See also the Time of Day Discounts section below.)

Connect time. The connect time is the actual time you spend communicating with the on-line service computer. Once you sign on with your name, password, and account number, the clock begins ticking. Only when you sign off will the clock stop. (You'll want to be certain to use the proper sign-off procedures or the computer may continue billing you after you've hung up.) Many services charge different rates for 300 and 1200 bps users. Even though theoretically the 1200 bps user receives four times the data in the same elapsed time, the 1200 bps rate is usually only twice as high. However, if the vendor's computer responds very slowly and thus negates the advantages of 1200 bps communication, you may wish to log on at the slower speed at half the price. Connect time costs anywhere from $15 to $300 per hour and averages $64. You may receive substantial discounts if you access some of the services during off-hours. (See the Time of Day Discounts section below.)

Long-distance telephone charge. Even though you may access the vendor through a toll-free telecommunications service such as Telenet or one provided by the vendor, the on-line service may bill you separately for the long-distance time. Some services fold this amount into the connect time charge and some don't. Make sure you know how they quote telephone charges, because adding $2 to $8 per hour for a separate long distance charge may influence your decisions about one service over another.

Per search charge. A per search charge is as easy to understand as the connect time charge. Basically you're charged for each search you conduct regardless of the number of "hits" you find. In some ways this penalizes the user who performs many simple searches and doesn't adequately charge the user who performs a single, long, complex search. However, it does ensure that the person trying to find "no hits" is paying an equitable share. Sometimes a "no hit" report is just what you're looking for. Just think how rewarding it would be to find out that no one has written a book on the subject you propose or that no patent exists for your newly invented device.

Computer resource charge. This charge attempts to fairly charge for the actual work that the vendor's computer performs during the search. The charge is calculated from the central processing time plus the input and output time to the disk and the terminal. For people who don't understand how computers "crank and churn," these charges can seem incomprehensible. Unless the vendor provides you with an estimated computer resource charge prior to running the search, I'd be leery of using it. Computer resource charges are more common with time-sharing services and with numeric databases.

Database resource charge. This charge isn't very popular with users and has been discontinued by several services. In essence, the user is charged for the number of occurrences of a particular term in the database; the larger the subject, the more you pay. In a way, this is similar to the computer resource charge.

On-line printing charge. This is a charge for each record "typed" on your terminal (either a CRT or printer output). Prices range from $.04 to $7.00 or more per citation. However, the typical bibliographic citation costs about 25 cents. Some type charges are calculated on the number of characters or lines printed. The person seeking a "no hit" answer benefits from this billing method.

Off-line printing charge. If you aren't in a rush for the information, you may request that the service print the citations on their printer and mail them to you. You'll usually get a letter-quality printout and you may even be able to specify the print format. Although there is a charge for off-line printing, you may save money by reducing the connect time (and searcher time) required to download the information to your own printer. Off-line printing is also used for SDI reports. Costs vary from $.01 to $11.00 per citation and average $.34. (See SDI Services section below.)

Royalty charge. The database provider makes its money through royalty payments from the on-line vendor. Sometimes this charge is folded into the on-line and off-line printing or type charges, and sometimes it's billed separately. It's important to understand the method used before comparing vendor rates.

Downloading charge. There's a great deal of controversy on the practice of downloading information onto magnetic storage media such as tape and floppy disk. With the influx of personal computer users, this trend will continue. The fear of database vendors is that the user can download all necessary files into their own database manager. After retrieving the data once, they can consult their own files instead of logging onto the database and paying for subsequent searches. In response, some vendors have policies forbidding electronic storage of downloaded information. However, this policy defeats one of the major advantages of using on-line information sources: the ability to manipulate the data without having to reenter it into a database manager, word processor, spreadsheet, or statistical software package. Not only does this ability save time, but it also reduces potential errors. Progressive database services will charge reasonable fees for downloading and thus permit their customers maximum flexibility for utilizing their information. Besides, the time and expense necessary for downloading the entire database would be prohibitive. (See additional information in Chapter 11.)

On-line storage charge.   Some services allow you to store search strategies on their computers to reuse later. Find out what the storage charges might be. If the vendor offers electronic mail services, you may also be able to store mailing lists for sending letters. Some services don't charge for using their computer storage; some do.

Software usage charge.   Many of the numeric databases offer the use of sophisticated statistical software packages with which you can analyze their data or your own data. You'll be charged not only for the computer time, but also for the use of the vendor's software. Find out if you can purchase the software to use off-line in your own computer.

Time of day discount.   You can save quite a bit on connect time charges by logging onto the services after peak hours. BRS After Dark and Knowledge Index from Dialog are examples of discounted services available after hours. Although it isn't a formal discount, you may also save money by using the services after users in several time zones have gone home. When usage is low, the computer response time is faster and thus reduces your connect time. For example, the users in the Central time zone report much faster response times after the East Coast users leave their offices. Likewise, the East Coast users have almost exclusive use of the services early in the morning.

SDI services.   You may wish to repeat a search every time a database is updated. For example, 25,000 articles are added to MEDLINE each month. If you want to stay informed on <INFERTILITY>, you can store your search strategy on Dialog and each time the database is updated, they will automatically produce an off-line printout of the new citations, which will then be mailed to you. Some on-line services allow you to request special formatting for the printout. Although this saves you on-line charges, you do pay for the off-line printout and citations.

Training, manuals, and newsletters. You'll find that your subscription fee may cover the costs of training materials, a set of manuals, and a monthly or quarterly newsletter subscription. Services with no subscription fees or guaranteed minimums may have separate charges for these materials. Also there may be charges for the extra copies you need if your organization is decentralized.

Several of the supermarket services provide training programs that may be conducted at your company or at a central location such as a public library. Service representatives may periodically call on large users to answer questions, to resolve problems, and to conduct informal training sessions. Find out from the service what's available and what it costs. You may also wish to check with other companies to assess the quality of these services and materials.

Other considerations. Be sure to determine up front if your software and equipment is compatible with the service. The service has no obligation to modify its service so you can access it. If you haven't purchased software and equipment, find out what they recommend. If they don't recommend a system, talk to current users to find out what they are using and how it works.

It's difficult to anticipate problems that may arise as you're using the service; for instance, what happens if they drop a database from their "library"? If you've paid a guaranteed minimum based on your anticipated use of this database, you may run into difficulty. What if you have repeated problems getting through busy telephone lines? What if their computer's response time is so slow that you're paying unfair on-line charges? You probably can avoid many of these difficulties and more by talking to present and past subscribers. Don't purchase a service just because of its apparent size, its good prices, or its promotion by a fast-talking sales representative. Check them out.

SUMMARY

To determine which on-line services to use, you'll need to examine them in detail. You'll want to know what databases they provide, how frequently they are updated, what time span the data covers, what search capabilities they provide, and what customer support is available. In addition, you'll want to examine very carefully their charges and fee schedules. Many times significant costs are hidden or downplayed in the literature. After you've narrowed your choice, be sure to find out from other users how well the system responds, how supportive the customer service actually is, and what the other users recommend. If you want the service, it's up to you to provide hardware and software to access their computer. Find out what telecommunication systems you'll need before subscribing.

Chapters 8 and 9 describe more about telecommunications software and hardware. The next two chapters discuss ways to implement on-line searching in your organization.

6

Designing the On-Line
Search Operation

First, the task force determines how on-line searches can benefit the corporation and which database services would be most beneficial. Next, it must design a data delivery system to meet its objectives. The approach will depend on the needs of each department, of top management, and of the company as a whole.

Smaller companies, or those with minimum on-line information needs, may prefer a centralized approach. Training and supporting one professional searcher will minimize overhead and still offer good service. Large companies, or those with high on-line information needs, may require both a centralized organization and search specialists for selected departments. For example, a midsized oil company uses on-line searchers in the research and development library, in the petroleum-geology division library, in the public affairs department, and in the legal department. Each department's focus is different enough that their management feels a need for specialized search operations.

The task force will also need to decide if the search operation will be reactive or proactive; that is, if the searchers will simply respond to search requests or if they will actively participate in problem-solving activities. For example, the top management of a major manufacturer established its own in-house news service. In-house searchers keep top management informed of general business news and industry activities that could affect the company. The searchers have not only replaced the executive secretary who would circle articles in *The Wall Street Journal*, but they've also contributed to a quantum jump in the quality of information available to management.

A closer look at the different organization options will help you identify what will work best in your company.

ON-LINE SEARCH DEPARTMENT CHARTERS

The Centralized Reactive On-Line Search Department

A number of organizations have one on-line information department serving the entire company or location. On-line searches are usually performed by the corporate or technical librarians with technical and/or library science experience. As a rule, these search organizations *react* to day-to-day requests from managers and specialists by responding to specific search requests.

This type of operation minimizes overhead by utilizing existing library staff for on-line searching. In fact, on-line searching may actually allow the librarians to perform their work more efficiently. Training and quality control are also easier to manage. One supervisor—for example, the head librarian—can manage the entire operation. He or she can select the on-line database services, monitor costs, and standardize equipment and procedures. The centralized operation also lets searchers share their resources, experience, and information—thus increasing productivity.

It's very difficult for a centralized department to be intimately familiar with the company's entire operation. Therefore, the searcher may not use the best strategies for locating highly technical information. Centralized organizations often find that their services aren't fully utilized. Managers and specialists will try on-line searching but if the information they receive isn't relevant, they'll quit using the service. The problem may lie with the manager's inability to explain the need, with the searcher's inability to understand the need, or with the searcher's inadequate search techniques. Whatever the reason, these problems are usually not detected, much less resolved.

The search department should be *conveniently located* for all users. In this age of electronic communication, you'd think that a manager or specialist could simply send the search request over a computer network, and then within an hour or so, the search results would arrive at the requester's terminal and be printed on a printer. Not so. Typically, the requester must telephone the request or physically take it to the search department. When the search is complete, the printout travels to the requester by interoffice mail. Using internal mail services each way may add a day or so to the process. So the instant search may actually spend several days moving around company halls.

Electronic mail is another service offered by on-line database vendors. Electronic mail will probably never be popular or utilitarian if it's only available through a centralized search department like a special library. Communication isn't the library's charter. Electronic mail works best in a decentralized environment, in a centralized word processing center, or in a mail operation.

The Public Affairs Information Service Department

Some managers, especially top managers, need to keep their fingers on the pulse of government, industry, and business— whether or not there's an immediate need for the information. For instance, every day a major food distributor's searchers look for any information with a bearing on the food industry. Writers consolidate their findings into bulletins to be circulated at 8 A.M. each day to top management and selected individuals. The department also maintains detailed files for future reference.

The food company's public affairs department also provides information for public and community relations, the house organ editor, and the advertising department. Although this department will conduct specific searches on request, it doesn't advertise or encourage the use of its services to other departments. The public affairs department anticipates the needs of the company and its top management, but only in a narrow sense.

If this is the only on-line search service the company provides, the needs of the entire organization are not met. Searching for food industry trends requires a much different technique than searching for additive patents at the request of an R&D department. The staff may not be familiar with the methods or the databases used to perform technical searches. Also, if the public affairs department serves top management, then that is where its priorities will be, and other "clients" will often be forced to wait.

The Centralized Proactive On-Line Search Department

This type of organization not only responds to individual search requests, but also works actively with each department to supply the information needed to conduct daily business and meet department goals. Information consultants counsel managers on the advantages of using on-line searches with specific projects. And they identify alternate information sources that may be more economical, like materials available through interlibrary loans. This posture differs from the other services described in that the information service actively tailors its activities to meet the needs of the organization *before* being asked for assistance. It is an integral part of the planning and problem-solving process.

When a company takes this posture, it's saying that *management doesn't expect each manager or specialist to be an information resource specialist.* The company realizes that "information technology" has become so complex that only an information specialist knows where and how to retrieve the best information for the most economical price. The *information consultants* become vital resources to managers and specialists.

Multiple Specialized On-Line Search Centers

Some departments feel that they need a search specialist familiar with their technology and activities. They prefer an on-line search service within the department or division. This configuration is particularly popular in such technical divisions as legal and research and development departments. The specialized on-line search center may be either proactive or reactive to daily requests.

Specialized searchers not only become more familiar with the department functions and technology, but they also become more familiar with repeatedly used databases.

The Individual On-Line Search Workstation

Many feel that eventually everyone will be able to perform on-line searches from a personal computer at their desk. Indeed, this may be a viable solution for those specialists— such as legal or finance—who conduct frequent searches. However, the complexity of on-line search techniques suggests that at present *a personal workstation on every desk isn't the most cost-effective solution.*

If the company chooses the personal workstation configuration, each searcher must be trained in on-line search techniques. Since each on-line database service uses different commands, search vocabularies, and codes, the user may have to learn a number of different systems. If users don't perform searches regularly, they tend to forget the intricacies of each database system. Keeping up with the rapidly changing database industry is almost a full-time job in itself, so I doubt that many managers and specialists will want to add these duties to their regular responsibilities.

Individual workstations will be a boon to electronic mail applications, whether they are limited to intracompany/facility communications or expanded to intercompany communications. The computerized, electronic mail workstation may soon become as useful as the telephone since it has many features the telephone doesn't. For example, sales representatives can send back written orders even if there isn't an attendant at the home-office workstation. The field computer electronically transmits the data over common telephone lines to the home-office computer. Salespersons can take advantage of cheaper long-distance telephone rates by transmitting at night, and they won't have the frustration created by time zone differences. Recording the orders on the home office computer's floppy disk eliminates the labor needed for entering handwritten data and reduces the possibility of errors. After the salesperson uploads the order, important messages can be transmitted to the field. New price lists, customer inquiries, and interoffice memos can be forwarded without having to wait for the U.S. mail.

In-house electronic mail systems can also connect the independent workstation to a company-operated on-line search department. The user sends the electronically generated search request to the special library staff, and within a few hours the results are sent to the workstation. Neither person must be at the terminal to receive the message. Electronic communications will save time and reduce the inherent delays of interoffice mail facilities.

Electronic mail promises work-saving capabilities that extend beyond the realm of the subjects covered in this book. Just imagine what it would be like to send within minutes a 10-page report to 15 people—without ever printing it on paper, duplicating it, stuffing it into envelopes, or licking any postage stamps. Electronic mail offers greatly improved communications without the use of paper, without the use of traditional mail services, and without confusion and delay. Electronic mail is indeed a revolutionary advance in communication.

CONTROL, COORDINATION, AND THE ORGANIZATION CHART

Positioning the centralized on-line search department in the organization chart shouldn't be done haphazardly. If the search organization primarily serves top management, for example, other users may get second-class service. Placing the search department in the corporate library may limit electronic mail services. Since the library tends to be a reactive group, they will have difficulty assuming a proactive information consultant role. And, placing the group in the management information services department may intimidate users who aren't computer literate.

Ideally, the information services department should have an identity of its own, apart from the images associated with libraries and with electronic data processing departments. Beginning with a clean slate, an information services department can address both on-line information retrieval and electronic communications, and it can assume a proactive role in the organization. Since information retrieval is as essential to decision making as long-range planning or financial management, the information services department probably should share a similar status in the organization. The department should report directly to an administrative vice president or general manager responsible for providing such support services as legal, financial, computer, personnel, and plant maintenance. From this vantage point, the information services department will be able to serve the needs of the entire organization.

If a decentralized approach is chosen, the corporation will still need a coordinator: someone who can standardize procedures and equipment, evaluate information sources, coordinate training, and monitor expenses. Without this control or coordination, the company will again be faced with the wasteful purchasing of duplicate services. And, should the company ever wish to consolidate a helter-skelter arrangement of independent workstations into a computer communications network, they'll be faced with overwhelming problems stemming from hardware and software incompatibility. See also Chapters 8 and 9, which discuss telecommunications hardware and software.

SUMMARY

The company will not only have to determine *what type* of information the organization needs, but also, *who* will access that information. The company may choose from a number of configurations, including centralized, decentralized, and individual workstations.

In addition, the company needs to decide if the information service will just be reactive to user requests, or if the service will actively participate in the organization's problem-solving processes.

The status or position of the information services department in the organization chart will greatly influence its ability to serve the company. Positioning the service in existing departments may limit its charter and effectiveness.

If the organization chooses a decentralized configuration, it will need to coordinate information retrieval activities and standardize procedures, equipment, and software. Control of on-line database usage will prevent expensive duplication of services.

The methods chosen will vary from company to company and from department to department, depending on the information needs. One solution will not fit all circumstances.

7

Implementing the On-Line Search Operation

In the last chapter you examined various configurations companies use for gathering on-line information. The centralized reactive on-line search department responds like a special library, performing searches on request for people throughout the company or location. The public affairs information service is a proactive organization primarily serving top management and performing communications activities. The centralized proactive on-line search department is a consulting group that actively plans with management how to incorporate the "best" information into projects and management plans. Multiple specialized on-line search centers serve specialized departments such as the legal department, patent department, and research and development department. The individual on-line workstation design allows managers and specialists to perform searches from their own desktop computers.

In addition, you learned how the centralized, decentralized, reactive, and proactive postures can either enhance or detract from their effectiveness. Once the company has decided on the basic form of the service, then the details of its operation must be determined.

This chapter will discuss staffing, budget requirements, and planning. You'll learn more about how the chosen configuration will affect the selection and purchasing of equipment, software, and on-line services. (Chapters 8 and 9 will cover the features and benefits of these items in detail.) Installing the service will also require the development of policies and procedures for its use. You'll need to decide such things as who will pay the overhead, who will control the usage, and who will perform document retrieval.

The task force can make these decisions. However, most companies find it beneficial to hire the information service department manager first so he or she can participate in the planning process. The new manager must not only understand how the operation will work, but should also have some "ownership" and say in its design.

STAFFING REQUIREMENTS

The Searcher

Whether you select a centralized or decentralized organization, the requirements of an on-line searcher will be similar. The person should be well organized and analytical and should enjoy solving puzzles or problems. Since the searcher will interface and communicate with people throughout the department or corporation, he or she should have good communication and interviewing skills. Library science skills are not essential; however, they are often handy. A searcher must have good memory, judgment, imagination, flexibility, thoroughness, patience, persistence, as well as high standards for accuracy.

Searchers who write article synopses or news bulletins for management will need writing skills. Familiarity with the industry and company will help the searcher identify relevant information.

Searchers who primarily access technical databases such as CA SEARCH, CLAIMS/U.S. PATENT ABSTRACTS, and WESTLAW should definitely have a technical background. Knowledge of technical vocabulary, spellings, and relationships will aid the searcher in interviewing clients, determining sources, and formulating search strategies.

In the proactive organization, information consultants must be active listeners, must be able to build credibility and trust, and must understand planning processes. They should be self-confident, secure, and know their limitations and impact on others. They'll also need a good understanding of business operations and problem-solving techniques. Information consultants should be familiar with a wide range of information sources beyond on-line database services.

The Centralized Reactive Information Services Operation

The head librarian. Frequently the manager of the centralized, reactive search operation is the special library head librarian. With library science training, the librarian will not only be able to utilize on-line searches, but will also be familiar with alternative information sources. And he or she will know how to retrieve documents from document services and through interlibrary loans.

If the search demands are low, the librarian or a member of the library staff can perform the searches part-time. If search demands are high, the librarian can train and supervise a group of searchers.

The Public Affairs Information Service Department

The public information research manag3r. The public information research manager is a consultant who can anticipate and satisfy the information needs of top managers and of critical personnel. This job requires consulting skills, a good knowledge of business management, and an understanding of employee communications and community relations. He or she should be able to establish a cataloging and filing system for storing newspaper and magazine clippings, search results, and other materials for future reference. An information manager must also be able to write and edit newsletters and information synopses.

Searchers in this department should be familiar with both the industry and business in general, so they will be able to recognize information useful to the organization. Searchers who write article synopses or news bulletins will also need writing skills.

The Centralized Proactive On-Line Search Department

The manager of this department should have consulting skills like the public information research manager. However, instead of working only with top management, this person must be able to work with all levels in the organization. Depending on the company, the job may require a strong background in technical areas.

Multiple Specialized On-Line Search Centers

Each search center should be operated by an experienced search specialist familiar with that organization's (department's) technology (for example, law or chemical research). If the search center is quite large, as it might be for an R&D operation, several searchers and a supervisor may be needed. Independent search centers may be either proactive or reactive. As discussed earlier, the qualifications of the search specialists should support the role.

The company may want to designate one person in the corporation to coordinate the activities of the specialized on-line search centers. The *coordinator* will ensure that each center meets company policies and standards, serve as a central contact point with the on-line database services, monitor expenses and search usage, and coordinate training. The coordinator can assist the search specialists with complex search problems and facilitate communication between search centers, as well. The coordinator might be the special library head librarian since he or she may also perform document retrieval for the search centers.

The Individual On-Line Workstation

The company will need a coordinator and possibly a consulting group to support individual on-line workstations. The size of this group will depend on the number of individual users and their needs for training and assistance. The manager of on-line support services will serve as an information consultant to managers and specialists who wish to perform their own on-line searches. The support person or group must not only be familiar with on-line search sources and search strategies, but also be able to train and assist managers and technical specialists attempting to use on-line services. In fact, the support group may actually perform the more complex searches. Chapters 8 and 9 discuss the hardware and software necessary to support individual workstations.

BUDGET REQUIREMENTS

Budget requirements and budgeting processes will depend on whether a centralized or decentralized configuration is chosen.

Centralized Services

Centralized organization budgets should include monies for facilities, staff, equipment, software, and supplies. Budgets will also have to include on-line service charges—the charges for connecting to and downloading information from on-line database providers. Some database services may not be available through toll-free telecommunication utilities, so long-distance charges may also have to be considered.

Since at first usage rate may be hard to predict, estimating these charges may be difficult. A reactive organization will tend to perform fewer searches than a proactive organization. Because the proactive group actively "sells" its services, managers and specialists will be more likely to use them.

If the centralized on-line service offers *electronic mail*, the company will have to estimate the extent of its usage. If electronic mail is confined to internal communication, the expense will be far less than using external services such as MCI Mail, Western Union, CompuServe, and The Source. Electronic mail is a cost-saving option because it tends to lower traditional expenses such as the costs of stationery supplies, mail handling, and postage.

Equipment and software expenses will be lower in a centralized department because several searchers may share equipment and software resources. One printer can usually support several search terminals. And a centralized unit can utilize the same manuals and reference materials. The chapter on equipment will cover these needs and expenses in more detail.

Searchers in a centralized department may not need to be as experienced as they would in a decentralized organization. The supervisor can help searchers with more complex tasks and with problems. Hiring less experienced people usually saves payroll costs. Multitalented searchers who can write, who have consulting skills, or who have technical training will be more expensive to hire.

Document retrieval may best be performed by the special library staff, since they are already in the business of securing documents through interlibrary loans, through document retrieval services, and from their own reference materials. Although on-line document ordering is convenient and fast, it's quite expensive compared to other alternatives. Special librarians are most familiar with document retrieval options.

Decentralized Services

Each decentralized unit will need its own equipment, software, manuals, and staff. The center will need at least one searcher proficient in search procedures. That person may also need expertise in the department's function (for example, a legal or engineering background). Centers with a proactive charter will need searchers with consulting skills. Finding someone with all of these qualifications may not only be difficult, but also expensive.

When multiplied by the number of centers throughout the company, the total overhead for a decentralized operation may be higher than that of a centralized operation. But positioning specialized services within the departments may prove to be more effective.

Individual Workstations

If the workstation is created *only* for on-line search activities, this is probably the most expensive configuration. However, if the personal computer workstation is established for other operations, such as word processing and database management, adding on-line communications is a relatively inexpensive proposition. Basically, the existing workstation may only require the addition of a communications software package and a modem (the device that connects the computer to the telephone line).

The most significant expense will be the training and support services needed by the individual managers and specialists searching on-line database services. They will need to attend classes, receive private tutoring, and have an expert available to answer questions. Each workstation will need manuals and literature updating vendor services and procedures.

POLICIES AND PROCEDURES

Centralized Service

For the centralized service to function efficiently and profitably, a number of policies and procedures will have to be established. Methods for requesting searches, receiving results, and paying for charges are just a few. The department must establish record-keeping procedures to account for department services, costs, and performance.

Search requests. Search requests should be submitted in writing on a standard form. If submitting a written request is an unreasonable burden, the information may be taken over the telephone. Ideally, the request should be forwarded to the searcher over electronic mail. Following is a list of items companies use on search request forms:

Date and time of request.

Requester's name, department, purchase order number, etc.

Urgency of the need (how soon a response is needed).

Nature of information needed (background and problem description).

Purpose for which the information will be used.

Search request description.

Suggested key words.

Foreign language citations (yes/no?).

Pertinent journals, authors, or known sources.

Amount of information needed (everything, highly relevant only, general overview, specify _____).

Cost limits/expense authorization.

Search results. Results should be reported in a written form that is easy to reference and to read. This may mean that the searcher or a member of the search staff will need to edit the downloaded information before forwarding it to the requester. Downloading information onto a dumb terminal (printer) doesn't give the searcher the flexibility to edit without retyping the information. However, downloading the information onto a personal computer does provide this capability.

Ideally, the results should be forwarded to the requester over electronic mail. This would give the requester the opportunity to manipulate the data further: to incorporate it into a report, for example.

Regular follow-up procedures should be instituted to ensure that clients receive the assistance and information they need. Once the requester sees the search results, he or she may wish to redefine the problem, much as a searcher might do when the database service computer responds with the number of "hits" (matches to the search parameters). Maybe the client defined the problem inadequately. Maybe the searcher didn't fully understand the application for the information. Maybe the requester now wants additional information. Follow-up is a good quality control check on the department's performance and will help ensure its relevancy.

Payment for services. Some on-line search departments fear charging for their services. They believe that managers and specialists won't use their services (and put them out of work) if they have to pay. However, I contend that if users see on-line searching as a time-saving, money-saving service that gives the company a competitive advantage, they'll gladly pay. If users won't pay for on-line searches, they haven't been sold on the benefits of searching, or else search service quality is lacking. (See the discussion on implementation below.)

In a centralized environment, a charge-back system for search expenses should be implemented (provided that the company uses this type of accounting system). The amount should include actual on-line expenses as well as an hourly rate for the searcher's time. The search department may choose to absorb the costs of short, inexpensive searches, since the accounting and record-keeping expenses might be higher than the search costs. A list of authorized users and "credit limits" should be retained. As indicated, searchers should advise requesters of unusually high costs—say over $100. The requester may appreciate the opportunity to refine the search, perhaps seeking only citations listed for the past two years instead of the past five, for example.

When the search center is located in a department, the

department will pay search costs. The search center may want to keep usage records by individual work groups. These expenses may eventually be charged to a client or contract.

Quality control/performance feedback. For any department to survive, it must justify its existence. An on-line search organization provides many intangible services difficult to quantify and measure. Therefore, the on-line information service department should establish goals and criteria for measuring its performance. Tangible measures might be the number of requests filled per day/week/month, the average turnaround time for search requests, or the number of people trained to use on-line search facilities. These criteria may not accurately represent department performance and effectiveness, though. For example, the number of requests processed depends in part on the nature of the searches. Simple searches may be processed much more quickly and easily than complex searches. Or if undue emphasis is placed on volume or speed, the quality of information may be sacrificed for reduced turnaround time.

Subjective measures may actually be more meaningful. Questionnaires for requesters and training program participants, for example, can give valuable feedback. If the goals and measures are established early, then the data can be recorded, feedback can be monitored, and adjustments in procedures can be made to head off potential problems and improve performance.

INSTALLING THE ON-LINE SEARCH DEPARTMENT

Assimilating the on-line search function into the organization requires managers and specialists to rethink their traditional ways of procuring information. Hanging a sign over a door will probably not be sufficient incentive for employees to use the on-line search department resources. Some corporate libraries have visibility problems even though they occupy thousands of square feet.

Use a Sound Sales Approach

Promoting any service requires matching the features and benefits of the product to the needs of the customer. Making a "sale" to the manager or specialist depends on the on-line search department's ability to do the following:

1. *Identify* the customer's information *needs* and current methods for satisfying those needs.
2. *Tell* the customer how on-line searching can meet those needs.
3. *Demonstrate* how an on-line search will satisfy a specific information request.
4. *Compare* on-line search features and benefits with alternative information sources.

Conveying these points to managers and specialists can be accomplished in a number of different ways:

1. Classroom instruction—workshops and demonstrations.
2. Individual instruction—tutorials and demonstrations.
3. Written communication—newsletters and memoranda.
4. Management directives—management plans and memoranda.

At times it may be necessary to utilize all of these methods in one form or another. The most effective method for bringing about organizational change is to first have a management directive (preferably in the form of the management plan) followed up with instruction and support for implementing the change. The directive provides the motivation for the change and the instruction and support provides the means for accomplishing the change. Demonstrations reinforce the advantages of making the change.

Individual resistance to change can often be managed better in a group environment. There's nothing like peer pressure to move an "immovable object." By introducing the new information resource methods to a group and convincing key individuals to accept and use them, you'll bring strong pressure on others in the group to follow suit. No one likes to be less effective than a peer. Managers should reinforce the use of on-line searches by rewarding those employees who use it to the department's and company's advantage.

Centralized Versus Decentralized—The Credibility Gap

Selling the centralized search service may be more difficult than selling the decentralized service or individual workstation service because few people like to depend on a distant, unfamiliar person for an important resource. The requester may have doubts about the searcher's competence. By relying on the searcher, the requester takes the chance that a search-er's ineptitude will be reflected in the end product for which the manager or specialist is held responsible. This type of skepticism is less prevalent the closer in the organization the searcher is to the end-user. A decentralized search center will tend to foster more confidence in the validity of search results.

When managers and specialists try to perform their own searches, they may develop a false sense of security. While they may think they've used the proper search strategies, they may not have found all relevant citations. Trained searchers usually produce better results than inexperienced ones. Letting these skeptics perform searches in tandem with an experienced searcher may convince them that on-line in-formation retrieval is a highly developed skill, one not easily mastered.

SUMMARY

This chapter discussed staffing, budgeting, and planning required to implement an on-line information organization. The policies and procedures needed to operate the service were also discussed, including such things as who will pay the overhead, who will control the usage and who will per-form document retrieval.

8

How to Buy
Telecommunications Software

The general-purpose personal computer performs a number
of different functions, including word processing, database
management, spreadsheet analysis, and telecommunications.
The instructions that tell the computer what to do and when
to do it are called *software* or *programs*. The software that
tells a personal computer how to use a modem to communicate over common telephone lines with another computer is
called *telecommunications software* or *terminal software*.
(Chapter 9 discusses personal computer hardware in more
detail.)

Usually software comes recorded on a floppy diskette.
The floppy disk stores information in much the same way as
an audio recording tape stores sound. The computer *reads* or
senses the recorded instructions and stores them in its active
memory, called RAM (Random Access Memory). Once the
telecommunications instructions reside in memory, the computer "knows" how to operate the modem: when to dial the
phone, what number to dial, when to hang up, and what
codes the remote computer will understand. (Chapter 9 also
discusses modems in detail.) The communications package
should occupy as little RAM as possible, since you will also
want to use the computer's memory for storing the data you
send and receive.

[*Note:* Some modems come equipped with telecommunications software already stored in nonerasable memory (Read Only Memory, ROM): for example, the Paradyne FDX 2400. If you buy this type of modem, you must also evaluate the software. Since you may one day wish to upgrade your software capabilities, you will want the ability to turn the internal software "off" and use other commonly available packages.]

In your information needs analysis you determined if novices or expert searchers would be performing on-line searches. If you've chosen novices, you'll want to consider *menu-driven* communications software, which simplifies searching by offering help, choices and prompting: for example, Smartcom II from Hayes.

Experienced searchers often prefer *command-driven* software, which is fast and efficient but more difficult to learn. Instead of operating from menu to menu, the searcher directly enters the commands.

Gateway software provides a friendly interface with a particular database provider; for example, In-Search is designed for searching Dialog. Since these packages are database-specific, you must know which services you plan to use.

Integrated software packages offer additional capabilities. As illustrated in Figure 8–1, along with telecommunications functions, Peachtree Software's Decision Manager includes a word processor, spreadsheet, data manager, business graphics program, and a micro/mainframe link. With these companion programs you can prepare data to transmit and manipulate data you've received. Other integrated packages are designed to perform tasks such as analyzing stock portfolios and business trends.

Telecommunication software prices vary from $35 for PC–Talk III, an excellent "freeware" program, up to $400 or $500. Gateway and integrated software packages tend to cost more than simpler command-driven systems. You'll learn more about gateway, integrated, and command-driven software in this chapter.

If you plan to use services and/or to install an internal electronic mail system, you'll want additional software features. For example, some communications software like BLAST are especially adept at "talking" to dissimilar computers, including minicomputers and mainframes.

Make sure the data communication speed options serve

FIGURE 8-1 Decision Manager (an integrated software package)

SOURCE: Courtesy of Peachtree Software Incorporated.

your requirements. On-line services run 300 bits per second (bps), 1200 bps, or 2400 bps (30, 120, or 240 characters per second); local networks (internal communication systems) often operate at much faster speeds, up to nearly 2,000 characters per second.

Look for communication packages that are fairly "intelligent." For example, you want software that displays at least an 80–column (character) line and breaks the right margin at a natural word division. Believe it or not, some programs automatically start a new line when they reach the 80th character. This makes the text difficult to read. Also, you'll want a program that both stores the information you receive on a data disk and prints it on a printer.

Because the communications software has to "talk" to so many devices—the personal computer, the modem, the printer, and the remote computer—the software must be selected very carefully. If you already have a personal computer and a modem, be sure to buy software compatible with that equipment. That is, the software must be designed to work with your computer, printer, and modem. If you haven't selected your equipment, you'll have more flexibility for selecting the software that best fits your needs. Once you've chosen the software, you can then buy the equipment that supports it. Software manufacturers specify which equipment operates with their programs.

(Note: The modem and computer must be able to perform the software commands if all are to work together. For example, buying software with automatic dialing capabilities and a modem that cannot auto-dial will negate the software's feature. Appendix A contains detailed reviews of popular communications software packages.)

This chapter discusses the many features and benefits of telecommunications software. A single software package may not possess all of these characteristics. You'll need to decide which features you must have and which you can live without. Then you'll know which software package will do your job.

FEATURES AND BENEFITS OF TELECOMMUNICATIONS SOFTWARE

Auto-dial. The auto-dial feature allows you to dial a telephone number from the keyboard, from a stored telephone directory, or from an automatic log-on command file (see below). With Lync, for example, you enter <CALL MCI> or <DIAL 1–800–555–5555>. Lync's CALL command looks at a previously entered phone list file for the MCI Mail telephone number. The DIAL command lets you type a telephone number from the keyboard. PC–Talk III and Crosstalk XVI display a phone directory. You dial the phone number by entering the number listed beside your party's name; for example, you enter <1> for the first party listed in the directory. If you wish to edit or add to the list, you simply update the directory.

Some software packages limit the number of services you can dial. For example, Naturallink, a gateway program for Dow Jones News/Retrieval, will only dial that service. Source Link and Telmerge will only dial a limited number of services. However, PC–Talk III, Smartcom II, and Crosstalk XVI allow you to enter a large number of telephone numbers, including local bulletin boards (amateur and computer club databases) and individual personal computer users. I prefer a package with the flexibility for entering the services and personal numbers I want. The telecommunications field is growing so rapidly, I wouldn't want to be limited.

When you dial a service, the software should alert you if you haven't made a successful connection. A bell and/or screen display should tell you when you've connected with your party. In addition, you'll need an AUTO–REDIAL feature, which will disconnect from a busy line and continue dialing the same number or alternate numbers until your party is reached. For example, Crosstalk XVI will call Telenet; if it's busy, it will call Tymnet; and if that's busy, it will call Uninet. PC–Talk III will repeatedly dial the same number until you've connected.

If you're using software that automatically performs a search, you may want to connect during off-hours when rates are less expensive. If your computer has an internal clock, you can tell the software to dial the service after a period of time or at a certain time. As directed the unattended computer will dial the number, log onto the service, perform the search, and log off. The next day you'll find your information stored on the disk and/or printed on your printer. This feature also comes in handy for communicating between time zones. See also the discussion of autosearch, below.

Handshaking. When the two computers connect with each other, they must speak the same language (protocol). The two software packages (yours and the remote computer's) will automatically exchange messages to verify good communication. Some personal computer packages adjust protocols (baud, stop bits, parity, etc.) automatically and others have to be manually preset. If your software allows you to change parameters after you've connected on line, you'll be able to resolve handshaking problems as they occur. You may also need to FILTER outgoing or incoming data to remove unwanted control characters such as sending a carriage return/line-feed at the end of each line.

Automatic log on (macros). On-line services require a number of sign-on formalities: for example, entering your password and account number. Many software packages (for example, ASCOM, Lync, and Crosstalk XVI) offer the ability to write simple command files (macros) that transmit your sign-on information automatically. The computer executes macros without keyboard input; for example, the computer recognizes a request for your password and sends that information to the service. You'll want software "smart" enough to recognize what information the service is asking for. Otherwise, you'll have to enter the log-on information in the exact order it is asked for by each service. One service may ask for your password and then your account number, and another may ask for this information in reverse order. "Smart" software will provide the appropriate information in response to the service's prompts.

Auto log-on can save you much time and effort because you won't have to remember or look up phone numbers, passwords, or account numbers in order to access the service. Also, auto log-on is a must if you're performing unattended, after-hour searches.

(Note: Be sure that your passwords and account numbers aren't available to unauthorized personnel. It's usually a rather simple matter to read this information stored on the disk.)

Autosearch. The macros (instructions) used to automatically log onto a service may be expanded into intricate command files that actually perform a search. With stored macros you can repeat searches from your workstation instead of having the on-line service do it with an SDI. Although it may take you several hours to design a complex search procedure, you will ultimately save both personnel and on-line time if you let the computer conduct routine searches automatically.

Command mode. In the command mode, you can instruct the computer and the modem to perform such functions as DIAL a phone number, SAVE a file to disk, or PRINT a message on the printer. Commands are not data and are not transmitted to the remote party. You may be able to select commands from a menu (a list of choices) or you may have to type them in. For example, Lync and Crosstalk XVI recognize commands after you press the ESCAPE key: Pressing ESCAPE and typing < DIR B > will display the disk directory (table of contents) for the data disk in B drive. Or, pressing ESCAPE and typing < TYPE FILENAME > will display your stored text file on the screen. The number and types of commands available vary considerably from program to program. Some of the command functions you'll want to look for are the ability to look at either disk directory, to look at a file, to change data disks, to turn the printer on and off, to use DOS (disk operating system) commands, to change communications parameters, and to reprogram function keys.

Help. Many software packages offer HELP when you type < HELP > or type a command after HELP. For example, < HELP SAVE. > Sometimes the screen will tell you to press a function key for help, like FUNCTION 1. In response, the definition for the software command or a help menu will appear on the screen to assist you. The program should also display the definitions for various function keys, such as BREAK, COMMAND MODE, and so forth. Computerized help will save you costly time while you're on-line.

Gateway software may not only help you with software documentation but may also offer information about the on-line provider itself. (See below gateway software.)

Status line. The status line keeps you informed of information you'll need during transmission. It should display the elapsed time since you logged onto the service and what percentage of a file being transmitted has been sent or received. Error messages should inform you if blocks of information are being resent due to poor connections or telephone line noise. The status line should also tell you if the printer is turned on or off. This may sound silly since you can see if the printer is printing, but it may not be so obvious if you're using a printer buffer that can send the printer previously received information while the computer is doing something else. (The buffer receives the information at a rapid rate and forwards it to the slower printer as it can print. Chapter 9 explains more about printer buffers.)

Status screen. At any time, you should be able to view your current communication parameters or defaults: for example, baud, parity, communications port, stop bits, and data bits. You should have the flexibility of resetting your parameters and redefining your function keys, even while you're on-line. (See the discussion of communication protocol later in this chapter.)

Upload. The software should allow you to send text files to the remote computer: for example, a letter you wrote with your word processor and stored on your data disk. A number of programs—for example, Lync and Crosstalk XVI—allow you to send more than one file by issuing a simple command. You could send all of the letters stored on your disk by pressing ESCAPE and typing <SEND *.LTR>. This command would send all of the files with the file name extension <.LTR>. (The asterisk is a wild card, which stands for any combination of characters—in this case, any file name.) *Multiple file transmission* capabilities are especially useful for electronic mail applications. The software should alert you with a screen status display and with a bell when the file transfer is complete or when there's a transmission problem. (See also the discussion of error checking below.)

Download. This feature allows you to receive files from the remote computer. Be cautious of programs that only allow you to receive the information in RAM (Random Access Memory) or on your printer. If the file is very large, you may run out of memory and lose some of the information. Better packages will let you automatically store incoming information onto the data disk. Make sure you have the option of turning your printer on or off during the download process.

Retrocapture. The retrocapture feature allows you to view and/or save previously viewed data to your disk. For example, Source Link, PFS:ACCESS, and Crosstalk XVI will let you capture (save) a series of news bulletins you just finished reading on the screen. Many software packages will store downloaded text into a memory buffer. Even after you've signed off of the service, you can display the buffer contents, print the data, and/or download it to disk.

Throughput. The actual data transmission speed is called throughput. Because of error-checking procedures, mainframe delays, and other factors, throughput won't average 300 or 1200 bits per second. Throughput during file transfers may be improved by using more efficient error-checking procedures (see below) and by data compression.

For example, TRANSEND software *compresses* the data enough to improve throughput by 15 to 30 percent. Data *encryption* methods used for security may increase file size and adversely affect throughput.

Error checking. When you transfer data to or from a service, you want to be certain there are no errors. A number of different systems have been developed to ensure that transmitted data are correct. To work, both computers must use the same error-checking procedure. Since the XMODEM error-checking protocol is in the public domain (free), it is used by many on-line systems, including electronic mail and computer bulletin boards. Kermit, a popular error-checking procedure developed by Columbia University, was designed to work with the UNIX operating system.

XMODEM (or MODEM 7) sends the file in 128–byte (128–character) blocks. At the end of each block, the sending computer calculates and sends a *checksum* byte. The receiving computer also calculates the checksum and compares the figure to the checksum received. If the checksums match, the receiving computer sends an ACK (acknowledge) signal which tells the sending computer to transmit the next 128–byte block. If the checksums don't match, the receiving computer sends a NAK signal and the block is retransmitted. The block will be retransmitted a preset number of times, after which the program will notify you that the connection is too poor to continue. Sometimes you can reduce the baud rate and overcome noisy line problems. If the telephone line is too noisy, you may want to redial the service and begin again.

The pause required for sending the checksum is relatively short, approximately one tenth of a second. At 300 baud it takes approximately four to five seconds to send the 128–byte block, so one tenth of a second is relatively insignificant. However, as faster modems enter the scene, the percentages aren't as good. For instance, a 2,400 bps modem sends 128 bytes eight times as fast or in less than a half a second. Now one tenth of a second occupies 20 percent of the transmission time. In response to this problem, software developers have implemented different error-checking methods.

One method increases the size of each block to reduce the number of verification pauses; ASCOM software allows you to increase the block size to up to 512 characters (one fourth as many checksum pauses). This works well unless you have to retransmit blocks, since resending a 512–byte block will take four times as long as resending a 128–byte block.

Third generation communications software has taken a different tack. BLAST from Communications Research Group and Relay from VM Personal Computing don't pause between sending blocks. They take advantage of *true full duplex* mode and send the verifying checksums while the transmitting computer is still sending data. This procedure works because the modem is quite capable of sending and receiving data simultaneously. If a checksum doesn't match, the affected block will be retransmitted later. Bidirectional file transfer will become more popular with the proliferation of high-speed modems.

A number of companies offer their own error-checking techniques. However, you can only use these procedures if you're communicating with a computer using the same software.

Printer control. If you don't have a printer buffer or a fast printer, the printer may reduce the speed at which your computer can accept information from the service. You will be "printer bound." To avoid this inconvenience, some people download information to disk and print later. (See also the section on buffers in Chapter 9.)

When you first log onto a service you may wish to turn the printer on to record sign-on messages, special bulletins, instructions, and menus. Later you can refer to these printouts instead of returning to and rereading menus on-line. Your software should allow you to turn the printer on and off as needed.

Keyboard programming. Some communication packages allow you to redefine the functions of various keys and combination of keys. For example, Crosstalk XVI lets you change the key used for sending the BREAK signal as well as redefine any of the function keys to include text, commands, and control characters. For example, you might define F6 to toggle the PRINTER ON/OFF or F4 to include your sign-on information. If your communications software doesn't offer this flexibility, you may wish to consider using a *keyboard utility* such as ProKey and SuperKey. For example, ProKey allows you to define up to 300 function keys when used in combination with unshifted, shifted, CONTROL, and ALTERNATE keys. The definitions (macros) for each function key may be as long as 12,000 characters. And you can redefine a key while you're connected on-line. The key definitions may contain text, commands, time delays, and the names of other macros. The definition file may be viewed and edited with ProKey's commands or with a word processor in the non-document mode. RAM–resident keyboard utility programs run transparently in the background.

Keyboard utilities are particularly useful for standardizing commands between a variety of programs. So if the text editor for your communications package uses the CONTROL–X command to delete the character to the right of the cursor and your word processor uses CONTROL–G, you can change CONTROL–X to CONTROL–G. In essence, you tell the utility program that when you press CONTROL–G, it should send a CONTROL–X command signal to the telecommunications program. The communications package text editor will appear to be operating with the word processing commands you're most familiar with.

Keyboard utilities help you enter automatic log-on sequences; for example, you may define function 1 as your password, function 2 as your account number, and so on. As the on-line service makes these inquiries, you simply press the function key instead of typing in the full answer.

Security and encryption. Make sure that your password and account numbers cannot be read from your communications software disk. Although most programs don't display your password on the screen as you send it to the remote service (or as it's sent by the automatic log-on file), the information is readily available to anyone looking at the log-on file stored on your disk. Locking the disk in a cabinet may be the only practical way to secure this information.

Also, you may wish to encrypt sensitive messages before they're sent on public or internal electronic mail systems. A few communications software packages like PFS: ACCESS provide encryption capabilities. However, you may have to use a separate utility program for coding and decoding. Separate encryption/decryption software has an added advantage that coding and decoding are performed before delivering the data to the in-house electronic mail service for outside transmission. SuperKey will encrypt files before they are transferred. It will also lock your keyboard so it's tamperproof, and after a specified time lapse, it will turn your monitor off to prevent images from burning into the screen phosphor. SuperKey's features are particularly useful for unattended computer operations.

PIC Privacy from MCTel, Inc., illustrated in Figure 8–2, is an encryption/decryption program that you run before transmitting a file. Since all encrypted characters are printable, they won't interfere with electronic mail protocol. In addition, PIC Privacy inserts a carriage return/line-feed every 65 characters and automatically removes control characters, another electronic mail requirement. The disadvantage to using PIC Privacy is that it increases the file size by about 50 percent, which will increase the transmission time and the number of characters (bytes) transmitted. The electronic mail costs and long-distance connect times will increase proportionally.

PIC Privacy also provides an interesting program utility called PURGE, which permanently erases a file from your

---

FIGURE 8–2   PIC Privacy Encrypts Files to Maintain Security on Public Electronic Mail Systems

---

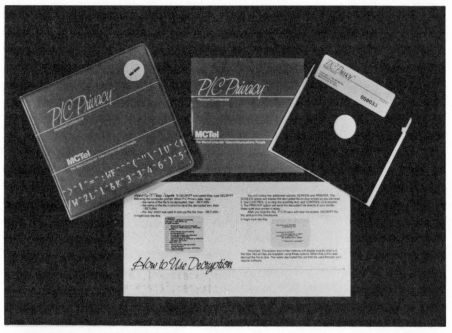

SOURCE: Courtesy of MCTel, Inc.

disk. When you use the disk-operating system ERASE command the computer doesn't actually ablate the data on the disk. In fact, there are utility programs designed to restore files accidentally erased in this manner. However, PURGE overcomes this security shortcoming by first writing data over the file and then erasing it. The original file can never be recovered.

Gateway software. Many professional quality, on-line services are difficult to learn and cumbersome to use. So many software companies have developed telecommunications packages that provide a "friendly" interface between the user and the database service. These packages allow the user to enter a search statement written in "plain English." The software then translates the statement into the cryptic codes required by the specific on-line service. Gateway software is especially valuable for training new users and for helping infrequent users who haven't mastered search procedures. Gateway software tends to be rather expensive ($300–$500) and usually can only be used to access one database or one supermarket service. For example, Naturallink from Texas Instruments can only be used to access data from Dow Jones News/Retrieval.

When you're selecting gateway software, you should look for a program that is easy to use and has cost and time-saving features. As in Figure 8–3, In-Search uses menus to help you preprogram your search strategy before accessing Dialog. The program "knows" what databases are available on Dialog. Therefore, without having to resort to the Dialog manual, you can formulate a search strategy that will work once you log on. This will obviously save connect-time charges.

Instead of using menus, experienced searchers may want the option of directly entering commands. They'll want a gateway package that is flexible enough to utilize their knowledge, that offers *less* help, and that utilizes all of the on-line service's search capabilities.

Sometimes gateway software is bundled with auxiliary software that allows you to manipulate downloaded data: for example, stock market analysis, word processing, or database management programs. Winning on Wall Street from SUMMA Software Corporation, shown in Figure 8–4, will download data from Dow Jones News/Retrieval or Dial/Data (Remote Computing Corporation) and create a database on selected

FIGURE 8-3 In-Search Gateway Software Provides Menus to Access Dialog

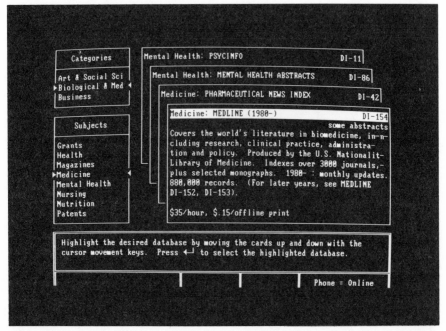

Menlo Corporation's In-Search software uses a "card catalog" presentation of over 200 on-line databases. A user identifies the most appropriate database for the search by scrolling through general categories, subjects, and detailed descriptions of individual databases.
SOURCE: Courtesy of Menlo Corporation.

stocks and securities. Winning On Wall Street's auxiliary programs let you print graphic and tabular displays, perform technical analyses, perform bookkeeping chores, and write reports. Other gateway packages include Sci-Mate Universal Online Searcher, microDISCLOSURE, and Search Helper. Make sure these auxiliary programs are as effective as the stand-alone programs you're used to, or they may be frustrating to use.

Ideally, the telecommunications software should be capable of downloading the data into a powerful, stand-alone software package such as WordStar, SuperCalc or dBASE III. (See also integrated packages discussion below.)

Integrated packages. Many of the new multifunction software packages include telecommunications software. Decision Manager from Peachtree Software comes with a word

FIGURE 8–4 Winning on Wall Street Analyzes
Downloaded Stock Market Data

SOURCE: Courtesy of TM Summa Software Group.

processor, spreadsheet, data manager, business graphics program, micro/mainframe link, and telecommunications program. Ashton-Tate's Framework, The Software Group's Enable, and Lotus's Symphony offer similar features. Many of these programs may be used to manipulate data before uploading or after downloading. Since you generally don't get something for nothing, you cannot expect a $700 integrated package to offer communications software (or other applications) with the sophistication of individual programs costing from $300 to $500 each.

Text editing. You may want a telecommunications package with a built-in text editor or rudimentary word processor so you can prepare electronic mail, edit downloaded information for distribution, and write search strategies. TRANSEND 2, Smartcom II, and ASCII PRO all offer built-in text editors.

Terminal emulation. A number of communications packages link with mainframe computers and on-line services by

FIGURE 8–5   PC/InterComm Emulates the DEC
VT–100

SOURCE: Courtesy of Mark of the Unicorn.

making the personal computer act like a terminal. In essence, the software tells the personal computer how to behave like a standard terminal. Crosstalk XVI can emulate the DEC VT–100, the IBM 3101, and Televideo 900; PC/InterComm (shown in Figure 8–5) and BLAST can emulate the DEC VT–100 terminal. Software companies specify emulation capabilities in their literature.

Communication protocol. The software must be capable of "speaking" the same code (communication parameters) as the remote computer. Some software must be preset with the communication parameters, some can be readjusted after logging on, and others can automatically adjust to match the remote computer's parameters. If the parameters are preset, the computer invokes the appropriate protocol each time you dial that service. Less intelligent packages cannot "remember" the parameters for each service, so you'll have to manually set them each time you log on. I'd avoid buying software that must be reset each time.

A rather technical discussion of the different communication parameters, including baud, word length, and parity, follows. You don't need to remember the details because the on-line service manual and your software user's manual will tell you how to set the parameters.

Baud is the commonly used term representing the speed of data transmission. The more accurate measure is bits per second (bps). A bit is a single signal representing a one or zero in the binary code that personal computers operate with. It takes roughly 10 ones and zeroes to represent one character (a number, letter or punctuation mark). The most commonly used transmission rates are 300 and 1200 bps. 2400 bps is becoming more popular, especially for data and electronic mail communications. 300 bps send approximately 30 characters per second, 1200 bps send approximately 120 characters per second, and 2400 bps send approximately 240 characters per second.

Data or word length refers to the number of bits (ones and zeroes) required to represent one character. Actually, the ASCII code used by personal computers requires only seven ones and zeroes to represent each character (often called a byte). However, some computer systems use eight bits. When these signals are traveling single file over the telephone line, the remote computer needs to know how to tell when each character starts and stops—that is, it must be able to recognize the character boundaries. So, before transmission a *start bit* and a *stop bit* are added to each character. Some error-checking procedures also add a *parity* bit used to perform checksums. (See discussion of parity bit below.) So the seven- or eight-bit word length is extended at least three more bits by the time it leaves the modem. (*Note:* Received data must have these extra bits stripped off before they can be utilized by the computer's processor.)

Parity bit is the extra one or zero added to each character (byte) for performing error-checking procedures. The parity bit is added to each binary character (byte) so as to make the total number of ones in the character either an even or odd number. Thus we speak of even or no (odd) parity. If the remote computer is "looking" for even parity and spots a byte with odd parity (an odd number of ones), it "knows" that a transmission error occurred. The remote computer will request that the block of data be retransmitted. (See also the discussion of error checking.)

Break key. Most remote computers allow you to tell them to stop. If by accident you tell the remote computer to download 5,000 abstracts at 25 cents each instead of only 1985's 200 abstracts, when you detect your error you can press a BREAK key (a key defined by the software) to tell the remote computer to stop downloading. The BREAK key actually causes a momentary cessation in the modem carrier signal. The length of this signal break must be very precise. If the BREAK signal is too short, the remote computer will not sense it, and if the signal break is too long, the remote computer will think you've hung up. Each on-line service's documentation will tell you which key sequence it recognizes as a BREAK key.

Unattended operation. Software that at a predetermined time can dial, log on, perform a preprogrammed search, and log off may offer unique cost-saving opportunities. Often on-line services offer lower rates after peak hours. Additional savings may be gained when usage is low, because the remote mainframe responds faster. Unattended operations offered by software such as Smartcom II (see Figure 8–6) and Lync may be just what you need.

If you have both the manual and the software, make sure that the procedures work. Sometimes the manual will omit steps or contain inaccuracies. A simple mistake like telling you to back your program disk up with the PC DOS command < COPY*.* > may cause grief. The correct command puts a space between the word COPY and the first asterisk:

FIGURE 8-6 Hayes Smartcom II Communications Software

SOURCE: Courtesy of Hayes Microcomputer Products, Inc.

<COPY *.*>. A few frustrations like this discourage even the best-intentioned newcomer.

Cost/purchasing considerations. The generally accepted copyright practice is that one software package may be used on one computer by one operator at a time. So if your operation requires three computers with three operators who may all be on-line simultaneously, you should buy three licensed software copies. Find out what extra copies of the software and manual cost. Sometimes you can get sizable discounts for multiple-user operations. If you plan to install the software on a hard-disk computer system, make sure the software is designed to work in that environment. If you purchase different brands of software packages for different users, you'll have to support each user with training and technical help. Standardizing software and hardware between work stations may be helpful.

Check with several vendors before writing the purchase order. You'll find that prices and services vary considerably.

Modem self test. Some software packages will run a diagnostic routine to see if the modem is functioning properly and if you have a reliable transmission connection. Both Smartcom II and Lync offer this feature.

Tutorials. Some software companies provide computer-aided instruction programs, audiotapes, and videotapes for training users. Naturallink from Texas Instruments comes with a built-in computerized tutorial. Gateway programs, in effect, train the novice by leading him or her through menu-driven steps. Some manuals will have a special tutorial section that gives step-by-step examples for set-up, dialing, and log-on procedures. Find out what type of training support the software provides and if there are additional charges for training aids.

Documentation. Request the manuals before buying the software. You may have to pay $10 to $35 for them but it will be worth it. When evaluating the manuals, keep in mind the expertise of the people who will be using them. If they are computer novices, the manual must explain *everything*. Even simple statements like "boot the computer" may confuse the novice. Make sure that the manual is well organized, logically divided, and adequately indexed. Being able to find information quickly is a big plus. Illustrations and examples should show the user how procedures work. If the manual is printed in two colors to highlight important information, that's also a plus. A quick-reference command summary is essential for the user at any level.

SUMMARY

Selecting and purchasing the "right" communications software is complex and time-consuming. I encourage you to read the reviews in Appendix A of this book, to read magazine reviews, to write for software manufacturers' literature and manuals, and to talk to other on-line searchers before buying. If possible, watch a demonstration and use the software yourself. Read the manuals to be sure they're relevant for your end-user. Most of all, make sure that the software satisfies the needs identified in your needs analysis.

9

How to Buy
Telecommunications Hardware

The telecommunications workstation may be as simple as a "dumb" terminal with a communications keyboard and a built-in matrix printer. When it's connected via common phone lines to the on-line service, the remote computer system senses the terminal as one of its own. For the past 10 years, special librarians have been accessing on-line services with this relatively primitive equipment. Clinging to dumb terminals, however, is equivalent to using the old mechanical typewriter instead of opting for the modern word processor.

The personal computer telecommunications workstation promises many more capabilities than those offered by terminals. As you've already learned in the telecommunications software chapter, you can automatically log onto the database system, preprogram a complex search, upload previously written information, and download and store retrieved material. In addition, you can print a hard copy of the information and/or forward it through an internal electronic mail network. With a personal computer you can manipulate downloaded data with word processors, database managers, spreadsheets, and statistical analysis programs.

In this chapter, you'll find out what kind of equipment supports the general-purpose personal computer telecommunications workstation. And you'll learn how to select the equipment best suited to your application.

Basically, you need a personal computer with either two floppy-disk drives or a hard disk drive for information storage. You also need a modem to communicate with the telephone system and a printer to produce typewritten copies of retrieved information. You can purchase the entire system for as little as $1,500. For another $1,000 you can even get letter-quality printing and one of the sophisticated software packages discussed in Chapter 8. Considering the added capabilities, these prices compare quite favorably with the cost of dumb terminals. (*Note:* Some on-line services only support certain hardware and software: for example, NEXIS and LEXIS from Mead Data. Before buying, check with the services you plan to access.)

THE ADVANTAGES OF PERSONAL COMPUTER WORKSTATIONS

Many librarians and terminal users question the necessity of a personal computer when terminals have sufficed. To answer this question, I'd like to point out some of the major advantages of using a personal computer for accessing on-line database services:

1. *Automatic log-on simplifies and speeds up initial contact with the database service.* The personal computer can automatically dial the on-line service, redial a busy number, and change to and dial an alternate number without any user supervision. Once the modem establishes connection with the remote system, the personal computer can automatically enter codes, passwords, and account numbers as well as perform other "handshaking" operations to establish communication with the database service. With software support, an unattended computer can even log on at a preset time and perform the search automatically.

2. *Automatic uploading of search parameters saves connect-time charges.* Usually it takes an experienced searcher to prepare a complete search strategy prior to logging on. However, using predesigned searches will usually save connect-time charges. Automatic searching is especially helpful when requesting a long list of patent numbers, for example. Rather than using the connect time to manually type in the patent numbers, the list can be prepared before logging on and then uploaded at 1200 bits per second to the system. Gateway software packages like In-Search will even help the searcher pre-

pare the search off-line. (See the section on gateway software in Chapter 8.)

3. *Electronic storage of downloaded information allows the user to manipulate the data with other software programs, including spreadsheets, database managers, word processors, and statistical analysis packages.* This feature is particularly useful for manipulating numeric information. Dow Jones Spreadsheet Link helps you analyze downloaded financial data with Lotus 1-2-3, Multiplan, or Visicalc. The program automatically connects you to Dow Jones News/ Retrieval, collects the information you want, and enters it directly into your spreadsheet. Downloaded files can also be edited by most word processing software. Instead of having to retype downloaded information into newsletter-styled summaries, you can merely edit and reformat the material to fit your company requirements. And downloaded bibliographic information can be incorporated into a company's computerized card catalog. The possibilities are endless. However, take care not to violate copyright laws and on-line service policies. (See Chapter 11 for a discussion of copyright issues.)

4. *Uploading data files to electronic mail services saves connect time and allows the user to utilize efficient word processing software.* You can use your personal computer's word processor to prepare correspondence and reports for transmission via electronic mail services. The prepared information is stored on the personal computer's floppy or hard disk. Once connected to the electronic mail service, these files are transmitted at 120 or 240 characters per second—far faster than you can type. Incoming mail can be downloaded and saved to the disk, and after disconnecting from the service, they can be read, edited, or printed. If the company has an in-house electronic mail system, incoming mail can be electronically forwarded through that network.

5. *A general-purpose personal computer justifies its expense better than a dedicated terminal.* The dedicated communications terminal will perform only one function. However, when the personal computer isn't engaged in telecommunication tasks, it may be used in a number of other ways, including word processing, database management, task management, spreadsheet analysis, trend analysis, and report preparation.

WHICH PERSONAL COMPUTER IS BEST?

The Hardware Must Work with the Software

If you've already purchased a communications software package, you'll have to buy a computer system that will run that software. Fortunately most software has several versions available for the popular hardware/operating system configurations, including IBM PC, IBM AT, Apple Macintosh, Apple II, CP/M, and MS–DOS compatibles. Venture outside these well-established areas and you'll severely limit your software choices.

Standardize Computer Hardware Throughout the Organization

Almost any personal computer can connect to and communicate with an on-line service, even an Atari or a Commodore. They do it every day. However, before buying the computer system, you'll want to consider what other personal computers are being used in the company. If the company uses "compatible" computers throughout the organization, the transfer of data between workstations will be greatly facilitated. For instance, a data disk prepared on a computer in the marketing department can be slipped into a "compatible" telecommunications computer for transmission to an electronic mail system. Likewise, downloaded data can be forwarded via disk transfer from the telecommunications computer to the finance division. The telecommunications system should serve the most commonly used computer system. (Note: Because of the differences in serial port configurations, many communications software and hardware packages are not as transportable between "compatibles" as other programs. In a way, the compatibility of telecommunications software is the acid test.)

"Compatible" computers must use the same operating system (PC–DOS, CP/M, etc.) and have the same floppy-disk size and format, so disks can be easily exchanged between machines. Sticking an IBM PC 5¼–inch disk into a so-called IBM PC–compatible Hewlett-Packard 150 that takes 3–inch disks is a bit difficult. And, a 5½–inch Apple disk can't be read by an IBM PC. It isn't enough to be IBM- or Apple-compatible, you must be machine specific: IBM AT–compatible or Apple Macintosh–compatible. Even within one brand, not all disks and software packages can be used interchangeably.

If the telecommunications personal computer is "compatible" with other systems throughout the organization, you'll have much greater flexibility; you may be able to get volume price reductions, and you will get better service arrangements. Also, by standardizing equipment, the company can better support personal computer users with training and technical assistance.

Two Disk Drives Are Better than One

I recommend getting two disk drives so your programs can reside on one drive and your data files on the second. This will give you maximum capacity for downloading without concern for filling up your data disk.

Serial and Parallel Ports

The computer must have a *serial port* (RS–232C) to connect to an external modem and preferably a *parallel port* to connect to the printer. (Internally installed modems don't require a serial port. Modems, printers, and ports are discussed in more detail later in this chapter.)

Monitor

The screen should be an amber or green monochrome capable of displaying 80–column-wide text. A word-processing quality screen will be easier and less tiring to read.

Keyboards

If you require heavy numerical input, you'll want a *keyboard* with a *numeric keypad*. A keyboard with *function keys* will simplify certain operations by allowing the user to press a single function key instead of a complex sequence of keys. One function key might be "programmed" to enter your password and account number, saving a dozen or more keystrokes. (See also the discussion of keyboard utilities in Chapter 8.)

Service Contracts

Some companies don't buy service contracts on personal computers because solid-state devices are quite reliable. However, since disk drives and printers are mechanical, you may wish to cover them with a service or maintenance policy.

Probably any personal computer with at least two disk drives or a hard disk drive will serve your basic telecommunications needs. However, by matching it to your software needs and to other personal computer applications throughout the company, you can increase its utilization and your flexibility.

WHICH PRINTER IS BEST?

The printer must be compatible with both the computer and the telecommunications software you choose. Many software packages provide an installation procedure which allows you to designate which port (plug) the printer is connected to and which model and brand of printer you're using. If in the software installation procedures the printer you want isn't listed as an option, you may have difficulty using that printer.

Most printers are designed to work with the IBM PC and its compatibles: some are Epson, Okidata, Juki, C. Itoh, Diablo, Brothers, and Texas Instruments. Some computers, such as Apple and Commodore, may require special interfaces (circuits), software, and cables to work with "standard" printers. Even then, the printer may not work at its full capacity.

Printers may be connected to your computer through a serial or parallel port. The most common method (and usually the least expensive method) is through the parallel port. This works quite nicely since the external modem connects to the serial port. Most telecommunications software packages are set up for this type of computer/printer/modem port configuration.

For those with technical curiosity, in *serial* transmission data travels single file through one wire from the computer to the printer. That is, each bit (the signal representing a binary one or zero) travels sequentially through the wire. In *parallel* transmission, eight bits (one character or byte) travel simultaneously through eight wires. Thus one character at a time travels from the computer to the printer. Parallel transmission is potentially much faster; however, few printers can actually take advantage of this transmission speed. (See the discussion of printer buffers below.)

The best proof that a software package will work with your computer, modem, and printer is to see them working together.

There are basically two types of printers: matrix and letter-quality. The *matrix printer* prints a pattern of dots that form individual characters. The dots may be formed by tiny hammers striking a ribbon *(impact printer)*, by tiny wires heating up and discoloring heat-sensitive paper *(thermal printer)*, or by tiny jets of ink squirting onto the paper *(ink jet printer)*. Only the impact printers can produce carbon copies, but they tend to be noisy. Thermal printers are inexpensive and almost silent, but, the heat-sensitive paper can be odd-sized, expensive, hard to find, and messy. And, in time the image tends to fade. Ink jet printers are silent, but, at this time the image tends to blur (a situation which seems to be improving with the use of special paper).

Matrix printers tend to be less expensive and faster than letter-quality printers. However, double-striking and other image-enhancing techniques, substantially slow down matrix printers. In the dot matrix (draft or data processing) mode, matrix printers range in speed from 120 to 180 characters per second. In the almost letter-quality (double-strike) mode, they average 40 characters per second. Matrix printers offer a wide range of printing techniques, including underlining, bold, compressed (up to 17 characters per inch), expanded (up to 5 characters per inch), super/subscripts, graphics printing, multiple fonts. Some matrix printers like the Texas Instruments Omni 855 produce letter-quality images and offer a choice of several fonts (type styles). Popular dot matrix printers include Epson, Okidata, C.Itoh's Prowriter, Gemini, Texas Instruments, and Mannesman Talley.

Letter-quality printers produce typewriter-quality characters. The *daisywheel* print head resembles a daisy with petals radiating from a solid center. At the end of each spoke you'll see a raised character. In operation, the daisywheel spins at a very high speed. A single hammer strikes the "petals" to produce the typewritten text. A few electronic typewriters use

FIGURE 9–1   Juki 6300 Daisywheel Printer

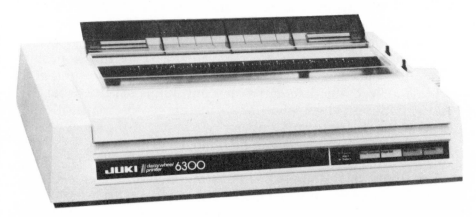

Juki's new Model 6300 daisywheel printer provides letter-quality printing at a fast 40 charac-
ters per second! At under 60 dBA, it's quiet . . . and at under a thousand dollars, it's reasona-
bly priced, too.
SOURCE: Courtesy of Juki Office Machine Corp.

this same technique. Instead of daisywheels, some letter-quality printers use balls (like the IBM Selectric typewriter) or thimbles (elongated balls) covered with alphanumeric characters.

Since most letter-quality printers are impact printers, like the Juki shown in Figure 9–1, they will produce carbon copies. Different fonts may be selected by changing the daisywheel, ball, or thimble. The noise levels vary considerably depending on sound dampening techniques used by the manufacturer. Letter-quality printers tend to be much slower than their dot matrix counterparts, ranging from 12 to 45 characters per second. Underlining and bold print slow letter-quality printers down considerably. Popular letter-quality printer manufacturers include Diablo, Brothers, Juki, C.Itoh, and IBM.

The methods used to move the paper through the print mechanism include pin feed, tractor feed, and friction feed.

The *pin-feed* mechanism is similar to that used to move film through a 35-mm camera. The continuous feed paper, bordered by thin strips of hole-punched paper, matches the sprockets on the pin-feed mechanism which holds the paper in line. Most pin-feed mechanisms are not adjustable to different paper widths. The pin-feed printer may not have a roller (as in a typewriter), so smaller or individual sheets of paper such as company letterhead, index cards, and package labels cannot be inserted into the printer.

Tractor-feed mechanisms perform the same function as the pin feed; they are also usually adjustable to different widths to accommodate narrower, continuous mailing labels. As with the pin feed, the tractor maintains the registration needed for multiple strike operations and mailing label production. Usually tractors can be removed or bypassed so you can use friction feed to print on letterhead, envelopes, and other single sheets. One advantage of a tractor or pin feed is that the operating printer may be left unattended for periods of time without concern that the paper may crawl from side to side.

Friction feed squeezes the paper between a roller and the printer body. As with ordinary typewriters, twisting the roller moves the paper past the print head. With most friction-feed mechanisms the paper tends to crawl both back and forth and up and down, losing the correct margins.

Telecommunication workstations are served well by matrix printers that range in price from $300 to $1,000, averaging $400. If you require a carriage able to produce more than 80 columns of print at 10 characters per inch (pica type size), the cost will be substantially higher.

The matrix printer is usually fast enough to keep up with the transmission from the on-line service. At 1200 bps, the computer receives approximately 120 characters per second; a typical matrix printer can print 160 characters per second. If the end-user requires printing quality better than draft, reprinting the material in the double-strike mode should be adequate. (*Note:* 2400 bps modems will probably transfer data faster than the printer can operate.)

If you require letter-quality print, consider these options: (1) You can use a letter-quality printer to print from information downloaded to disk; (2) you can use a faster matrix printer on-line and a letter-quality printer off-line; (3) you can use a *printer buffer* to store the information until the slower letter-quality printer can catch up. Waiting for a slow printer will increase your connect-time charges as well as your frustration level.

The *buffer* is a memory device that retains the information and feeds it to the printer as it is able to accept it. Some printers offer (optional) internal buffers to serve this purpose. Stand-alone buffers are installed between the computer and the printer. You'll want a large buffer so your computer will not become printer bound (to slow down throughput to wait for the slower printer). Buffer memory capacity is measured in Ks (kilobytes). 1K is equal to approximately 1,000 characters or 200 words (one double-spaced page). I recommend a 32K or 64K buffer for most applications. The buffer will also come in handy during other printing operations since once the computer has sent all the data to the buffer, you can use the computer for other jobs. The buffer and printer perform their tasks independently of the computer.

Since printers are mechanical devices, they tend to require more service than solid-state computers. Some companies purchase service contracts on printers even though they don't on personal computers. Your decision depends to some extent on the original cost of the unit and the projected use. Your best "insurance" may be a spare printer.

A multitude of inexpensive printers are available for personal computers. Based on your needs for print quality, speed, and durability, you should be able to locate the right printer for the right price. You may also wish to consider a tractor-feed mechanism so the printer can operate unattended.

WHAT MODEM IS BEST?

A *modem* (modulator/demodulator) is a device that converts (modulates) the computer's data signals into a form that can be transmitted through common telephone lines. On the receiving end, a modem converts (demodulates) the telephone signal into a form the computer can understand. The two computers may be sitting next to each other, or they may be thousands of miles apart. An *external modem* (stand-alone modem) connects to the personal computer through a serial (RS–232C) port. The Visionary 1200 stand-alone modem is shown in Figure 9–2. An *internal modem* is installed inside the computer housing. Figure 9–4 is a photograph of the Racal-Vadic VA212PAR internal modem. (See the discussion of ports in printer section above.)

The *direct-connect* external modem connects to the tele-

FIGURE 9–2   The VISIONARY 1200 Stand-Alone
1200 bps Modem from Visionary
Electronics

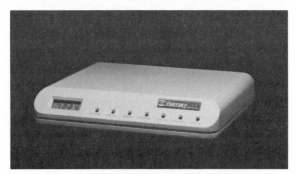

SOURCE: **Courtesy of Visionary Electronics Inc.**

FIGURE 9–3   The Radio Shack TRS–80 Acoustic Modem

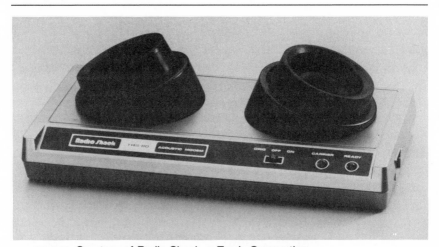

SOURCE: **Courtesy of Radio Shack, a Tandy Corporation.**

phone system with a wire and a modular plug. The modem
electronically generates and transmits the signals. In contrast, the *acoustic* external modem converts signals to sounds
or tones that are detected by a standard telephone handset
mouthpiece. Figure 9–3 presents the Radio Shack TRS–80
Acoustic Modem. Although acoustic modems have rubber

FIGURE 9-4   The Racal-Vadic VA212PAR Internal 300/1200 bps Modem

SOURCE: **Courtesy of Gamma Technology Inc.**

cups that seal the phone headset to the modem, environmental noise may interfere with and disrupt data transmission. In the past, acoustic modems were less expensive than direct-connect modems. However, the price gap has diminished considerably.

Internal (direct-connect) modems are plugged into slots (connectors) located inside the computer. *Modem boards* or *cards,* as they are sometimes called, must be specifically designed for a particular computer model. A modem card for an Apple II will not fit or operate in an IBM PC. Before buying an internal modem, make sure your computer has an open slot (an unused plug) into which you can install the card. Internal modems are frequently less expensive than their external counterparts. Personally, with internal modems I miss being able to see the external modem status lights, which reassure me that transmissions are proceeding normally.

The communications software package (discussed in Chapter 8) sends instructions to the modem. The software package and the modem must be compatible for all features of each to be utilized: for example, auto-dial, auto-answer, auto-redial, and auto-protocol selection. The installation procedures for the software should list the modem you plan to use. If the modem isn't supported, you may run into difficulty (Note: Some modems, like the Paradyne, have built-in communications software.)

The most common transmission rates used by personal computers are 300 and 1200 bps (30 and 120 characters per second). The relatively inexpensive 2400 bits per second (bps) modems entering the market will soon promote more on-line services to offer this faster rate. Better 2400 bps modems like Hayes and Racal-Vadic will automatically fall back to a slower transmission speed if they develop communications difficulties. Easylink, Dow Jones News/Retrieval, Delphi and News-Net already offer 2400 bps service.

Rates up to 12,000 bits per second are feasible; however, it will be a few years before ultrahigh-speed modems become commonplace. The main advantage of faster communication rates is that more information can be transmitted in less time. This technology is a must if we are eventually to receive graphics and video images such as photographs and animated, television-like transmissions.

Since most companies use touch-tone dialing, the modem should support this service. Most users will want a direct-connect modem with auto-dial (and perhaps auto-answer) capabilities. The auto-dial modem allows you to dial a number from the keyboard and to have a number dialed automatically under software control. Depending on your software, you can type the command <DIAL MCI>, or you may select MCI from a menu of dialing choices. The computer then sends dialing instructions to the modem. On an external modem, a carrier-detection indicator (LED) will tell you when you've connected with the on-line service. Some modems have speakers that allow you to monitor the activity on the line; for example, you can hear a busy signal or a puzzled party dialed by mistake.

If you plan to use a multi-line telephone, you may need special switching capabilities to connect your modem to the phone system. For example, the EasyCom/1 from Computer Business Solutions, shown in Figure 9–5, is a simple switch that connects to the telephone via the headset modular plug.

FIGURE 9-5   EasyCom/1 from Computer Business Solutions

SOURCE: Courtesy of Computer Business Solutions.

The headset and the modem are both plugged into the Easy-Com/1 module. Flipping the switch one way or the other connects and disconnects each peripheral.

The industry modem standard has been set by Hayes, so you'll hear many claims from manufacturers that their modem is "Hayes compatible." These claims must be taken with a grain of salt—as should claims about computer compatibility, such as IBM PC compatibility. When you're selecting a modem, make sure that it's recognized in the installation procedures for your software package. If the modem is listed, it should work.

Hayes modems tend to be more expensive than their clones. 300/1200 bps modems cost from $250 to $700 and 2400 bps modems run from $700 up. Popular modem manufacturers include Hayes, Anchor Automation, Novation, U.S. Robotics, Multitech Systems, Universal Data Systems, and Racal-Vadic.

THE ADVANTAGES OF STANDARDIZATION

Whatever software or hardware configurations you choose, purchase the same ones for *all* telecommunications workstations. I suggest this for several reasons:

1. You can use the same vendor and get a volume discount.
2. If something fails, you can use a spare.
3. You can send everyone to the same training program.
4. Searchers can help one another with problems and questions.
5. Your equipment will all use the same supplies.
6. You can buy a maintenance agreement for all equipment from the same vendor.

Some people may object to standardization, but it will pay off handsomely in the long run.

SUMMARY

Three pieces of equipment are required for a personal computer telecommunications workstation: a personal computer, a printer, and a modem. Almost any personal computer and modem will communicate with the on-line services. However, there are many factors to consider in your selection: (1) the equipment must support the software you selected in Chapter 8, and (2) the equipment should be compatible with equipment used elsewhere in the company. Standardization will enhance your ability to exchange software, disks, and data between computers. In addition, the company can provide better support for training and maintenance.

10

Planning and Designing Search Strategies

Throughout this book, you've caught glimpses of what it's like to log onto a database service and perform a search. This chapter will acquaint you with some of the preparation, strategies, and procedures for retrieving information. When you've finished this chapter, you won't know how to log onto a service and perform a search because, unfortunately, no two services use the same procedures for retrieval. Only by studying a particular service's manual and/or attending training classes will you be able to learn the skills needed to retrieve on-line information.

It takes years of study and experience to learn what the best sources are for finding information—either on-line or hard copy. Learning search conventions and techniques requires additional skill and practice. It's important for you to remember that when you've performed a search, YOU HAVE NOT SEARCHED THE WORLD'S LITERATURE. If you don't find what you're looking for, try new keywords, try a different database, and try different search parameters to broaden or narrow the scope.

This chapter will acquaint you with the preparation you'll need prior to logging on and performing the search, and with some of the concepts used when searching most databases.

LEARN HOW TO USE YOUR
TELECOMMUNICATIONS SOFTWARE

If you haven't become thoroughly familiar with the telecommunications software you plan to use, do so before you ever
log onto an on-line service. Since during practice sessions
you don't want to pay $8 or more per hour for long distance
service plus on-line charges averaging $40 per hour, you'll
want to practice on a FREE database service. You can find
free services in almost any city. Many computer clubs, computer hobbyists, and computer stores run computer bulletin
boards which are absolutely free.

A bulletin board is a personal computer connected to an
auto-answer modem and the telephone line. The bulletin
board software (BBS) allows callers to read messages left on
the bulletin board, leave messages for other users, upload
(send) text files, upload public domain programs, and download (retrieve) public domain programs. You simply command your telecommunications program to dial the bulletin
board, and once you've logged on, follow the instructions.
Depending on the board, you may need a password to access
the message base. Some clubs require you to join before
they'll issue you a password. Usually the membership fee is
only $10 to $20 per year.

Most bulletin boards operate at 300 baud, and many operate at 1200 bits per second. If possible, contact the bulletin
board systems operator (sysop) before logging on. The sysop
will give you a password and tell you what communications
parameters the board uses: for example, 1200–N–8–1 meaning 1200 bps, No parity bits, 8 data bits, and 1 stop bit. Once
you know the correct settings, you can experiment with your
software's automatic log-on features. Enter the auto-dial telephone number, the communication parameters, and your
password according to the instructions in the software manual. Now you're ready to dial the bulletin board and see if
your automatic log-on file (script) works.

If you can't get the communication parameters in advance, once you log on, you can change your parameters to
match. In fact, this is a good opportunity to operate "on the
fly" as it were. You'll get a taste for the frustration you can
feel while fumbling to get your computer to "talk" with the

bulletin board. You'll find yourself flipping through manual pages, pressing HELP keys, and experimenting with different options. Fortunately, it isn't costing you anything. And there's nothing like experience to teach you the ropes.

Practice with several bulletin board systems to learn the many ways these on-line systems ask for information. Practice with your software until you're comfortable with transferring files, looking at your disk directories, downloading to disk, turning your printer on and off, and editing your text files.

Once you're familiar with your local bulletin boards, you may wish to log onto an inexpensive and relatively simple service such as MCI Mail. Since MCI Mail's long-distance charges are 15 cents per minute or less, you can get some inexpensive training while learning to use their electronic mail system. The MCI Mail commands are relatively easy to remember and use. Try sending a few letters to business associates or even to yourself.

Of course, if you're using a special, database-specific software package, such as In-Search designed to access Dialog, you won't be able to practice with bulletin boards. Many specialized packages, however, do have computer tutorials that simulate on-line search sessions. Practice with the tutorials before logging onto the services.

Most services will give you free or discounted time when you first sign up. Some software packages contain coupons or offers for discounted on-line service as well. Take advantage of these offers during your break-in period.

JOIN AN ON-LINE USER'S GROUP

Your community may have a group of on-line database users who meet regularly to discuss the field. Support groups can lend a helping hand with hardware, software, and on-line database information. You'll have someone to call if you get into a jam or if you want a reference about a specific product. The group may also be able to take advantage of volume discounts on floppy diskettes, and other supplies.

Check with local computer clubs, with the public library, and with the special library association to see if such a group exists. If your community doesn't have one, you may wish to form one.

PREPARE FOR YOUR SEARCH

The next sections will tell you how to prepare for an on-line search. First you need to define the problem you're trying to solve. Then you need to decide what type of information will help you with that problem: perhaps statistical data, magazine articles, or news releases. Once you have a clear idea of your goals, then you can examine the individual databases to determine where you are most likely to find the information you need. Having decided on a database service, you'll be able to formulate the exact search strategy (command statements) required to access the information. Although the steps I've outlined for preparing a search appear to be logical, you may not perform them in this exact order. For example, you may define the problem, look at your database resources, and then define the output and steps to obtain it. Experienced searchers simply sit down in front of the computer and sign on. At first, though, you may need to approach the task with a bit more structure.

DEFINE THE PROBLEM (INPUT)

A good problem definition will save you frustration and expensive on-line time. Not only do you need to know what keywords you might use, but also what your ultimate goal is—that is, what the big picture is.

Let's say you want to research letter-quality printers for use in your on-line operation. The purpose of your search might be stated as follows:

1. To locate overview articles on purchasing letter-quality printers used with personal computers.
2. To locate product review articles on specific letter-quality printers, including Juki, Diablo, Brothers, IBM, Texas Instruments, and others identified in #1 above.
3. To locate information on the use of letter-quality printers in on-line search operations.
4. To locate information on stand-alone personal computer printer buffers.

In contrast, let's state the problem from the point of view of an engineer who's developing a letter-quality printer design:

1. To locate all patents on letter-quality printers used with personal computers.
2. To identify all companies making letter-quality printers for personal computers.
3. To locate product review articles on specific letter-quality printers, including Juki, Diablo, Brothers, IBM, Texas Instruments, and others identified in #2 above.
4. To locate manufacturers and suppliers for printer parts, including printed circuit boards, rollers, dip switches, and membrane switches, and so forth.

As you can see, the purpose of the search will significantly influence the type of information you seek and the database(s) you'll search. A general observation shows that while managers want overviews and summaries, engineers want THE answer, or proof that they're correct, and research scientists want ALL the information available.

DEFINE THE RESULTS (OUTPUT)

If you have a retrieval plan before logging on, you'll save yourself time and money. You will want to determine the need for statistical reports, bibliographies, abstracts, and/or full text, for example. At first, you may wish to view only bibliographic information. At that time you may choose to log off to study the list. Later you can reenter the system to retrieve specific abstracts, retrieve full-text articles, or order document copies.

You'll also want to consider an overall plan for performing your on-line search:

What will you do if you get no "hits"? What if you get hundreds of hits?

Are you going to print the bibliography and log off to study it? Or, are you going to stay on-line and perform the document retrieval right away?

How soon do you need the information? Will you print the information or request an off-line printout?

Are you going to save your search strategy on-line so you can perform the search again? Or are you going to save your search strategy in an SDI so the service will automatically run it?

Have you memorized or written down all the software and database search commands you'll need?

How much money are you willing to spend?

If you've already answered these and other questions to your satisfaction, you're ready to begin designing the search steps. If you haven't answered these questions, do so before proceeding further.

STUDY THE ON-LINE SERVICE

Examine the Database Contents

Your first task will be selecting the database that will most likely have the information you're looking for. For example, does NEXIS or Dow Jones News/Retrieval contain the magazines and news sources covering your topic of interest? Does the service offer full text or only abstracts? Supermarket services provide brief descriptions of each database they offer. If you want detailed information, request manuals and materials directly from the database producer.

You can learn more about the database contents by studying the *thesaurus* or *controlled vocabulary* allowed for searching it. The thesaurus is similar to an index of terms you can use to find information in a book. When you design your search strategy, you'll need to know what terms the on-line computer can recognize and look for. If you don't find the terms you need in a written thesaurus or in the on-line thesaurus, you'd better consider searching a different database. I recommend that new users begin with a database with a thesaurus or with a full-text database like NEXIS. Once you've become familiar with the art of searching, you may wish to venture into more nebulous grounds.

If the database doesn't have full-text search or a thesaurus, you'll just have to experiment. You may want to refer to a lexicon (a topic-specific dictionary) or a book of synonyms for alternative wording. And you may want to study a few articles covering the topic you plan to search. By examining these works you'll discover the "keywords" that might be used in titles and in abstracts of articles on your topic. If you were researching personal computer printers, you might find terms such as matrix, dot matrix, letter-quality, typewriter quality, and daisywheel.

Learn the On-Line Service Commands

The searching task requires that you not only master your own software commands for uploading and downloading, but also that you master the on-line system commands. Switching from one on-line system to another adds even more confusion. (You'll learn more about the system commands later in this chapter.)

If the service and/or your company offer a training program, attend it. Many services provide free training to heavy users. If you don't have access to a training program, you may wish to perform your first searches together with an experienced searcher.

Prior to logging on, you should read the manuals, newsletters, and other documentation provided by the database vendor. You must be thoroughly familiar with both the on-line procedures and the commands required to operate the remote computer system. The following MCI Mail commands are very simple compared to the more abstract and cryptic commands used by many on-line services, but they'll give you an idea of what a command does:

CREATE: Originate an MCI Mail message.

FIND: Find if someone is an MCI Mail subscriber.

READ: Read your messages one by one.

SEND: Post (transmit) an MCI Mail message.

Perhaps the most important commands for you to learn are BREAK and the sign-off message. BREAK tells the remote computer to stop executing your last command; for example, stop printing 5,000 full-text articles. As you can see, BREAK is quite essential. Also, you need to know how to stop their meter from ticking. Since different services offer any number of sign-off commands, including BYE, QUIT, STOP, LOGOFF, and END; it's essential to know when it's appropriate to use what command. At first, you'll experience a steep learning curve. If you intend to use a major supermarket service, plan on spending 8 to 10 hours in supervised classroom or tutorial training and many more hours of on-line practice. You'll never stop learning, because database services never stop changing. Most experienced searchers find it's a full-time job just keeping up with two major supermarket services such as Dialog and SDC Orbit.

Infrequent users find keeping up their skills even more difficult. Usually infrequent users do best by accessing more user-friendly systems, such as the menu-driven portions of Dow Jones News/Retrieval, The Source, NEXIS, and Compu-Serve.

A BRIEF INTRODUCTION TO SEARCH STRATEGY DESIGN

The on-line service computer software offer a number of powerful tools for performing your search, including Boolean logic operators, positional operators, occurrence tables, and SIC codes. Their implementation may vary from system to system, so this discussion is designed only to introduce you to how these features can improve your search tactics.

Boolean Logic

Boolean logic operators let you combine keywords to focus the search on the precise information you need. For example, the Boolean operators on Dialog are AND, OR, and NOT. The following examples illustrate how you can formulate your search strategy using these operators:

PRINTER *AND* MATRIX = *both* PRINTER and MATRIX must be true; that is, you'll find only citations mentioning both terms.

PRINTER *OR* MATRIX = *either* PRINTER or MATRIX must be true; that is, you'll find citations mentioning either term.

PRINTER *NOT* MATRIX = you'll find all occurrences of PRINTER except those where MATRIX is mentioned.

If you use the keywords PRINTER AND MATRIX, you may omit a number of generalized articles such as "How to Buy a Printer" or "Printer Prices Hit All-Time Lows." However, these two parameters will zero right in on an article titled "Matrix Printers: How to Choose the Right One for You."

PRINTER OR MATRIX is more general and will find all of the article titles just mentioned. In addition, you'll locate an article titled, "Letter-Quality Printers for Your Office." You may pay too high a price if you choose this search strategy. A really good use for the OR operator might be to link synonyms: for example, HORSE OR MUSTANG OR EQUINE. By linking synonyms you'll avoid losing important data because you chose a search term slightly different from that used by the author or abstractor.

NOT can be used to omit unwanted data. If you want to research registered or purebred horses, you could search for HORSE OR EQUINE NOT MUSTANG. This will delete citations that make reference to the wild mustangs.

Truncation and Wild Card Characters

You can also *truncate* key words to avoid missing their varied forms. Dialog uses a question mark (?), BRS a dollar sign ($), and NEXIS an exclamation point (!) to indicate a truncated word. For example, you may want to search for any word beginning with the prefix "infertil-", including such terms as infertility and infertile. You could do this by searching on NEXIS for <INFERTIL!>, on Dialog for <INFERTIL?>, and on BRS for <INFERTIL$>. The wild card symbols (!, ? or $) stand for the missing characters. [*Note:* The PC–DOS operating system uses the asterisk (*) wild card character in a similar manner.] You can also insert wild card characters to avoid misspelling words; for example, on NEXIS you can search for <NIN*TY> if you forget whether or not this word has an "e" in it.

Proximity (Positional) Operators

When you search abstracts and full-text articles, you may want to refine your search with positional operators. That is, you'll want to look at the position of one term relative to that of another. Let's say you wish to search for any reference to RONALD REAGAN within 10 words of MARGARET THATCHER. The odds are pretty good that articles meeting this criterion will discuss the relationship of the United States and Great Britain.

The proximity operator for BRS is ADJ for adjacent, while Dialog uses W for with. You could find articles on Apple computers by asking for APPLE(W)COMPUTER or APPLE ADJ COMPUTER.

BRS also utilizes AND, WITH, and SAME as proximity operators. AND means find the document if the two terms occur anywhere in the document. SAME means find the document if the two terms occur in the same subparagraph in the document. WITH means find the document if the two terms occur in the same sentence. BRS also uses NOT; however, NOT may unduly restrict retrieval.

SIC Codes and Other Classification Systems

In 1972, the U.S. Office of Management and Budget developed SIC (Standard Industrial Classification) codes to classify all economic activity. In 1977, a few minor revisions were made. The code created 11 major divisions (the first digit in the code) and 99 major groups (the second digit in the code). Additional digits represented individual groups (third digit), industry categories (fourth digit), and product classes (fifth, sixth, and seventh digits). This standardized, hierarchical code provides a good base for comparing many companies.

SIC codes are especially useful for finding competing companies for marketing, financial, and statistical studies. Over 30 databases loaded on Dialog use some form of SIC codes.

In the time since the SIC codes were created, many new industries have developed, including the on-line information industry and personal computer industry. Therefore, if a database uses the SIC codes to classify companies, it must invent new codes to fill in the gaps. For this reason, a company may be listed under one code in one database and under another code in a different database. Conglomerates and companies with diverse product lines are often difficult to classify.

There's no financial incentive for database producers to standardize codes. To use SIC codes as a controlled vocabulary, you must study the specific coding system used by the database you intend to search. To improve the consistency of coding across databases, sometimes you can truncate SIC codes. You'll sacrifice precision, though. Many database producers advise using SIC codes with other terms in a proximity or Boolean search statement.

Other codes are also used by databases. Disclosure II uses

the Dun & Bradstreet code developed for the Market Identifier 10 + database. Electronic Yellow Pages and Predicasts ARA (Annual Reports Abstracts) also use in-house developed codes.

WHEN TO SEARCH ABSTRACTS (OR FULL TEXT)

There are a number of ways to search for the information held in databases. For example, you can search for an article title, for keywords in article titles, for the first author's name (multiple authors usually are not retrievable), for keywords in the abstract, and, when available, for keywords in the full text. Since titles may not include the keyword(s) you're looking for, especially in proximity to other limiting words, you may have better success searching abstracts and full text. Searching abstracts will usually be faster (and less expensive) than searching the more massive, full-text database. The advantages to searching abstracts (and also full text) include the following:

1. *Searching abstracts gives the ability to search for terms, events, proper names, and companies not listed in the controlled vocabulary (thesaurus).* Let's say you want to find all news releases mentioning the current governor of Oklahoma. It's unlikely that his or her name will appear in the database thesaurus. Also, it may be difficult to locate all references to the governor by only searching article titles. But the article abstract will probably mention the governor's name if it appears in a substantive way.

2. *Searching abstracts gives the ability to identify all articles with a common theme.* As opposed to the controlled vocabulary used to find information in article titles, abstracts are likely to include a small number of common terms in all similar records. Since these terms reflect the same concepts, you will be able to find all articles on a given topic.

3. *Searching abstracts gives the ability to find current topics or topics that use jargon.* Since the controlled vocabulary probably will not contain references to very current issues and to jargon, searching abstracts will be a more effective method for finding these types of topics. One caution about jargon: *acronyms* (letters which are pronounced like NABISCO,

AMOCO and RAM) and *initialisms* (letters spelled out like TV, SEC and AT&T) may have many different meanings. Always qualify them with a substantive word; for example, use RAM with MEMORY to avoid references to male goats, pickup trucks, football teams, and so forth. You may wish to keep an acronym dictionary handy.

4. *Searching abstracts gives the ability to find ALL references, even minor ones.* If the user wants to review every mention of the Juki 6300 daisywheel printer, searching the abstract (or full text) is the only way to insure some references aren't missed.

5. *Searching abstracts gives the ability to search for special subjects such as surveys, collections of events, and techniques.* These subjects are often poorly treated in titles. Only by searching through abstracts or full text can you be sure you've located these data.

6. *Searching abstracts gives the ability to search databases that don't have thesauri or that have thesauri that don't address the subject.* If you aren't sure of the indexing terms (keywords), then search the full text or abstracts.

CONDUCTING SPECIAL SEARCHES

Searching for Someone Else

If you're performing a search for someone else, you'll need to find out as much about the nature of the information needed as possible. You'll want to interview the requester to find out the purpose of the search, the urgency for the information, the search scope required, and suggested sources: for example, authors, journals, and specialized newsletters. You'll also want to find out if the requester wants foreign-language citations. The more you know about the subject, keywords, and use for the information, the better equipped you'll be to find relevant answers.

The Trend Analysis

Some people reason that the frequency of a term in the literature determines the level of interest in that topic. During years when environmental interests were high, many more articles appeared about acid rain, toxic wastes, and nuclear power than in years when people were concerned about other issues. Thus, by querying a database for the number of times a subject appears per year, you can determine the importance of that topic to societal groups. Some caution should be taken to ensure that the database didn't grossly change its composition over the years compared. Also, the searcher must take into account that the terminology referring to a topic may change with time; for instance in the past literature might refer to Negroes whereas today they are referred to as blacks.

Using Occurrence Tables

When you're searching full-text articles, you may want to find out how relevant that article is to your subject. One hit doesn't necessarily indicate the article will provide a wealth of information. In response to this need, some databases like BRS provide occurrence tables, which are in effect document-specific indexes. The occurrence table will identify specific fields and subparagraphs in which your keyword(s) appear. With this information, you can decide if you want to retrieve the entire article or only portions of it.

Using SDIs

The SDI (Selective Dissemination of Information) tells the database service to repeat your search each time the database is updated. You automatically receive an off-line printout of the new references.

Some searchers prefer to run their own SDIs by either storing their search strategy on the service's computer or by storing it on their own personal computer. In this way, when they repeat the search they can determine whether they're getting too much or too little information. Performing your own search updates gives you the option of changing search patterns or even changing databases.

DOCUMENT RETRIEVAL

Many people hesitate to use on-line services because most provide only bibliographic information. After selecting the articles comes the task of procuring the magazines, newspapers, and/or article copies. Unless you have access to an extensive library, you will have to order the documents or document copies.

Most on-line services provide on-line document retrieval services. That is, for a fee the on-line service (or a third party) will send you the copies you need. This service is fast but it's also expensive, costing as much as $12 to $15 per citation. If you aren't in that much of a hurry, there are also sources for acquiring information at lower costs.

Most librarians in public and special libraries are familiar with these resources, their prices, and the quality of their performances. The sources for documents include local public libraries (approximately 10 cents per page), distant public libraries (interlibrary loans), city and state university libraries (one or two week delay), document retrieval services (several days—and they use the university libraries), Library of Congress (one month), and associations. As a rule you'll get the fastest service from local public libraries, next-fastest from document retrieval services, and third-fastest from interlibrary loans. Associations are also a good source for documents. The *Encyclopedia of Associations* from Gale Research Co. in Detroit, Michigan is an excellent source for association information.

If the documents are printed in a foreign language, you may need to contact local translators. Quite often you can find translators at universities.

SUMMARY

This chapter has introduced you to a number of elements involved in planning and designing search strategies. Before you even consider logging onto the database service, you should become thoroughly familiar with the capabilities of your telecommunications software. Practicing on free local bulletin boards is an inexpensive way to learn uploading and downloading techniques.

The first step in performing a search is defining the problem or input you'll make to the database computer system. You'll also want to define your desired results or output from the database. Only when you are thoroughly familiar with the database procedures, commands, and contents, will you be able to economically retrieve the information you seek.

This chapter has also acquainted you with some of the tactics searchers use, including Boolean logic operators, truncation, proximity operators, and SIC codes. The pros and cons of searching bibliographic data, abstracts, and full-text were also discussed.

11

What's in the Future?

So far on-line database services have only scratched the surface in their attempts to penetrate the market. Statistics indicate that on-line usage is increasing at 35 percent per year. As marketing analysts identify more and more applications, as the growing outside sales forces sell the problem-solving potential, and as competition increases, this figure will climb exponentially. Advances in telecommunications, changes in pricing strategy, expansion into foreign markets, and the proliferation of the personal computer in the corporate workplace will all contribute to the industry's success.

This chapter explores the influence that these and other factors will have on the growth and development of the on-line service industry.

Greater Utilization by Industries and Specialties

The "natural" markets for on-line database information include broadcasting, advertising, public relations, investment banking, law enforcement, and government intelligence. In fact, when the full-text database NEXIS first came on-line, the Secret Service, Department of Defense, and Internal Revenue Service soon became their largest subscribers. Ironically, many heavy on-line users resell their information at a substantial markup to corporations that wonder, "Where do they find out all of this stuff?"

Within corporations, selected groups took early advantage of on-line services. Lawyers use services like Mead Data's LEXIS to research cases and to ensure that the company adheres to regulations and laws. Long-range planners analyze economic indicators, examine industry trends, and study the competition. Corporate development specialists use on-line information to study mergers, acquisitions, and investments. Investor relations professionals log on to keep abreast of the corporate image and to monitor broker relations. Daily, controllers and treasurers tap into databases to learn foreign exchange rates, stock market information, and comparative information for debt management.

Other specialties are getting in on the act. Public relations firms use services like NEXIS and Dow Jones News/Retrieval to research speech writing assignments. They research materials for publishing house organs, as well. On-line generated briefings prepare company representatives to visit foreign countries by educating them on the nation's economy, customs, and political environment.

Compliance directors research regulations, legislation, and standards. Safety managers use information like that provided by Hazardline to set standards and design emergency procedures. Government relations researchers keep up with legislative activity by using BILLCAST to determine the probability that bills will reach the House, to study political candidates, to analyze voting records, and to assess the status of issues before Congress.

Sales and marketing professionals use on-line information to develop plans, to study the competition, and to prepare advertising. On-line information will not only help identify potential customers but will also help familiarize the sales representative with the client before making the call. Prior to their first meeting, the sales representative can research such topics as the customer's credit rating, areas of expansion, new patents, and key executive names.

On-line services report that many of their customers won't disclose how they use the service because they want to maintain their competitive edge.

On-line services are expanding into foreign countries. Mead Data has offices in London, Paris, and Japan. Since the penetration of personal computers into the corporate environment trails that of the United States anywhere from one to five years, foreign markets are just beginning to flourish.

Higher Emphasis on Meeting Customer Needs

On-line information services will begin to change their focus from providing a full spectrum of information to *packaging solutions*. To help the customer get the entire answer to a problem or question, services will have to "walk users through the world of information." To accomplish this goal, the services will have to anticipate the many ways companies can utilize the information. Given this perspective, the services can plan what information to offer, how to organize the information, and how to present the information in a useful form.

Services are beginning to *organize information* into more relevant categories. For example, instead of listing database names such as Medical and Exchange, NEXIS introduced additional menus such as business, finance, government, news, and trade and technical. You'll also see the introduction of more electronic clipping services like Mead's ECLIPSE, which highlights important news items every day.

Full-text databases such as *The Wall Street Journal*, NEXIS, and LEXIS will become the standard. You'll no longer be limited to bibliographical references and abstracts. Declining costs for data storage and the introduction of faster and less expensive data input have accelerated the availability of full text. Now many database providers send updates to the service via telecommunications lines or magnetic tape. Electronic data transfer not only increases the rate of putting data on-line but saves a great deal of work.

Friendly access will be another industry trend. Gateway software and better on-line system software will provide the user with a number of "intelligent" aids. Even now some systems correct the user's typing and spelling errors. Within the next three to five years, artificial intelligence will allow you to enter your questions in ordinary English instead of having to master a cryptic code and syntax. The goal of on-line services is to make it possible for everyone to do their own searches. On-line services want the end-user to be as comfortable with dialing up information as they are with using the common telephone.

Competitive Pricing

Many on-line services are reexamining their price structures to accommodate high-speed modems and personal computer users. In the future, services will tend to charge more for answers rather than charging primarily for connect time. Mead Data reduced its charges for browsing through the system and increased its charges for information retrieval. Services don't want to discourage people from logging on and experimenting with the system. This is the way users learn and discover new applications for the information. Charging for solutions is not only more equitable to the service but also more meaningful to the end-user.

Flexible Guidelines for Screen-to-Disk Storage

Mention "downloading" to on-line providers and they cringe. This is probably similar to mentioning "copy machines" to book, magazine, and newspaper publishers.

Electronic publishers are the first to realize the advantages of retrieving digitized information. In fact, they'd like to sell users on the advantages of storing information on computer disk and manipulating it with software packages. They see a growing need for electronic transmission through company electronic mail networks as well.

At the same time, electronic publishers are troubled by this modern technology. In the past if 10 people wanted to retrieve today's top news stories, each person would log onto the system and print a copy of the report. If the company respected copyright laws, it would not reproduce and distribute this written report any more than it would copy an entire magazine. However, with a personal computer the company can retrieve and record the electronically coded information on disk, and then forward the news through the electronic mail system to anyone who wishes to see it.

Publishers realize that it doesn't make sense to repeatedly retrieve information, but, they want and deserve royalty payments for each "copy." The solution to this dilemma lies in an equitable agreement between database providers, on-line services, and end-users.

Current Copyright Restrictions

Now most contracts restrict the end-user from utilizing the full potential of the data. For example, in essence Mead Data's contract says that you can store electronic data for 30 days at the most, and then you must destroy the original data. You may not electronically search the recorded data to avoid logging onto the service. That is, you cannot use the FIND features of a database manager or word processor to locate specific items in the downloaded data file. You can print out the data and manually prepare indexes for the text.

Downloaded text may not be incorporated into documents used for resale or other commercial purposes. Text from TODAY (the *New York Times* On-line) cannot even be edited. So, forget printing a *New York Times* story in your company's customer newsletter. Simply giving credit for the source does not relieve your responsibility for copyright infringement any more than admitting you've stolen a car prevents you from being prosecuted. Before copyrighted information can be distributed to multiple users, the text must be completely rewritten to avoid copyright infringement. Many of these restrictions are not applicable to public domain information such as court case documents stored in LEXIS.

Services such as Dow Jones News/Retrieval have a more liberal perspective. In fact, they even provide software to help investors analyze downloaded stock market information. But I doubt they'd approve of blatant copying of text from *The Wall Street Journal.*

Check your contract to determine what policies and practices the on-line service you use recommends. If you have concerns or questions, talk to their representatives. Your feedback may help them formulate new policies which are more relevant to end-user applications.

Alternate Distribution Methods

Along with traditional data transfer techniques, on-line services will support remote on-site databases by supplying data on optical discs. An "electronic loose-leaf service" will allow users to search through and manipulate the information without incurring on-line and telecommunications charges. This service will be particularly useful for analyzing historical information: for example, conducting a five-year performance study for corporations in the chemical industry. Since these users don't require the most up-to-date stock quotes or market information, they don't really benefit from instant on-line information.

Advances in Telecommunications Technology

The Integrated Services Digital Network (ISDN) universal protocol converter promises to expand worldwide telecommunications at an unprecedented rate. Terrestrial fiber optic communications is growing at a tremendous pace with the result that long-distance services are becoming less expensive and more reliable.

In the near future we're going to see inexpensive teleconferencing, voice and data integration, facsimile transfers, interactive video, and graphics. On-line services will be able to support real-time conferencing, in which a number of people can view written reports on computer screens while discussing them over the telephone. Patent information will be accompanied by drawings and illustrations. Facsimile transfers will replace many postal services. Interactive video will allow people to buy and sell products from electronic catalogs. And advertisers will help defray the costs of on-line services to end-users.

SUMMARY

Even though it's a billion dollar industry, and it developed in the 1960s, the on-line industry is still in its infancy. It has barely penetrated 5 percent of the market. With recent advances in mainframe data storage and telecommunications, and with the incorporation of personal computers into the workplace, the industry expects to expand and develop at unprecedented rates. You'll see more full-text databases, an increased exchange between foreign countries, specialization to provide solutions, the use of artificial intelligence to make access easier, more competitive pricing, better sales and service support, and user agreements that provide for electronic manipulation and retransmission of downloaded data.

Within a few years the companies and managers that haven't taken advantage of these possibilities will fall behind. As one manager aptly put it, "It's amazing how often I use my personal computer for on-line information retrieval; and, it's amazing how many people have information within 15 feet of them and don't know it."

PART TWO

Appendixes

APPENDIX A
On-Line Services in Review

A–1 Mead Data Central—NEXIS

DATABASE NAME: NEXIS

VENDOR/PROVIDER NAME: Mead Data Central

ADDRESS: 9393 Springboro Pike, P.O. Box 933

CITY, STATE, ZIP: Dayton, OH 45401

TELEPHONE: 513-865-6800

CARRIERS/TOLL–FREE LINES: MeadNet, Telenet, WATS

COMPATIBILITY:

  HARDWARE: IBM PC, XT, AT, PCjr, and 3270
                IBM Displaywriter and 3101 terminal
                Wang PC, AT&T PC 6300, Compaq, NCR PC 4, NBI 4100, and ITTxtra
                Apple IIe, IIc, III, Macintosh
                DEC VT–100/220 terminal, TeleVideo 924/950
                FREE customized LEXIS/NEXIS Terminal (UBIQ)

  SOFTWARE: Communications Session Manager (Mead)
                Crosstalk XVI (Microstuf)

GENERAL DESCRIPTION:

NEXIS's goal is to provide up-to-date financial and business information that managers need to make decisions. Many NEXIS databases are cover-to-cover and full text: for example, the *New York Times*. Some of the specialized databases may contain selective coverage, full text, cover-to-cover abstracts, or selective abstracts. (See descriptions below.)

NEXIS contains nearly 20 million documents (more than 87 billion characters) from more than 130 foreign and domestic newspapers, magazines, professional and trade journals, newsletters, and wire services—and approximately one billion characters per month are being added. In 1983 NEXIS incorporated the full text of the *New York Times* and *New York Times* Information to provide a popular library of abstracts from major publications.

The *NEW YORK TIMES* contains the full text of the *New York Times,* including news stories, feature articles, editorial page items and columns, letters to the editor, articles from all special sections, main news summary of the day, business digests of the day, corporate and bank earnings reports, and Votes in Congress. This database extends back to June 1, 1980 and is updated daily. Complete editions are added within 24 to 48 hours of publication.

ADVERTISING & MARKETING INTELLIGENCE (AMI) keeps you up to date on key changes in the marketplace including new products, product safety, test marketing, market research, consumer behavior, and FTC, FCC, and FDA regulations. AMI consists of 125,000 selected article abstracts from more than 60 trade and professional journals since September 1979.

DEADLINE DATA ON WORLD AFFAIRS contains geopolitical data on the 50 states, over 250 countries of the world, Canadian provinces and territories, and major world intergovernmental organizations. Profiles of each country include population statistics, economic data, health care, transportation, communication, embassies, culture, descriptions of armed forces, government, political parties, and more. World organizations include the Arab League, Comecon, European Communities, International Monetary Fund, NATO, OPEC, Organization of African Unity, Organization of American States, and the United Nations.

THE INFORMATION BANK, prepared by the New York Times Company, contains over 2 million selected abstracts from 60 newspapers, magazines, scientific and financial periodicals. The database contains salient facts on current affairs, business, economic, social and political information since 1969. Approximately 15,000 items are added each month. The editorial page and business section of the New York Times are added within 24 hours of publication. Other abstracts are gathered from the Chicago Tribune, Christian Science Monitor, Los Angeles Times, Washington Post, Advertising Age, Barron's, Business Week, Forbes, Fortune, Harvard Business Review, The Wall Street Journal, Foreign Affairs, Science, the Atlantic Monthly, the New Yorker, Time, and the Washington Monthly.

TODAY provides concise summaries of today's news in three capsulized reports. The News Summary, available each morning at approximately 9 A.M. Eastern time, is a condensation of the top international, national, and metropolitan New

York news stories from the morning *New York Times.* The Business News Summary, also available at 9 A.M., highlights news of companies, international business, litigation, regulation, and the markets. The Business News Update available at 2 P.M. Eastern time is a more comprehensive business news summary taken from a variety of sources in addition to the *New York Times.*

NEXIS also provides access to instant newswire information including such services as Associated Press (AP), Business Wire, KYODO, PR Newswire, and United Press International (UPI). Most of these files extend back five or more years.

GOVDOC (Government Documents) contains text from The Federal Register, Code of Federal Regulations, Federal Reserve Bulletin, as well as a weekly compilation of Presidential Documents.

ECLIPSE (Electronic CLIPping SErvice) keeps you up to date on any topic you choose from NEXIS, EXCHANGE, and LEXPAT. The ECLIPSE service automatically conducts searches of your choice on a daily, weekly, or monthly basis, printing only the updated materials since the last report.

NEXIS also offers LEXPAT, which provides the full text of U.S. patents issued since 1975. The database is expanding at a rate of 70,000 patents each year. In cooperation with the American Institute of Certified Public Accountants, NAARS, the National Automated Accounting Research System, was introduced to provide annual reports, proxy information and authoritative pronouncements of the AICPA, FASB, and SEC on 20,000 annual reports.

NEXIS added THE REFERENCE SERVICE to provide The Aerospace Database, BIOSIS (Biosciences Information Services), ABI/Inform, Management Contents, BILLCAST, and Hazardline. In addition, THE REFERENCE SERVICE provides BMA (Bank Marketing Association), DOE (Department of Energy) Bibliographic File, INDASO (Industry Data Sources), NTIS (National Technical Information Service), AMPOL (Almanac of American Politics), DDWA (Deadline Data On World Affairs), EXPERT (Forensic Services Directory), FORBAD (Forbes Annual Directory), FRIP (Federal Research In Progress), and WORLD (World Information).

For full-text research reports on companies, industries, and national economies, NEXIS provides the EXCHANGE International database produced by major financial services including Merrill Lynch, ABECOR, Paine Webber, Argus Research, Drexel Burnham Lambert, and Yamaichi Research Institute. Hundreds of analyses of smaller U.S. companies with the potential for development are also included. In addition, the EXCHANGE's EARN service reports on what Wall Street is saying about the consensus earnings estimates for over 3,000 U.S. corporations. The full text of 10-K and 10-Q filings from the Securities and Exchange Commission are incorporated within 24 to 48 hours of their filing.

COMMENTS:

For the very latest news, no service even approaches the timeliness and completeness of NEXIS. Many NEXIS services are updated within 24 to 48 hours of the publication. Even though the service is expensive, having full-text articles at your fingertips will ultimately save you time and money. You won't have to mess with going to the library or with waiting for expensive document retrieval services to respond to an order.

Full-text searches are also convenient and easy to construct. You aren't restricted to keywords or to an index of terms. For example, I decided to do a search regarding my next project, a book on infertility. So I entered < INFERTIL! > and NEXIS quickly searched the entire text database to inform me there were 208 articles on-line. Not wanting to view that many, I restricted the search by asking for dates after 1984. NEXIS quickly reported it had 11 stories. The first search cost $15, and the narrowing search cost an additional $3. At this point, I hadn't actually seen a word of text. My connect time was accumulating at $20 per hour, and my telecommunication charges at $8 per hour.

Now I could choose to see bibliographic references, the full articles, or the text within a given number of words of the search term. A CITE search will display a list of bibliographic references for the retrieved documents. A KWIC search will show the highlighted keyword in a 25–word window on either side of the term. A VAR QUIK search will allow me to vary the size of the window from 1 to 999 words. With a simple command you can shuttle back and forth between full text and the KWIC format.

If I'd known ahead how to search for my topic, I could have entered the entire search string at once:

< NEXIS;PAPERS;INFERTIL! AND DATE AFT 1984 >

If I'd been looking for a particular author's byline, I could have entered < LINDA PRE/2 CHRISTIE >. This would find "Linda" within the previous two words of "Christie." That way, I'd also find "Linda Gail Christie."

The NEXIS UBIQ terminal makes searching much easier with keys labeled NEXT PAGE, PREV PAGE, TRANSMIT, ROLL UP, ROLL DOWN, FIRST PAGE, NEXT DOC, PREV DOC, and PRINT DOC. Although I didn't personally try the software Mead provides for the IBM PC, I understand that in essence it redefines the PC keyboard to perform many of the UBIQ functions. From examining the manual, I don't believe that at $225 this software package is nearly as versatile or powerful as Smartcom or Crosstalk. However, it will take some doing to configure third party programs to perform like the UBIQ terminal.

The occasional user will find NEXIS's $50 per month minimum too expensive. However, the heavy user will appreciate the convenience and speed of using a full-text database. Because of its user-friendliness, the manual is rather short. It does appear to cover most salient points in a clear, well-written style. A quick reference sheet highlights most of the terminal capabilities. Mead prides itself on quick customer service turnaround, and this is reflected by good reports from their customers.

NEXIS offers toll-free, 24-hour, year-round customer support. In addition, NEXIS provides a free 3-hour formal class, and local sales/service representatives will provide user assistance as needed.

A-2 Mead Data Central—LEXIS

DATABASE NAME: LEXIS

VENDOR/PROVIDER NAME: Mead Data Central

ADDRESS: 9393 Springboro Pike, P.O. Box 933

CITY, STATE, ZIP: Dayton, OH 45401

TELEPHONE: 513-865-6800

CARRIERS/TOLL–FREE LINES: MeadNet, Telenet, WATS

COMPATIBILITY:

HARDWARE: IBM PC, XT, AT, PCjr, and 3270
IBM Displaywriter and 3101 terminal
Wang PC, AT&T PC 6300, Compaq, NCR PC 4, NBI 4100, and ITTxtra
Apple IIe, IIc, III, Macintosh
DEC VT–100/220 terminal, TeleVideo 924/950
FREE customized LEXIS/NEXIS Terminal (UBIQ)

SOFTWARE: Communications Session Manager (Mead)
Crosstalk XVI (Microstuf)

GENERAL DESCRIPTION:

LEXIS is the world's leading computer-assisted legal research tool. LEXIS contains major libraries of federal and state law, codes and regulations, and special libraries of law. With LEXIS you can search the full text of federal cases, the case law of all 50 states and Washington, D.C. as well as perform citation searches in Shepard's, Auto-Cite, or LEXIS itself. With the Federal Register, Encyclopaedia Britannica and Mead's general news and business information service NEXIS, you'll have all the information you need right in your office. (See also Appendix A–1 NEXIS.)

LEXIS offers a comprehensive collection of specialized law libraries including tax, securities, trade regulation, bankruptcy, communications, labor, public contracts law, Delaware Corporation Law, United Kingdom Law, French Law, and patent, trademark, and copyright law. Slip options are added shortly after receipt from the courts, so LEXIS is far more current than printed sources. The complete, original text is at your disposal so there is no third party to stand between you and the law as originally written.

LEXIS is also fast. The average search takes under 15 seconds and the average search session requires 15 minutes. You can locate cases or statutes that contain particular terms or phrases, that discuss the language contained in a standard contract, or that cite an earlier decision, statute, treatise, or article. Also you can locate a case by the name of a party, docket number, or other limited information. You can determine how federal circuit or district courts have applied U.S.

Supreme Court decisions in subsequent cases and identify opinions written by a particular judge or in which a particular counsel appeared. The variety of uses depends mainly on your own ingenuity.

Other LEXIS databases useful to the legal profession include The General Federal Library Files (GENFED), The Federal Tax Library Files (FEDTAX), Commerce Clearing House Library Files (CCH), The Federal Securities Library Files (FEDSEC), The Federal Trade Regulation Library Files (TRADE), The Federal Patent, Trademark (PATCOP), The Federal Communications Library Files (FEDCOM), The Federal Labor Library Files (LABOR), The Federal Bankruptcy Library Files (BAKRTCY), The Federal Public Contracts Library Files (PUBCON), The Admiralty Library Files (ADMRTY), The International Trade Library Files (ITRADE), The Military Justice Library Files (MILTRY), The Baldwin-United Library Files (BALDWIN), Delaware Corporation Law Library Files (DECORP), American Bar Association Library Files (ABA), Law Review Library Files (LAWREV), U.S. Patent and Trademark Office Library Files (LEXPAT), and Mathew Bender Library Files (BENDER).

LEXIS documents include STATES Library Files and STATE Library Files. UNITED KINGDOM LAW Library Files include English General Library Files (ENGGEN), United Kingdom Tax Library Files (UKTAX), English Industrial Library Files (ENGIND), United Kingdom Intellectual Property Library Files (UKIP), English Local Government Library Files (ENGLG), Admiralty Library Files (ADMRTY), and European Communities Library Files (EURCOM). The FRENCH LAW Library Files include Public Cases Library Files (PUBLIC), Private Cases Library Files (PRIV), Laws and Regulations Library Files (LOIREG), International Library Files (INTNAT), and Library Files (REVUES).

LEXPAT provides the full text of utility patents issued by the U.S. Patent and Trademark Office since 1975, and plant and design patents since 1976. You can search quickly through thousands of patents for a term, feature, or characteristic. Attorneys use LEXPAT for documenting the validity of a new or existing patent. Executives review LEXPAT to define the particulars about a patented product line, including who owns it and whether any similar patents have been issued.

The Encyclopaedia Britannica Library Files (EB) include

the Micropaedia, Macropaedia Book of the Year, Medical and Health Annual, and Science and the Future. With the exception of law schools, court and government agencies, and department libraries, personal computer users may not have access to these files due to downloading restrictions.

COMMENTS:
For the very latest in legal information, no service even approaches the timeliness and completeness LEXIS offers. Even though the service is expensive, having full text at your fingertips will ultimately save you time and money. You won't have to go to the library or wait for expensive document retrieval services to respond to an order.

Full text searches are also convenient and easy to construct. You aren't restricted to key words or to an index for terms. The glossary of index terms is as large as any standard legal reference.

The following illustrate frequently used search formats:

(1)   Finding a specific case—
      NAME (CONTAINER AND FRANCHISE)

This means find a case name containing both the terms "container" and "franchise."

(2)   Finding cases citing a specific case—
      CONTAINER W/15 FRANCHISE

This means find a case where the term "container" appears within 15 words of the term "franchise."

(3)   Finding decisions from a specific court—
      UNITARY BUSINESS AND COURT (2ND)

This means find a "Unitary Business" case for the 2nd Court.

Many other search parameters may be designed to locate data. With LEXIS you can check virtually any type of citation. Displaying the retrieved documents in the KWIC format (see NEXIS in Appendix A–1), allows you to see how the cited material is discussed within the context of the retrieved document.

You can automatically display Tax Analysts, Inc.'s TAX NOTES TODAY (TNT) by typing the file name TNT. TNT is an electronic tax service which provides comprehensive coverage of all federal tax developments including IRS letter rulings, tax-related correspondence between Treasury and Congress, comments on regulations from private practitioners, and reports on tax issues from Congress, federal agencies, and the private sector. By pressing the UBIQ terminal NEXT PAGE key, you can browse throughout the file document by document.

Searching LEXPAT is equally as easy. For example, you can find patents that discuss the use of artificial sweeteners in tooth paste by performing the following search:

ARTIFICIAL! OR SYNTHETIC! W/7 SWEET! W/30
TOOTH PASTE OR TOOTHPASTE

The wild card exclamation point allows you to find variations of the term: artificially, synthetics, sweeteners, and so forth. In addition, the two forms of the words "tooth paste" may be linked with the Boolean operator OR. The W/# proximity operator allows you to find these terms relative to their position in the full text.

If you already know a patent number, you can simply enter that number: PATNO = N,NNN,NNN. You can find all patents related to a certain company (assignee) by entering ASSIGNEE (XXXXXX).

The custom designed NEXIS UBIQ terminal makes searching much easier by providing keys labeled NEXT PAGE, PREV PAGE, TRANSMIT, ROLL UP, ROLL DOWN, FIRST PAGE, NEXT DOC, PREV DOC, and PRINT DOC. Although I didn't personally try the software Mead provides for the IBM PC, I understand that in essence it redefines the PC keyboard to perform many of these same functions. From examining the software manual, I don't believe that at $225 this communications package is nearly as versatile or powerful as Smartcom or Crosstalk. However, it will take some doing to configure third-party programs to perform like the UBIQ terminal.

The occasional user will find the $100 per month plus $10 per professional (up to 20) minimum too expensive. But the heavy user will appreciate the convenience and speed of using a full-text database. Because of LEXIS's user-friendliness, the manual is rather short. It appears to cover most salient points in a clear, well-written style. A quick reference sheet highlights most of the terminal capabilities.

Mead prides itself on quick customer service turnaround and this is reflected by good reports from their customers. Mead offers a toll-free, 24-hour, year-round customer service line. Training costs $75 per professional when the account is set up; afterwards training is free to new personnel. With the combination of the training course, Mead's personal sales and service representatives, the documentation, and the toll-free customer service, any serious user should be able to turn LEXIS into a powerful and profitable tool.

A–3 Dow Jones News/Retrieval

DATABASE NAME: Dow Jones News/Retrieval

VENDOR/PROVIDER NAME: Dow Jones & Company, Inc.

ADDRESS: P.O. Box 300

CITY, STATE, ZIP: Princeton, NJ 08540

TELEPHONE: 1-800-257-5114; New Jersey 609-452-1511

CARRIERS/TOLL–FREE LINES: Tymnet, Telenet, Uninet, Datapac (Canada)
DowNet (free service for limited cities)

COMPATIBILITY: Most standard time-sharing terminals and personal computers. Call 800-257-5114, in New Jersey 609-452-1511, for answers about a particular model. Modems must be compatible with Bell 103, 113, or 212A.

GENERAL DESCRIPTION:

Dow Jones News/Retrieval connects you with the most up-to-date financial and business news information available. In-depth coverage of companies, industries, the stock market and the economy will help you make many different types of monetary decisions; for example, you can track investments and industry trends, examine corporate histories, keep an eye on your competitors, study current legislation, analyze mergers, and keep track of current U.S. and world news. Figure A3–1 demonstrates the breadth of information offered by Dow Jones News/Retrieval.

The *Wall Street Journal* Highlights Online provides headlines and summaries of the major stories from *The Wall Street Journal's* front page, section 2 front page, editorial pages, the Heard on the Street column, and Abreast of the Market col-

FIGURE A3-1   Dow Jones News/Retrieval Main Menu

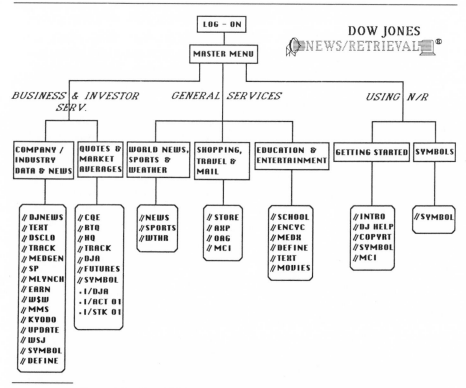

umn. You'll get a quick look at the day's major stories at 6 A.M. (Eastern time) each day. If you want an executive summary of the week's economic news and the most recently released economic indicators, search The Weekly Economic Update. This database is compiled by the News/Retrieval editorial staff from *The Wall Street Journal*, the Dow Jones News Service and *Barron's*.

Within 15 minutes, the Current Quotes provides continuously updated stock quotes from the floor of the exchange for companies listed on the New York, American, Midwest and Pacific Stock Exchanges, and NASDAQ OTC–traded companies, as well as composite quotes. When used in combination with custom designed stock market analysis software and spreadsheets, you can store downloaded data such as market quotes, chart price, and volume data and maintain a portfolio for making buy and sell decisions. Historical Quotes provides daily high, low, volume and closing stock prices for common and preferred stocks for the past year. Monthly summaries to 1979 and quarterly summaries to 1978 are available. Historical Dow Jones Averages provide daily summaries of the transportation, industrial, utility, and 65 stock composite indexes. The database contains high, low, close, and volume information for a full trading year.

The Corporate Earnings Estimator, compiled by Zacks Investment Research, Inc., provides consensus forecasts of earnings per share for 3,000 companies. Estimates from over 1,000 research analysts at more than 60 major brokerage firms contribute to the forecasts covering the next two fiscal years. In addition, you'll get the average high and low of the latest earnings per share estimates. You can see what analysts think about a company's earnings prospects and you can compare their previous predictions with current performance.

The Disclosure II database compiles data on 9,400 companies from updated filings with the Securities and Exchange Commission including corporate profiles; balance sheets; income statements; line-of-business data; five-year summary of revenues; income and earnings per share; names of officers, directors, and subsidiaries; management discussions; and a two-year list of documents filed with the SEC. This is the perfect place to see the "corporate picture." This information can be supplemented with data from The Economic and Foreign Exchange Survey (provided by Money Market Services, Inc.), which offers a consensus of analyses and forecasts by leading economists about the nation's major economic indicators, such as the money supply, unemployment, federal funds rates, consumer price index, and retail sales. These forecasts are also compared with previously released government figures. Media General Financial Services provides weekly-updated access to price, volume and fundamental data on over 4,300 companies. This database includes reports on revenues, earnings, dividends, price-earnings ratios, and stock market performance relative to market indicators.

Merrill Lynch Research Service provides seven databases including Market Analysis, Recommendations for Investment Action, Company Comments: Highlights, Industry Comments: Highlights, Revised Earnings Estimates, Investment Ratings Changes, and Explanation of QRQ Investment Ratings. With this broad range of information, you'll be more informed about investment decisions, you'll be able to track market activities, and you'll have access to earnings estimates from a firm with a worldwide reputation for its expertise.

Taken from the wires of United Press International, NEWS/RETRIEVAL WORLD REPORT provides a continually updated "front page" summary of the top five news stories of the moment. Within 90 seconds of its appearance, THE DOW JONES WIRE electronically captures data. Before going on-line, each story is read and edited by the DJN/R editorial staff. For a more comprehensive look at today's business, the full-text *The Wall Street Journal* database includes every news article scheduled to be printed in every edition of *The Wall Street Journal* since January 1984. This is an exclusive service of DJN/R. Since this data is provided by *The Wall Street Journal* production tapes, you have the WSJ "on your screen" by 6 A.M. (Eastern) each day. *The European Wall Street Journal* and *The Asian Wall Street Journal* were added in 1985 as well as the full text of the *Washington Post*. Dow Jones News brings you selected articles from *Barron's*, Dow Jones News Service (Broadtape) and *The Wall Street Journal* since June 1979. Updated daily, the articles are added to Dow Jones News within 36 hours of publication. For those interested in the strength of the Japanese economy and the Tokyo markets, the Japan Economic Daily provided by Kyodo News International, Inc., offers major economic, political, and business news from Japan.

You can gather background information for speeches, studies and reports from Grolier Electronic Publishing, Inc.'s Academic American Encyclopedia, which contains more than 30,000 articles on a broad array of subjects. Words of Wall Street provides over 2,000 definitions, mathematical formulas, and examples used in the securities industry including new financial techniques and corporate finance terms. Traders, investment professionals, and serious investors will appreciate this extensively cross-referenced lexicon.

Dow Jones News/Retrieval offers additional services for the busy business professional. The Official Airline Guide (OAG) lists flight schedules and fares for over 650 airlines worldwide. In the near future DJN/R will let you make reservations and order your tickets on-line, too. Cineman Movie Reviews, News/Retrieval Sports Report, and News/Retrieval

Weather Report will help you keep up with your outside interests. In addition, the COMP-U-STORE service will let you use your credit card to order over 60,000 brand name items which are discounted up to 40 percent. You'll also have access to MCI MAIL's electronic mail services. (See the review of MCI MAIL in this Appendix.)

DOW JONES SOFTWARE:

As a software publisher, Dow Jones & Company, Inc. offers several packages that automatically download market information and provide tools for data manipulation and analysis. The Dow Jones Market Analyzer automatically collects and stores market quotes so you can chart price and volume data and construct standard technical analysis charts. Dow Jones Market Manager is a portfolio management program for accounting and system control. The Dow Jones Market Manager maintains one or more security portfolios of stocks, bonds, options, mutual funds and Treasury issues. Dow Jones Market Microscope collects and stores information on extensive lists of companies and industries so you can print data on individual companies or industries. This software will automatically alert you at critical price points. Dow Jones Investment Evaluator helps you keep track of investments. Many other third-party software packages are supported for Apple, Atari, Commodore, Hewlett-Packard, IBM, and Radio Shack computers.

DJN/R management reports that in the near future, its 200,000 users will be seeing more interactive transaction services, including airline reservations, and brokerage and banking services.

COMMENTS:

Dow Jones News/Retrieval is the unquestioned leader in on-line financial information, but some have criticized the service for having rather unsophisticated system software. For example, the system doesn't recognize a break signal to start and stop screen scrolling. If you access the service with Tymnet, you can use CONTROL–X (^X) for BREAK except for the full-text databases, on which you must wait for all requested text. If you access DJN/R with Telenet, ^S and ^Q will control scrolling.

To overcome some of the system shortcomings, Dow Jones

has published a number of data retrieval and analysis software packages (see above). Unfortunately, most of these packages were purchased from separate vendors, so you cannot exchange databases between them. If you need stock market quotes for 20 companies in your portfolio, you'll have to download them into each software package requiring that data.

The DJN/R Master Menu provides a comprehensive listing of all available services. Used in combination with DJ HELP, the user can access the system command documentation and database descriptions. System commands are preceded by the double slash <//>; for example, you can return to the main menu by entering <//MENU>. The user can either utilize the menus or skip menus and prompts by entering a dot <.> and a designation: for example <.category> or <.stock symbol>.

You can read a free on-line subscribers newsletter by entering <//INTRO>. INTRO contains new developments in DJN/R, how-to guides, new software products, tips on using the service, and schedules for software and DJN/R seminars. You will also learn of free time offers made by various database services.

You can maneuver through the financial databases by looking for any company stock symbol or industry category. An on-line symbols library helps you select the one you want. Let's say you want to search several databases for information on Phillips Petroleum in Bartlesville, OK: You would simply enter its stock symbol <.P>. Or, if you want to search for information on the telecommunications industry, you'd enter <.I/TEL>.

Full-text searches in *The Wall Street Journal* and similar full-text databases is somewhat more complicated. The manual provides very good explanations and examples of search procedures using Boolean and proximity operators, truncation, and other limiters. For example, you can use NEAR to retrieve those documents in which one search term appears next to a second term. By adding a number <NEAR6> you can specify the maximum number of words or characters that can appear between two search terms. SAME indicates that your search words must appear in the same paragraph. For the average user, many of the advanced search features may be more difficult to learn.

Most screens are presented in a 14-line by 32-character format. If you're looking at a multiple-page document, a page header will indicate which page you're viewing: for example, page two of six. You must press ENTER each time you want to proceed to the next page. If you want, later you can use your word processing software to change the page column width and to reformat the text. However, you'll find numerous control codes in your down-loaded file, so be prepared for quite a bit of editing, including the removal of page header and footer information.

I found the system responded fairly slowly at 3 P.M. (Central Standard Time) and somewhat faster after the East Coast logged off at 4 P.M. Even at night The Official Airline Guide (OAG) seemed slow. The menu-driven medical database (MDEX) was cumbersome to use and of limited value. Not only did the system become confused—for example, mistaking <INFERTILITY> for <INTESTINAL>—but it also required frequent and cumbersome re-routing through the main menu.

To display full-text documents from *The Wall Street Journal* I could use the <..P> printing command which then pauses at the end of each page. This required my constant attention at the terminal and the downloading task became quite tedious and time-consuming. However, I could interrupt the printing and return to the main menu if I wished. If I used the continuous printing command <..CP>, I wouldn't be able to exit from the printing process until all documents had been viewed. Unfortunately, even the best designed search strategy will result in finding extraneous articles; for example, the search <ABORT AND HUMAN AND LAW> resulted in an article on South Africa's attempt to abort a particular law instead of a treatise on abortion laws I'd expected. I wanted to print five of the six articles found; however, there was no simple way to skip this unwanted 24-page document. Some of the advanced viewing document features allow this; but they are difficult to learn and use. I found NEXIS's QUIK scanning techniques much more efficient; however, I do prefer DJN/S's straight on-line connect charge to NEXIS's per search fee.

The manual is well written and well illustrated with examples. However, the quick reference sheets aren't as clear and helpful as those provided by Mead Data for LEXIS and

NEXIS. This is in part due to the increased difficulty of using the DJN/R service.

Dow Jones News/Retrieval is available under three pricing plans. Blue Chip Membership requires a $75 password fee or the purchase of one Dow Jones–supported product for each workstation and a $100 annual subscription fee. Executive Membership requires a $50 monthly subscription fee. Both of these services provide a 33⅓ percent discount on nonprime usage and a half hour of free usage each month on selected databases. The Executive Membership also qualifies you for a 33⅓ percent discount on prime time usage. A Standard Membership requires a $75 password or the purchase of a Dow Jones supported package per workstation.

For Dow Jones Text-Search Services, Financial and Investment Services, and Dow Jones Business and Economic News, prime time rates are billed at $1.20 per minute and nonprime time rates are at $0.20 per minute (not including the discounts mentioned above). Dow Jones Quotes prime time costs $0.90 per minute and non-prime $0.15. General News and Information Services are billed at $0.60 prime time and $0.20 nonprime time. If you use 1200 bps service instead of 300, double these rates. A detailed pricing sheet listing individual databases is available. At these rates, you aren't encouraged to browse at your leisure. However, unlike Mead Data's NEXIS, you aren't charged extra for each search procedure. At $15 per search, NEXIS can get expensive very quickly.

A–4 Dialog

DATABASE NAME: Dialog

VENDOR/PROVIDER NAME: Dialog Information Services, Inc.
A wholly-owned subsidiary of Lockheed Corporation

ADDRESS: 3460 Hillview Ave.

CITY, STATE, ZIP: Palo Alto, CA 94304

TELEPHONE: 800-227-1927; In California 800-982-5838

CARRIERS/TOLL–FREE LINES: Tymnet, Telenet, Uninet, DIALNET, inbound WATS

COMPATIBILITY: Any personal computer and 300/1200 bps modem compatible with Bell 103, Bell 212A, or Racal-Vadic 3400 series

GENERAL DESCRIPTION:

According to the corporate searchers interviewed for this book, Dialog is the most used information system, for several reasons. Dialog's 200 databases provide the strongest source for business information and for current events. The state-of-the-art searching system is both powerful and flexible. With Dialog for business information, SDC Orbit for technical information, and an instant news service such as NEXIS or Dow Jones News/Retrieval, a company would have access to almost all the information it could want.

Itemizing the databases Dialog provides would require 60 printed 8½ by 11 pages—the size of the *Dialog Database Catalog*. The catalog gives a brief explanation of each database, including the nature of its contents, number of records, costs, and provider. Along with this well-written catalog, Dialog has an on-line DIALINDEX service to help you determine which database provides information on your search topic.

The 90 million items of information stored on Dialog computers include summaries from trade journals, newspapers, news services, and corporate literature as well as new product announcements and historical information on product introductions. Dialog's access to information on 12 million companies around the world will help you target companies for new business, compile mailing lists, develop company profiles, find new markets, locate suppliers, and analyze sales territories. If you're interested in registered trademarks, patent descriptions, and technical information from major scientific journals, Dialog offers that, too.

Dialog will also help you manage your investment portfolio, target companies for mergers and acquisitions, investigate joint venture opportunities, and compile company and industry financial reports. You'll get informative summaries from key business journals such as *Fortune, Forbes,* and *Business Week,* as well as data from the U.S. Bureau of the Census and U.S. Department of Labor on price indexes, employment levels, consumer characteristics, population, exports, and much more.

For the corporate librarian who has printed material or interlibrary loan services at his or her fingertips, Dialog provides a vast reservoir of reference information. For the desktop personal computer user, finding Dialog's bibliographic information may only be the first step in an arduous document searching process. The Dialog "information super-market" contains bibliographic references and/or abstracts from some 60,000 journals, plus dissertations, research and conference reports, patents, government documents, books, pamphlets, and corporate financial reports. If you need the full documents, you'll have to acquire them elsewhere or through Dialog's document retrieval service.

The only full-text databases are the UPI Wire Service, Drug Information Full Text, Magazine ASAP, Trade & Industry ASAP, Investext, Academic American Encyclopedia, and *Harvard Business Review.* A number of numeric or reference databases such as Ulrich's Periodicals Directory contain detailed lists, reports, and statistics. For example, EIS Industrial Plants lists 160,000 industrial plants together with such data as the location, sales figures, products, and so on.

Although Dialog's DIALORDER service does provide on-line document ordering, it tends to be expensive; a 10–page article costs about $8. When you consider that the average search only takes 10 to 15 minutes and costs under $15, it's a bargain compared to spending a day at the library and only barely scratching the surface.

Dialog doesn't actually abstract, code, and enter printed information into the computer. The service purchases electronically stored data from individual database providers and offers the information on-line to Dialog subscribers. For this reason, each database has its own unique characteristics and pricing.

The following is a partial listing of business and financial databases offered:

COMPANY INFORMATION
D&B—Dun's Market Identifiers.
D&B—Dun's International Market Identifiers.
D&B—Million Dollar Directory.
Electronic Yellow Pages.
ICC British Company Directory.
Trinet Company Database.
Trinet Establishment Database.

COMPANY FINANCIAL DATABASES
Disclosure II.
Disclosure/Spectrum Ownership.
ICC British Company Financial Datasheets.

Investext.
Media General Databank.
Moody's Corporate Profiles.
Moody's News.
Standard & Poor's Corporate Descriptions.
Standard & Poor's News.

REFERENCE AND FULL TEXT—COMPANY INFORMA-
TION
ABI/INFORM (business and management journals).
Adtrack (advertising from 150 consumer magazines).
CLAIMS (patent abstracts).
Derwent World Patents Index.
Commerce Business Daily (U.S. government contract
awards).
Management Contents.
Marquis Who's Who.
PTS Annual Reports Abstracts.
PTS F&S Indexes/PTS Promt (specialized industry ar-
ticles).
Trade and Industry ASAP/Trade and Industry Index.
Trademarkscan (600,000 pending and active trade-
marks).

In addition you can get information on any number of
subjects. This is illustrated in Figure A4–1.

With over 100 million records, Dialog offers unequaled
subject balance and variety. However, since the majority of
these records are bibliographic (with abstracts) or numeric in
nature, you'll have to be prepared to retrieve the full documents using other methods.

COMMENTS:
The Dialog computer search system is both powerful and
flexible; however, this strength makes it difficult for the novice to use. Being a command-driven system, the user must
learn not only how to drive the program but also how to construct search strategies. Many of the commands are not mnemonic so they can be difficult to remember; for example, SE-
LECT(S) means to search a database for a specified term, SE-
LECT STEPS (SS) means search a database for more than one
term and produce sets of data, and SELECT FILES (SF) means
select files to search in DIALINDEX.

FIGURE A4-1 Dialog Database Subject Categories

Agriculture—Food, Biological Sciences, Marine Sciences.	Industrial Regulations.
Associations.	Information Science.
Biographies.	Labor.
Biosciences.	Language and Linguistics.
Books.	Law.
Business—Companies, News, Market Research, Statisitics.	Leisure.
CAS Registry Numbers.	Marine Science.
Chemistry—Chemical Literature, Chemical Substances.	Medical Engineering.
Computer Science.	Medicine.
Current News—Standard & Poor's, Newsearch, AP News, UPI News.	Metals.
Defense Technology.	Market Research.
Education.	Nutrition and Foods.
Energy.	Patents.
Engineering.	People.
Environment/Pollution.	Petroleum, Oil, and Gas.
Electronic Yellow Pages.	Pharmacology.
Food Sciences.	Physics.
Foundations/Grants.	Psychology.
Geology.	Public Affairs.
Geophysics.	Regulations.
Government.	Science—Technology and Applied.
Humanities.	Social Science.
	Software.
	Toxicology.
	Water.

According to many professional users, the $50 *Guide to Dialog Searching* is superb. Dialog regularly issues update sheets that keep searchers posted on system changes and unique, efficient ways of accessing information. The monthly newsletter, "Chronolog" contains price changes and searching tips and highlights user experiences. The newsletters are also stored on-line in database #410. Along with written support, Dialog offers an excellent one and one-half day training program for $145 for each participant. Corporate customers report that the Dialog sales and service representatives and the customer service personnel (available through toll-free numbers) are very responsive and helpful.

Dialog also provides on-line help for finding the best database(s) to search. For $35 an hour (58 cents a minute),

DIALINDEX evaluates your search statement against its master index of the databases and gives you the number of records in each chosen database. This is less expensive than logging onto a more expensive (and perhaps an inappropriate) database and doing the same thing. Once you've decided on a search strategy and a database(s), you can save your search and move to that database. You can then recall the search commands and execute the search for each database chosen.

New users get $100 of free search time; however, an inexperienced person can use that up in a flash. When you first log onto Dialog, you enter the Education database (#1) which charges $25 an hour. You can save $10 an hour by changing the default database to one of the practice databases (#201, 216, or 290) or to Dialog's publications (#200 or 410), which only cost $15 an hour. Once you've designed your search statement, you can temporarily save it, switch to the database you wish to search, and execute the instructions. Should you be interrupted during a search, you can save your search and log off of the system. When you return, you'll continue from the place where you exited. The typical search takes 10 to 15 minutes, and costs from $5 to $25.

Dialog's off-line printing service can save you time and money. Off-line printing usually costs around 15 to 20 cents a record. In contrast, the cost for connect time plus on screen viewing will be more.

An SDI service is available for selected databases, not for all. Dialog's electronic mail service allows a company's centralized search service to enter the search and have the results printed on an end-user's terminal located elsewhere in the company.

Many professional searchers said the Dialog system is "state-of-the-art" and always improving. The searching provides truncation, proximity operators, Boolean operators, and a number of other techniques. And you can view the results of your search in a number of different forms. To save time, you may wish to see only the titles of the articles. Once you've determined which ones you're interested in, you can ask to see the citations as the full record without the abstract, the bibliographic citation only, the title and indexing terms only, or the Dialog record identification number only.

Dialog offers an after hours on-line service called KNOWLEDGE INDEX (KI). Many of the Dialog databases are available on KI for a flat hourly rate of $24, including communications charges. The KI searching techniques are easier to learn than Dialog's and yet they are similar enough that many people find it easy to learn KI's techniques first and then move up to Dialog. A review of Knowledge Index appears in this appendix.

The IN-SEARCH gateway software package allows you to design Dialog searches off-line and then to automatically log on and conduct your search. The IN-SEARCH software is menu-driven and also contains enough information about the Dialog databases that you'll have a good idea of what information you'll find once you've logged on. A review of IN-SEARCH appears in the software review appendix that follows.

Although Dialog users are predominantly professional searchers, that complexion is gradually changing. Before you subscribe to Dialog, you may wish to have a demonstration or attend one of their classes.

A–5 Knowledge Index

DATABASE NAME: Knowledge Index

VENDOR/PROVIDER NAME: Dialog Information Services, Inc.
A wholly-owned subsidiary of
Lockheed Corporation

ADDRESS: 3460 Hillview Ave.

CITY, STATE, ZIP: Palo Alto, CA 94304

TELEPHONE: 800-227-1927; In California 800-982-5838

CARRIERS/TOLL–FREE LINES: Tymnet and Telenet (no extra charge)

SPECIAL HOURS: Monday through Thursday to 6 P.M. to 5 A.M. local time;

Friday 6 P.M. to midnight; Saturday 8 A.M. to midnight;

Sunday 3 P.M. to 5 A.M. Monday.

COMPATIBILITY: Any personal computer and 300/1200 bps modem compatible with Bell 103, Bell 212A, or Racal-Vadic 3400 series

GENERAL DESCRIPTION:

Knowledge Index (KI) is Dialog's answer to the personal computer user. Available only on weekends and during the evening hours, KI provides access to over two dozen Dialog databases in a number of popular subject areas: agriculture, computers, electronics, engineering, business news, business, magazines, general news, books, medicine, psychology, law, education, and government.

For a one-time $35 joining fee and a flat rate of $24 per hour, including telecommunications charges, KI provides access to over 17 million *summaries* of articles, reports, and books on thousands of topics drawn from over 10,000 sources. The initial fee qualifies you for two free hours of connect time within the first 30 days and a complete, self-instructional *User's Workbook*.

Many professionals are attracted to the databases offered. Computer enthusiasts enjoy the Computers and Electronics section, which provides indexing of technical journals, microcomputer software, and popular microcomputer press. IN-SPEC provides comprehensive coverage of physics, computers, and electronics and includes over 1,200,000 references to 2,300 journals, conference proceedings, technical reports, books, patents, and more. The International Software Database indexes and describes over 12,000 commercially available programs for micro- and mini-computers. And, Microcomputer Index and Computer Database provide indexes and abstracts from over 500 microcomputer publications.

If you don't have time to catch up with Corporate News and Business Information until the day's work is done, you can search Newsearch indexes for daily updates of the *New York Times, Washington Post, The Wall Street Journal, Los Angeles Times,* and *Christian Science Monitor* plus PR Newswire and more than 1,000 magazines and journals. The National Newspaper Index offers cover-to-cover indexing of these major newspapers, over 700,000 articles published since 1979. Standard & Poor's News contains full-text coverage of corporate news including financial reports on more than 10,000 publicly held U.S. corporations. The ABI/INFORM database offers over 300,000 articles and conference reports, since 1971. You'll find that the monthly updated Trade and Industry Index is a prime source for business information relating to all major industries and trades since it indexes over 500,000 journal and newspapers articles, columns, letters to the editor, books, and the complete text of PR Newswire press releases since 1971.

If you have a technical interest, the Engineering Literature Index, with over 600,000 items drawn from 3,000 publications, will be invaluable. Medical professionals will appreciate Medline, a database specializing in biomedicine, dentistry, and nursing, containing references to over 4 million publications since 1966. The International Pharmaceutical Abstracts provide comprehensive coverage of pharmacy and drug-related literature. Biosis Previews gives worldwide coverage of biological and biomedical research from over 9,000 U.S. and international journals, books, proceedings of meetings, monographs, reports, symposia, and research communications published since 1969. Psychologists will enjoy browsing through two databases providing comprehensive coverage of psychological literature including PsycINFO, which corresponds to the *Psychological Abstracts* and *Mental Health Abstracts*.

COMMENTS:

A low-cost, abbreviated alternative to Dialog, Knowledge Index provides a wealth of information for corporate businesspeople and professionals. At 40 cents per minute, a simple search will cost about a dollar and a more complex search only $4 to $5. In contrast to Dialog and many other services, you aren't charged extra for telecommunications connect time, for each search, or for the number of citations displayed. Your credit card is billed only $24 per hour for connect time.

Users report that the system responds quite rapidly so you won't pay excessive amounts to wait for the KI computer. You can order articles on-line for $6.25 plus 20 cents a photocopied page, or you can check with your company or public library.

Because the search system is more user-friendly than Dialog's, many new users begin with KI and, if necessary, graduate to Dialog's huge resources. The KI workbook is far superior to that provided by BRS After Dark. It's written in a simple-to-understand style and provides many examples and sample searches. The commands are easy to understand and use. Although somewhat simplified compared to Dialog's, KI's search system allows you to search by author, by journal name, and by field. KI also offers on-line help messages to guide you to the appropriate database, but this on-line help costs $24 per hour. You should try to design your search before logging on so you can prevent unnecessary delays. A toll-free customer service number is available to KI users as well as a quarterly newsletter.

Since it is primarily a bibliographical database, KI won't replace your library. However, detailed article summaries from such databases as the Computer Data Base and brief abstracts like those in the Microcomputer Index will provide you with enough information to know if retrieving the entire article is worthwhile.

If you're an after-hour searcher, Knowledge Index is certainly worth strong consideration.

A-6   The Source

DATABASE NAME: The Source

VENDOR/PROVIDER NAME: Source Telecomputing Corp.
Subsidiary of the Reader's Digest Association, Inc.

ADDRESS: 1616 Anderson Road

CITY, STATE, ZIP: McLean, VA 22102

TELEPHONE: 703-734-7523

CARRIERS/TOLL–FREE LINES: Telenet, Uninet, Sourcenet, WATS

COMPATIBILITY: Most terminals and personal computers; 300 and 1200 bps

GENERAL DESCRIPTION:

You can get financial databases and up-to-the-minute news from a number of other services, but if you also want state-of-the-art electronic communications, The Source may be your answer. Designed as a user-friendly, menu-driven system, The Source is easy to use and reasonably priced. Over 60,000 personal computer owners subscribe to The Source.

SOURCEMAIL is an electronic mail system that allows you to create messages, send messages, address mail to more than one recipient, receive confirmations that your messages are received, and even send hard-copy messages to non-computer owners. You can either use The Source text editor to write your messages on-line or you can upload files from your computer disk. All Source subscribers have their own personal mailbox and can voluntarily list themselves in the DiSearch subscriber database, which indicates their interests. So if you want to contact all subscribers who are electrical engineers, you can do so with ease. The MAILGRAM Message Service allows you to send MAILGRAM messages to anyone in the continental U.S. or Canada with next business day delivery guaranteed.

Participate is The Source's dynamic electronic roundtable. As an open-forum service, Participate allows you to conduct conferences on topics of your choice. If a roundtable topic already exists, you can join in. Users report that Participate conferencing is far superior to that provided by CompuServe. If you want to visit with other Source members, the CHAT mode allows keyboard-to-keyboard communication. If you want to exchange ideas and sell merchandise and services much as ham radio operators do, you can leave up to 23 lines of text for 14 days on POST, the electronic bulletin board. Private Sector allows you to create your own "private" bulletin board for disseminating information to selected members such as your sales force or branch offices. In addition, you can create and save your own text files, membership lists, and directories.

Electronic communications isn't the only reason to become a Source subscriber. STOCKCHECK gives you updated Associated Press figures from the New York and American Stock Exchanges; over 10,000 stocks and bonds tables are available for analysis. With The source software you can create and update your very own investment portfolio. For on-line trading, you can use Spear Securities' discounted investor service. You receive instant transaction capability, confirmation, real-time and delayed stock quotations, automatic portfolio updating and recordkeeping, and a variety of investment information databases, including The Media General Financial Service. For historic stock analysis, you can consult with UNISTOX Market Reports, Commodity World News, The *Donoghue Moneyletter*, and the *Washington Post*.

BIZDATE is a popular service for corporate users who need access to the most current business and economic news events. Updated 70 times a day from 8:30 A.M. to 7 P.M., from the Source's own news room, BIZDATE lists financial stories, commodities indexes, economic indicators, foreign exchange rates, and editorials. BIZDATE also provides access to the *U.S. News Washington Letter*. In addition, United Press International (UPI), posts international, national, and state news stories broken down into general news, sports, weather, business, and features. UPI retains historical information for one year. And, BYLINE provides syndicated reports from leading columnists on a wide variety of topics, including leisure, lifestyles, the arts, health, and technology.

If you need in-depth background information, the Management Contents database provides 250-word abstracts from some 30 leading business and financial publications including *Business Week, Forbes, Harvard Business Review, Dun's Review, The Banker, Fortune, Inc., Medical Economics, Mergers & Acquisitions, Venture, Wharton Magazine, Sloan Management Review, Journal of Retailing*, and much more. Abstracts are retained for one year.

CONSUMER SERVICES allow you to shop for airline tickets, hotels, and restaurants. The Official Airline Guide (OAG) is updated daily and lists nearly 300,000 flight schedules and fares in North America. OAG will help you find the best fare and the most convenient schedule. USREST, provided by the Mobile Restaurant Guide, lists more than 6,000 dining facilities in 1,800 cities and towns across the U.S. and Canada. USROOM is a travel guide to over 16,000 hotels, motels, and inns. And AIRSCHED provides information on all domestic and most international air routes. The Source Travel Club can handle all your ticket, travel, hotel, and car reservations. You can also learn of money-saving charter trips and special tours. To help plan your trip, the ACCU-WEATHER database provides weather reports worldwide, nationally, regionally, and for the largest 15 metropolitan areas in the United States. And, you'll get the latest highway travel advisories.

The discounted catalog-shopping Comp-U-Store lets you use your credit card to save up to 40 percent on 50,000 brand-name products including appliances, cameras, cars, stereos, tableware, luggage, sporting goods, video equipment, electronic equipment, computers and accessories, and much more. CSTORE is a gateway service that connects you to the Comp-U-Card of America system. Membership in this service costs an extra $25 per year.

Other outside services include market and technical research services, document delivery services, document translating services, and current awareness services to provide you with regular, concise, timely information summaries. For example, MICROSEARCH provides over 15,000 current reviews and descriptions of over 6,000 microcomputer products including hardware, software, peripherals, and accessories.

If you're a frustrated author or publisher, PUBLIC is a self-publishing arena where you'll have an opportunity to start your own electronic magazine. With electronic publishing you don't have expensive typesetting or printing expenses. You will have an opportunity, however, to be paid for your knowledge and information.

The Source doesn't bring a library into your office, but it does provide creative electronic communications capabilities, up-to-the-minute news, portfolio management, electronic catalog shopping, and travel information and services—all at a competitive price. The on-line charge is $20.75 per hour during the day and $7.75 evenings and weekends *including* telecommunication charges. In contrast, many services charge The Source's evening rate for telecommunications charges alone. There is a $5 per hour surcharge for 1200 bps access during the day and $3 during off-hours. You'll be charged a one-time $49.95 membership fee and a $10 per month minimum whether you use The Source or not. In addition, there is a 25 cent minimum access fee for each time you connect. Some value-added services such as the OAG and Media General Financial Analysis are priced at $39.75 per hour weekdays and $34.75 all other times. Individual users are billed on a major credit card, and individually itemized company accounts are available.

COMMENTS:

The Source is primarily designed for easy access by personal computer end-users. The menu-driven system is quite user-friendly: easy to learn and easy to use. When you log onto the system you'll be offered the following menu selections:

WELCOME TO THE SOURCE
1   USING THE SOURCE (INTRO) **FREE**
2   MENU OF SERVICES (MENU)
3   MEMBER INFORMATION (INFO) **FREE**
4   TODAY FROM THE SOURCE (TODAY)

This menu provides both direct access to electronic news (Business Update, Today and What's New) and to other programs (The Main Menu and Command Level). If you enter #2, the MAIN MENU appears:

THE SOURCE MAIN MENU OF SERVICES

1 TODAY FROM THE SOURCE (TODAY)

2 NEWS, WEATHER AND SPORTS (NEWS)

3 BUSINESS AND INVESTING (BUSINESS)

4 COMMUNICATION SERVICES (COMM)

5 PERSONAL COMPUTING (PC)

6 TRAVEL SERVICES (TRAVEL)

7 SHOPPING, GAMES AND LEISURE (HOME)

8 MEMBER INFORMATION (INFO) **FREE**

You can proceed to any subsection of the service by merely entering the menu category number and pressing the RETURN. The direct command names are now listed in the menus, so you can learn them easier and faster. To exit the menu-driven mode, you can type <Q> at any prompt. Many experienced users prefer this more direct method. If you enter HELP followed by a specific service—for example, <HELP MAIL>—The Source computer will tell you about using SourceMail. Likewise, <HELP SERVICES>, <HELP COMMANDS>, and <HELP MANUAL> will provide more on-line assistance.

If that isn't enough, the manual provides clear explanations of the various commands and services. THE SOURCE MANUAL is well illustrated in two-color printing to highlight what you type (in dark blue) versus what text the system responds with. Unfortunately, it's sometimes difficult to distinguish between bold dark blue and bold black print, especially in dim lighting often found around a personal computer terminal. Although the manual seems complete, it's disorganized. For example, the explanation for on-line help appears on page 211 even though it's probably one of the first major features you need. And the command summary at the back of the manual isn't alphabetized: a quick reference it's not. The command guide booklet is conveniently sized and a needed aid. However, the number of commands is rather

mind-boggling to the uninitiated. For those who get too confused, The Source does provide a toll-free customer support
number and free on-line assistance (see the menus above).

Several system features show The Source's responsiveness
to personal computer users. For example, you can configure
your screen display to 80 columns by 24 lines; 40 × 24; 40 ×
16; and 32 × 16. Even an Atari or Commodore with a television set for a monitor can access The Source.

The system commands also support personal computers. For example CONTROL–S and CONTROL–Q stop and
continue scrolling. The NOCTR command allows continuous scrolling for downloading. Not having to pause every
24 lines is a nice convenience and does save time and
money. Also you can store an automatically executed command file on line. For example, if every time you log onto
the system you wish to view BIZDATE, your stored SID
(command) file will enter the steps necessary to take you
directly to that part of the system. You can change this file
any time you wish.

The Source doesn't rival the breadth and depth of Dialog,
Knowledge Index, or BRS; however, for the money, you can
gain access to a number of useful features. You'll enjoy the
varied communications methods The Source provides, but,
some users complain that the user communication areas are
too full of classified ads.

A–7 CompuServe

DATABASE NAME: CompuServe

VENDOR/PROVIDER NAME: CompuServe Information Services
An H&R Block, Inc. Company

ADDRESS: 5000 Arlington Center Blvd.; P.O. Box 20212

CITY, STATE, ZIP: Columbus, OH 43220

TELEPHONE: 800-848-8199; In Ohio 614-457-0802

CARRIERS/TOLL–FREE LINES: Tymnet, Telenet, Datapac
(Canada)
CompuServe Network (25¢/hour)

COMPATIBILITY: Almost any type of personal computer or
terminal

GENERAL DESCRIPTION:

CompuServe is especially designed for the personal computer end-user. Everything from financial information and news to industrial hygiene can be found in some 800 different services. However, discovering the nature of these services is a trick in itself. You won't find the details in the standard brochures—or the manuals, either. To really find out what CompuServe is all about, you may have to buy a $39.95 starter kit with five free hours and explore for yourself.

CompuServe isn't trying to be sneaky or deceitful; it's just hard to describe the vast number of selections and do them justice. Basically CompuServe offers two types of service: the Consumer Information Service (CIS) and the Executive Information Service (EIS). EIS is an expanded version of CIS and charges a $10 monthly minimum. The following will illustrate their chief differences.

Consumer Information Service (CIS). Both CIS and EIS subscribers have access to the CIS services and menus. If you enter the CIS area of CompuServe, you'll see the following main menu:

CONSUMER INFORMATION SERVICE MAIN MENU

1. Home Services
2. Business & Financial
3. Personal Computing
4. Services for Professionals
5. The Electronic Mail (tm)
6. User Information
7. Index

9. Executive Information Service

Selecting an option from this menu leads you through a number of sub-submenus until you find the exact information you're looking for. For example, if you select #4, SERVICES FOR PROFESSIONALS, you'll be presented with the following submenu:

SERVICES FOR PROFESSIONALS MENU

1. Aviation
2. Communications/Data Processing
3. Engineering/Technical
4. Legal

5. Medical
6. Jewelers
7. Real Estate
8. Military Veterans Service

If from this submenu, you select option #3, ENGINEER-ING/TECHNICAL, you'll proceed to the following menu:

ENGINEERING/TECHNICAL MENU

1. Communications Industry Forum
2. Environmental Forum
3. Firenet
4. News-A-Tron Commodity Quotes
5. Information Retrieval Service
6. NWWA—Waterline
7. Mining and Energy Services
8. Industrial Hygiene Forum
9. DECISIONLINE/Energy

If you want to participate in an electronic forum in the Communications Industry, for example, you can select option #1, COMMUNICATIONS INDUSTRY FORUM. At this point you'd be welcomed into a specialized bulletin board which would allow you to leave messages, read messages, conduct real-time conferences, view a member directory, and so forth. If you want, you can further subdivide your forum discussion into General Interest, Radio, Television, Land Mobile, Tele-communications, Shortwaves, etc.

If you multiply the sub-submenus I've discussed above by all of the options available, you can picture the difficulty CompuServe has describing the breadth and depth of the CIS system.

Executive Information Service (EIS). For those in-terested in a broader range of business and financial informa-tion, the EIS offers additional possibilities. When you enter this system, you'll see the following menu options:

EXECUTIVE INFORMATION SERVICE MAIN MENU

1. Communications
2. Investments & Quotations
3. Decision Support
4. News

5. Travel
6. Shopping
7. Weather
8. Professional & Technical
9. Consumer Information Service
10. User Information

If at this point you select option #2, INVESTMENTS & QUOTATIONS, you'll proceed to the following submenu:

INVESTMENTS & QUOTATIONS MENU

1. Ticker Retrieval Reports
2. Expert User
3. Current-Day Pricing
4. Historical Pricing
5. Annual & Quarterly Reports
6. Estimates & Projections
7. Investment Analysis
8. Economic/Financial Outlooks
9. Specialized Software Interfaces
10. Financial Forums
11. Banking & Brokerage Services
12. User Information
13. Transaction Charges

If instead of #2 you selected from the main menu option #3, DECISION SUPPORT, you'd see to the following menu:

DECISION SUPPORT MENU

1. Demographics
2. Information on Demand
3. IRS Tax Information
4. *Donoghue Moneyletter*
5. U.S. Government Publications
6. DECISIONLINE/Issues
7. DECISIONLINE/Trends
8. Transaction Charges

If from the EIS Main Menu you'd asked for NEWS, you'd get the following submenu:

1. Executive News Service
2. *USA TODAY* Update HOTLINE

3. *USA TODAY* Update DECISIONLINE
4. AP Viewdata
5. CP Business Information Wire
6. The National Business Wire
7. The *Washington Post*
8. MMS Financial Forecasting
9. Stevens' Small Business Reports
10. InfoWorld
11. News-A-Tron Market Reports
12. Business & Law Review
13. Transaction Charges

A number of the EIS services charge premiums above the standard CompuServe on-line connect charges. You'll want to check the current price sheet before planning a search in these databases; for example, SUPERSITE Demographic Reports cost $25 and up each, and the Official Airline Guide (OAG) connect time surcharge is $32 per hour. In general CompuServe charges aren't unreasonable, but you should know the price before you buy.

A CompuServe Overview. CompuServe provides electronic mail, forums, manufacturer's newsletter, aviation and weather information, news and sports information, financial information, travel planning and services, banking and shopping services, educational resources, and much more. Professional forums and electronic conferencing put you in touch with experts across the country. In addition, the Executive News Service connects you with the *Washington Post*, Associated Press (AP) and a customized around-the-clock news clipping service. Interactive services provide Comp-U-Store for ordering discounted products as well as computer banking, brokerage, and travel services.

The optional EIS section offers a number of important financial databases, including Ticker Retrieval, Standard & Poor's, Disclosure II (SEC filings), Institutional Brokers' Estimate System, Historical Market Information, Portfolio Valuation, Money Market Services, and Up-to-the-Minute Quotes. In addition, stock quotes are continuously updated with a 20 minute delay from the market floor, and commodities are updated twice a day. EIS also offers tools for analyzing investments, loans, and depreciation.

SUPERSITE's ACORN (A Classification of Residential

Neighborhoods) database provides you with U.S. demographic and sales potential information needed to make decisions about locating your next franchise, designing your sales territories, and spending your advertising dollars. You can get even more background on a state or country by consulting the full text of Grolier's Academic American Encyclopedia.

COMMENTS:

CompuServe EIS (which includes CIS) offers a broad range of information and consumer services. The user-friendly, menu-driven system is easy to learn and to use. The optional command system is straightforward and efficient. For example, at the exclamation point (!) command prompt, you may enter T (TOP) to return to the main menu, M (MENU) to return to the previous menu, F (FORWARD) to move forward one page, B (BACK) to move back one page, H (HELP) to display documentation about the area you're using, S (SCROLL) to display pages continuously, and G (GO) to move directly to any page or database you wish to examine.

The manual was described to me as "worthless." That may be an exaggeration, but I wasn't overly impressed. Don't despair, because other resources are readily available. To help you navigate through the CompuServe information maze, an on-line INDEX lists all CompuServe services in alphabetical order and places an asterisk (*) beside those services in CIS. Each SIG group (IBM, Kaypro, etc.) has volumes of help stored on-line; for example, the IBM SIG Download Library 8 contains 40–50 pages of help. One of your first tasks might be to download these customized HELP files. Also, I'd recommend *How to Get the Most Out of CompuServe* by Charles Bowen and David Peyton (Bantam Books, 1984). They do an excellent job of teaching you how to explore the CIS section of CompuServe. *Online Today*, CompuServe's slick magazine, and the insert "CompuServe Highlights" will keep you posted on new services and applications. Occasionally you'll also receive quick reference cards and other bonuses.

The free on-line FEEDBACK service allows you to send your comments and questions directly to customer service. One user reported that the primary benefit to this service is catharsis—don't expect relevant, timely answers. The toll-free customer service number will generally result in helpful information. Many users prefer using the SIG bulletin boards for advice from their fellow users. The SIGS attract some pretty competent folks; for example, Ward Christensen, the father of the XMODEM transfer protocol, is on the IBM SIG almost every day. Also you'll find some of the most up-to-date information about computer products. If you're in the market for software, for example, just post on the Kaypro SIG a message like, "What's the best spelling checker for a Kaypro?" and see what happens.

CompuServe's electronic mail services are somewhat limited though inexpensive. You can send a 50-line by 80-character message (maximum size) for only 50 cents. Some users report that the conferencing mode isn't nearly as sophisticated as Participate on The Source.

You can design and store your own personal menu on CompuServe; for example, if you regularly access a half dozen services and a couple of SIGS, you can log onto your own custom-designed menu and make your selections from it. Any time you wish, you can go to the main menu and submenus for additional options or use the command mode. If you plan to perform XMODEM downloads, you'll need to change the system defaults by typing at the prompt <! GO DEFALT> (a six-letter command). Then you can change the values to 1200–N–8–1.

For 300 baud connect time CompuServe charges $12.50 per hour during prime time and $6.00 per hour on weekends and evenings. 1200 bps service is $15.00 and $12.50 respectively. CIS subscribers only pay for on-line time. EIS subscribers (who may also use CIS) pay a $10 monthly minimum which is applied to on-line charges. You can purchase several types of starter kits which provide you with documentation and free, after-hours 300 baud on-line time; for example, a manual and five free hours for $39.95. If when you first log onto the service, you answer "YES" to the credit card information, you can apply your five free hours of credit at 300 baud to 1200 bps service ($30.00's worth).

After hours, if you're just browsing through the system and reading screens, I recommend logging on at 300 bps (an average reading speed). When you're familiar with the system or when you plan to download files, you may wish to select the faster 1200 bps option. You'll find that the system begins to respond slowly around 9 P.M. Eastern Standard Time and is especially bad on Sunday evenings. 300 bps during busy hours may be more economical. Around midnight, the response time begins to improve. Along with connect charges, the CompuServe Network telecommunications service will bill you $0.25 per hour, a real bargain. If you use Tymnet or Telenet you'll pay $10 per hour prime time and $2 per hour evenings and weekends. Pricing for EIS premium services (mostly business and financial) are listed in a pamphlet provided by the service.

With over 140,000 subscribers, CompuServe obviously fills an information need. The menu-driven system makes searching a pleasure—almost an adventure—for even the most inexperienced novice. Anyone wanting to learn how to use an on-line service may want to begin on this relatively inexpensive and broad-based information service.

A–8 SDC Orbit

DATABASE NAME: Orbit Search Service Databases

VENDOR/PROVIDER NAME: SDC Information Services
SDC System Development Corp.
A Burroughs Company

ADDRESS: 2500 Colorado Ave.

CITY, STATE, ZIP: Santa Monica, CA 90406

TELEPHONE: 800-421-7229; In California 800-352-6689

CARRIERS/TOLL–FREE LINES: Tymnet, Telenet, and INWATS

COMPATIBILITY: Any Bell and Vadic modem protocols 300/ 1200 bps;
Software that emulates a teletypewriter, ASCII character set in asynchronous mode.

GENERAL DESCRIPTION:

Any company with a need for technical information will want to take a serious look at the 70 databases offered by SDC's ORBIT Search Service. With more than 55 million citations on-line, SDC Orbit provides bibliographic citations and abstracts from journal articles, patent records, books, conference papers, annual reports, contracts, government legislation, newspaper articles, specification sources, and statistical and tabular databases. The major subject areas covered include chemistry, engineering and electronics, energy and environment, patents, selected industries, life sciences, government and legislation, science and technology, social sciences, and business and economics.

If you need information on the oil, refining, and/or energy industry you will want to search databases such as APILIT and APIPAT. Prepared by the Central Abstracting and Indexing Service of the American Petroleum Institute, these databases cover worldwide refining literature and patents including petroleum refining, petrochemicals, air and water conservation, transportation and storage, and petroleum substitutes. Additional patent information may be found from the U.S. Department of Energy Energy Data Base which contains over 800,000 citations on all aspects of energy production, utilization, and conservation. In addition, ENERGYLINE provides comprehensive coverage of over 2,000 journals as well as reports, surveys, monographs, conference proceedings, and irregular serials. The American Geological Institute GEOREF database covers geosciences literature from 3,000 journals and other source documents. And Petroleum Energy/Business News Index covers sixteen major petroleum and energy industry publications.

Utility companies are especially interested in Edison Electric Institute's Electric Power Industry Abstracts, containing literature on electric power plants and related facilities. The POWER database contains catalog records for books, monographs, proceedings, and other material in the book collection of the Energy Library, U.S. Department of Energy.

The BIOTECHNOLOGY database includes information from 1,000 scientific and technological journals. Other technical databases include the CAS SERIES from Chemical Abstracts Service of the American Chemical Society contains millions of citations covering chemical sciences literature from over 12,000 journals, patents from 26 countries, new books, conference proceedings, and government research reports. The Chemical Abstracts Source Index is a compilation of bibliographic and library holdings information for chemistry sciences literature.

SRI International also provides annual supply/demand and price data for many of the 1,300 major commodity and specialty chemicals, chemical groups, chemical-related industries and U.S. economic indicators covered in the *Chemical Economics Handbook*. CORROSION contains data on the effects of over 600 agents on the most widely used metals, plastics, nonmetallics, and rubbers. COMPENDEX adds over 100,000 citations per year to its worldwide database of significant engineering literature from approximately 3,500 sources in industries such as aerospace engineering, bioengineering, civil engineering, electrical engineering, marine engineering, and nuclear technology. Other technical subjects covered include food science, forestry, physics, veterinary medicine, metals, pesticides and herbicides, paper and pulp, pharmaceuticals, psychology, and the environment.

The World Patents Index is a comprehensive and authoritative file of over one million patent families compiled by Derwent publications from 24 major industrial countries. In addition, Derwent prepares the U.S. PATENT OFFICE files which cover all U.S. patents, continuations, divisionals, and defensive documents from 1971 to present. USCLASS contains all U.S. Classifications, Cross-Reference Classifications, and Unofficial Classifications for all patents issued from the first U.S. patent issued in 1790 to date.

If you need to know what the government is doing, you can search THE FEDERAL REGISTER for rules, proposed rules, public law notices, meetings, hearings, and Presidential proclamations on a myriad of topics. Over 18,000 citations per year are added to this database. GRANTS contains thousands of references to grant programs offered by federal, state, and local government, commercial organizations, and private foundations in over 88 disciplines. NTIS (The National Technical Information Service) covers U.S. government-sponsored research and development from over 200 federal agencies, including technical reports, reprints, translations, and other documents. If you're a government contractor, you'll want to check the information in the U.S. Contract Awards database, which provides access to more than 39,000 contracts awarded by the federal government and its agencies to both public and private sectors, approximately 15,000 awards per year.

Orbit also provides a few news and business-oriented databases, including ACCOUNTANTS, which cites literature on accounting, auditing, taxation, financial management, and so forth. BANKER contains approximately 27,000 citations from the *American Banker*. In addition, the AMERICAN STATISTICS INDEX covers statistical publications of the U.S. government, including periodicals, annuals, biennials, surveys, analytical reports, statistical compilations, and special publications. This is a great place to find the entire spectrum of social, economic and demographic data.

Data Courier also provides ABI/INFORM which covers over 550 periodicals for business, management and industry. MANAGEMENT from Management Contents rounds out the business selections with extensive coverage of literature from both U.S. and non-U.S. journals on accounting, banking, commodities, economics, finance, human resource development, marketing, public administration, government, and social issues. Monitor and Newspaper Index put you in touch with the *Christian Science Monitor* as well as nine major U.S. newspapers and ten Black newspapers—over 200,000 citations per year. Since these databases are updated monthly, you won't find today's news on-line; however, you will find a wealth of historical data.

COMMENTS:

Many searchers using SDC have both a technical background—in chemistry or engineering, for example—and extensive experience in on-line search techniques. SDC Orbit is definitely a professional searcher's database. The command-driven retrieval system is designed for intricate in-depth searches. Although the search system isn't quite as sophisticated as Dialog's, searchers report that SDC is improving all the time. The system response time is very good and SDC does a better job of formatting the screen and printed reports than Dialog.

SDC charges a $100 per month minimum, which is applied to usage charges. You don't want to "play" or casually browse on many of SDC's databases since many of them charge upwards of $75 per hour for connect time. In addition, they assess a fee for each off-line printed citation that ranges from $0.20 to $1.00 each. You can obtain discounts up to $20 per hour by guaranteeing a sizeable minimum usage.

The Orbit User Manual costs $40 and is quite complete. A $15 Complete Quick Reference Guide is also available. For $7.50 each you can buy 30 or 40 different database manuals that discuss the details of specific databases. SDC provides a number of courses for searchers, but they tend to be geared for the experienced searcher more than the novice or small user.

If you require the full-text document, you can order it on line through the ORBDOC Online Ordering Service. Users report that their document delivery service is superb.

SDC's ORBIT is one of the best technical on-line services available. It is a must for researchers, engineers, and others working in technical industries.

A-9 MCI Mail

DATABASE NAME: MCI Mail

VENDOR/PROVIDER NAME: MCI Digital Information Services
                        Corporation
                        Subsidiary of MCI
                        Communications Corp.

ADDRESS: 1133 19th St. NW

CITY, STATE, ZIP: Washington, D.C. 20036

TELEPHONE: 800-MCI-2255; in Washington, D.C. call 833-8484

CARRIERS/TOLL-FREE LINES: WATS (15 cents per minute)
                            Tymnet (5 cents per minute)

COMPATIBILITY: Almost any terminal, word processing
                 equipment with telecommunications
                 capabilities, and personal computers with
                 modems

GENERAL DESCRIPTION:

Electronic mail can provide instant communication with branch offices, field personnel, and even to the building next door. You can communicate with customers, stockholders, vendors and many more.

How many times have you played telephone tag with someone? Or, how many times have you needed to instantly send information in writing to avoid confusion or mistakes? Electronic mail might have been an economic and efficient method for handling these situations. MCI Mail offers several types of services which could be used to make communications faster and less expensive.

Instant Mail. If both parties have an MCI "electronic mailbox," you can instantly send up to 500 characters (approximately 100 words) to each other, for only 45 cents plus

15 cents per minute for telecommunications charges. So, for less than a dollar you can send a written message across town or across the country. The addressee doesn't have to be at his or her workstation when you send the message. So, time zones, travel schedules, and business activities won't interfere with your ability to communicate. Over 130,000 MCI Mail subscribers have electronic mailboxes.

If you have more lengthy reports or contracts to send, you can prepare them with your word processor, connect to MCI Mail and upload the file to MCI's computer. At 300 or 1200 bps (30 or 120 characters per second), this procedures will save connect time charges. You can send 501 to 7500 characters (approximately 100–1500 words) for $1 plus WATS line charges. It doesn't matter that your computer and your addressee's computer are not the same or that the word processing software differs. Both computers will be able to "read" the messages. By electronically downloading the messages, the addressee gains the ability to electronically manipulate the information and print it: for example, multiple copies for intra-office distribution. The only hitch is that all control characters must be removed from the data, so no underlines and special formatting codes can be used.

Four-Hour Paper Delivery by Courier. If your addressee isn't an MCI Mail subscriber, you can still deliver information in a flash to 17 major metropolitan areas, including Atlanta, Boston, Chicago, Cleveland, Dallas, Denver, Detroit, Honolulu, Houston, Los Angeles, Miami, Minneapolis, New York, Philadelphia, Pittsburgh, San Francisco, St. Louis, and Washington, D.C. Regardless of your location, your message will travel electronically to one of these points and then be printed on a laser printer for delivery. If you pay an extra $20 to register your letterhead and signature, your correspondence will be personalized and custom printed. A four-hour, courier-delivered letter of up to six pages will cost $30.

Printed Overnight Letter. If overnight service is adequate, MCI guarantees laser printing and delivery before noon the next business day, hand delivered to over 20,000 cities and towns. You can type HELP *STATE* to find out what cities are supported. Sending up to six pages overnight for $8 is a bargain.

Printed First Class Letter. If your letter is going to or

178 / APPENDIX A

near one of the major metropolitan areas mentioned above, you may be able to get overnight service for "first class rates." The MCI Letter is printed at one of these nodes and then placed in the local U.S. Mail. First class letters mailed in this way frequently arrive the next day, and up to three pages cost only $2. Longer documents cost $1 for each additional three pages.

Overseas Mail Delivery. You can cut several days from overseas mail delivery by electronically transmitting your correspondence to MCI's European network in Brussels. For details about sending mail to a particular country, simply type HELP <COUNTRY>: for example, <HELP ENG-LAND>. For $5.50, a printed MCI World Letter from 7,500 characters to six pages may be delivered anywhere in the world. And, for $12 to $30, the same overseas printed letter can be hand-delivered by courier or delivered by the local postal system.

Telex Dispatch. MCI Mail messages can be delivered to any telex terminal in the U.S. or to 1.7 million telex subscribers in more than 200 countries. You can also receive telex messages in your MCI Mail electronic mailbox. By paying as little as 25 cents per minute, your company will save up to 33 percent over standard telex rates.

Additional Services. To become an MCI Mail subscriber, you simply pay an annual $18 mailbox fee which may be applied to your usage charges. These charges can even be billed to a major credit card. For $10 per month you can purchase advanced services that offer more capabilities. With advanced service, you can combine two commands in one step; for example, at the prompt you can enter <READ DRAFT> instead of <READ> and then at the next prompt <DRAFT>. This will save you some time and effort. In addition, you will qualify for extended on-line storage so your mail will remain on-line for five days. Also, you can create your own mailing list and use it to send messages to a number of addressees. The VOLUME MAIL service provides discounted mailings to hundreds and even thousands of recipients. By registering several letterheads and signatures plus all your business forms, you'll be able to meet most of your correspondence needs.

MCI's ON-LINE ADS let you take advantage of dozens of

special services and merchandise offers; for example, you can purchase software, legal forms, computer paper, investment services, travel services, and more.

MCI Mail also serves as a gateway to DOW JONES NEWS/ RETRIEVAL where you can read *The Wall Street Journal* and receive up-to-the-minute stock market quotes. See also the review on DJN/R which appears in this appendix.

If your company is willing to guarantee a $50 or $250 per month minimum, you will receive discounts and free access to Advanced Service. You can call MCI's toll-free number for the details.

COMMENTS:

MCI Mail provides a unique electronics communications system for both individuals and companies. MCI Mail can be used as an internal electronic mail system or it can supplement in-house systems by providing links to customers, suppliers, stockholders, and others.

As an in-house electronic mail system, employees can send correspondence to other departments and to field personnel; for example, if the Corporate Legal Department wants to send a contract to the California-based Branch Sales Office for signatures, MCI Mail is the fastest vehicle. If the Branch Office has an electronic mailbox, they can download the contract, use a word processor to insert the names of the parties involved, and print as many copies as needed. It doesn't matter that the word processor that created the document is a Lanier III in New York and the word processor editing and printing the contract is an IBM Display Writer in Los Angeles.

The menu-driven MCI Mail system is quick and easy to use. The manual explains what each command does, and since the commands are close to English equivalents, they are easy to learn. For example, selecting CREATE from the menu allows you to create a message using the MCI Mail text editor on-line. If you choose this method, you don't even need a word processing program; you just need telecommunications software to link you with the MCI Mail computer. Note that you'll be charged a 15 cents per minute fee if you compose your document during connect time. Creating your documents off-line on your word processor and saving them on a data disk is a more economical method. Once you've logged onto the MCI Mail system, you can then upload the text file(s) at 1200 bps—much faster than you can type.

Even though uploading process seems fast, don't dawdle. The connect time for uploading a five or six page document may cost as much as sending the document itself and thus double your expense. I sent a 1,000 word article to PICO magazine for a $3.00 delivery fee PLUS a $2.86 (19 minutes) access charge. I'm sure that a good portion of the connect-time charge was caused by my reviewing (reading) the uploaded text on-line to ensure that the transfer was successful. Even at $5.86, I was able to electronically transmit the article for half the price of overnight U.S. Mail service and without the expense of printing, paper and envelope.

Don't overlook the fact that your customers or clients will be impressed with your promptness. The extra expense and effort you make to get information to them fast may result in your getting the contract or preferential treatment. A case in point: I had been trying to sell a book proposal to an editor for a couple of months. After weeks of negotiation, my literary agent said the editor wanted me to rewrite the introduction and first chapter in a different style. Not wanting to blow the deal, I used MCI Mail to send a draft to my agent for her comments. In only a few days, I had the 3,000-word, rewritten proposal ready and laser-printed on MCI Mail stationery in New York. My agent decided to forward the proposal to the editor, saying to me, "This looks great. And, it looks like you busted your b— to get it here. That should impress her even more." The day the editor received the proposal, we received a top-dollar offer.

The advantages of using electronic mail service is only just beginning to be explored. And with the influx of personal computer workstations into departments and offices, the opportunities are growing.

A-10 Delphi

DATABASE NAME: Delphi

VENDOR/PROVIDER NAME: General Videotex Corporation

ADDRESS: 3 Blackstone Street

CITY, STATE, ZIP: Cambridge, MA 02139

TELEPHONE: 800-544-4005; In Massachusetts 517-491-3393

CARRIERS/TOLL–FREE LINES: Tymnet, Telenet, Datapac
(Canada)

COMPATIBILITY: Most personal computers with 300/1200 bps
modems

GENERAL DESCRIPTION:

If you're looking for a user-friendly, inexpensive on-line service for electronic communications, access to the daily news, and on-line financial and travel services, Delphi may be the answer. In addition to an on-line encyclopedia and technical services (described later), Delphi serves as a gateway to DIALOG, the largest on-line database service. (See complete description elsewhere in this appendix.) By using Delphi to access Dialog, you can save expensive monthly minimum fees.

Communications.   Delphi offers a number of communications options that allow you to share information with other computer users and to forward information to and from office and field staff. The BULLETIN BOARDS are both public (open to all users) and private (open only to members in a specified group). In fact, some boards may be READ ONLY and password protected. You can read up to three boards at once to save logging onto each board of interest. And you can search for specific messages by limiting your topic; for example, you can specify < BBOARD >COMPUTERS,SOFT-WARE > to access two bulletin boards and then enter a SUBJECT category < SPREADSHEET > to see messages on a specific topic.

If you're a frustrated writer, INFOMANIA is a member publishing area for prose, poetry, a collaborative novel, interactive executable programs, newsletters, product reviews (software, movies, cars, etc.), and opinion polls.

You can conduct real-time conferences with other Delphi users, and you can page specific users for a chat. The on-line schedule tells you what conferences and symposiums are currently active as well as posts future sessions.

The MAIL option is a comprehensive private messaging system you can use to send messages, read messages, store messages, and perform a topic search through your private stored message file. You can send TELEX messages anywhere in the world; and you can even send electronic mail directly to The Source and CompuServe users. However, they cannot send electronic mail to you.

APPOINTMENT CALENDAR and DIARY help you keep track of important information while you're in the office or on the road. Others can read your calendar, too, and post entries on it to keep you aware of upcoming events.

On-Line Oracle. If you have a burning question about computers or any other subject, the Delphi Oracle will do his or her best to answer your inquiries. If it's a quick question about Delphi or about computers, the Oracle's time and expertise are free. If your question involves more technical subjects, like whether you should use your company's stock purchase plan, the Oracle will quote you a consultation charge. The Oracle consultant uses videotex private conferences, telephone discussions, U.S. Mail exchanges, off-line studies, and audio tapes to provide personalized recommendations about how you can change your behavior and attitudes. The Oracle will also help you gain insight into your personality and problems. There's even an on-line addict's group for persons addicted to the machine, victims of the "Silicon Syndrome."

Financial Services. If you join a Delphi Member Bank, you can pay your bills, keep your bank balance, and reconcile your statement on-line. If you're in need of Brokerage Services, North American Investment Corporation and David N. Glassman will provide you with new stock ratings, a technical newsletter, financial research, and personal recommendations. When you open a brokerage account with them, you can enter buy and sell transactions of stocks, bonds, tax exempts, mutual funds, IRAs and money market instruments 24 hours a day, 7 days a week. You'll obtain discounts of up to 70 percent of their regular commission schedule, and you'll receive confirmation of your transactions at your terminal. You'll also have access to their quote system. North American's interactive brokerage service costs an extra fee. You can also get value-added investment advice from Security Objective Service.

Information Retrieval. The LIBRARY gives you access to Dialog, the Kussmaul–Encyclopedia and to other reference sources.

Dialog contains over 200 separate bibliographic databases; however, the system is rather complex to search and usually requires that you attend a 1½ day workshop-seminar to master it. The database fees range from $30 per hour to over $100, so this isn't a casual place to look for information. You'll also need to purchase separate manuals from Dialog to learn the details about how to use the system. Although you save Dialog's $100 per month minimum, Delphi charges a $25 per search minimum. (See the Dialog review elsewhere in this Appendix for the details.) For an additional hourly charge, the Colorado Online Information Network (COIN) will conduct on-line search and retrieval operations for you.

The Kussmaul-Encyclopedia is a general reference work that contains information on more than 20,000 topics. For example, by entering <KUSS MYTHOLOGY> you'll proceed directly to the reference on this topic. Many cross-references will lead you to other sources of information.

Currently there are two types of news services. You'll pay an extra $5 per hour surcharge to read the HOLLYWOOD HOTLINE, which is a collection of reviews, industry news, and upcoming events. The NEWS extra value service connects you to the major wire services for up-to-the-minute news releases.

On-Line Shopping. BAZAAR is Delphi's on-line user flea market. You can also read Delphi vendor ads on the CATALOG database as well as shop from SPECIALTY SERVICES and SOFTWARE EMPORIUM, which offer a variety of computer products. COMP-U-STORE offers some 35,000 other products, but this is a service you'll have to sign up for separately.

The TRAVEL databases provide you with information on airline schedules and fares and general travel information. You can make plane, car rental, and hotel reservations with the service. Delphi serves as a gateway to the Official Airline Guides (OAG), which provides you with complete up-to-date schedule and fare information. OAG is a premium service, charging an extra fee.

COMMENTS:

Delphi is a menu-driven system so easy to use you probably won't need to refer to the well-organized and plainly illustrated manual. In fact, almost everything you need to know is printed on a greeting card–sized, 10-page quick-reference chart. When you log on the first time, you'll receive a Guided Tour of the Delphi system. As you become more familiar with the system, you can change your beginner menu Profile option to two other levels, intermediate or advanced (a sleek single prompt). If you become confused, simply enter a question mark (?) and help appears on the screen. On-line help is frequently available from a human sysop.

If you wish, you can customize the menus to meet your own needs. You can also control your screen width, the type of terminal your computer is imitating, your password, and your own personal description, which may be seen by other users for conferencing purposes.

One of Delphi's most popular features is conferencing. One reason for its popularity is that messages are kept in order, and you can enter and leave the conferencing section with a single command.

Delphi's fees are quite reasonable if you're primarily interested in the communications features. They charge a one-time subscription fee of $49.95 which qualifies you for the handbook, all updates, and a subscriber newsletter. The hourly connect charge is as low as $5 per hour on evenings and weekends, and as low as $20 per hour during business hours, including telecommunications fees. Also, there is no premium charge for 1200 bps service. You'll have to consult the on-line fee schedule for value-added services, which cost varying amounts. A number of the services require that you establish separate accounts and passwords: for example, the financial, news, and banking services.

A–11 I.P. Sharp Application Software

DATABASE NAME: I.P. Sharp Application Software

VENDOR/PROVIDER NAME: I.P. Sharp Associates, Ltd.

ADDRESS: 2 First Canadian Place, Suite 1900, Exchange Tower

CITY, STATE, ZIP: Toronto, Ontario, Canada M5X 1E3

TELEPHONE: 416-364-5361

CARRIERS/TOLL–FREE LINES: IPSANET, Tymnet, Telenet, Telepac, Datex–P, Datapac, PSS, Transpac, and Telex

COMPATIBILITY: Most any business level personal computer and modem

GENERAL DESCRIPTION:

Established in 1969, the SHARP APS time-sharing service supports the largest APL (programming language) time-sharing operation in the world. I.P. Sharp offers customers an extensive library of application software, including the following:

Database retrieval and reporting.

Color business graphics.

Electronic mail.

Consolidation of budgets and plans.

Crosstabulation.

Project analysis, planning, and evaluation (critical path).

Actuarial analysis.

Econometric analysis.

Forecasting.

Statistical analysis.

Lease evaluation.

Financial analysis.

Capital budget analysis.

Most of these programs operate in a user-friendly, prompted mode that requires little orientation. For the more experienced user, many programs can also perform in a command-driven mode. I.P. Sharp also offers tools to assist the APL programmer with model building, graphics applications building, system maintenance, and documentation systems.

Along with applications software, I.P. Sharp maintains the world's largest collection of on-line numeric databases. I.P. Sharp offers over 100 different databases containing 50 million time series of public data, including data on economics, securities, banking, finance, energy, aviation, and insurance. Information from these databases as well as private data may be manipulated by their on-line applications software. See Appendix A–12 for a description of the public numeric databases.

Applications software is available free of any royalty charge; that is, the user is subject to only normal time-sharing rates. Below are synopses of the major applications software available on line:

MAGIC provides a consistent and easy-to-use method for access, manipulation, reporting, and plotting of data contained in the I.P. Sharp public numeric databases. This software allows you to calculate summaries over time as well as moving averages, year-to-year changes and percent changes, curve fitting, deseasonalization, and forecasting. A powerful report formatter provides a variety of flexible yet simple to operate output options.

MABRA is a general purpose record administration and database management system used to maintain personnel records, pension systems, inventory, conference registrations, prospect lists, and mailing lists—any application with fixed-length records. The powerful record-searching feature allows you to select records based on any combination of fields. You can also accomplish complex database operations and produce sophisticated data analyses and reports.

SUPERPLOT is a color business graphics package that plots on a wide variety of plotting devices and terminals. You can create straight- or curved-line plots, bar charts, pie charts, surface charts, histograms and stacked histogram plots, high-low-close plots, log plots, and web charts. You can control the color and size of textual information, including titles, footnotes, legends, and labels.

MAGICSTORE is a multidimensional time series data management system that lets you create a database, maintain it, and retrieve data in a variety of formats. MAGICSTORE can be used as an integral part of data modeling, forecasting, planning, consolidation, and reporting applications.

CONSOLE maintains data and produces business reports, including multinational financial consolidations, sales forecasting by product, acquisition analysis, budget preparation, inflation analysis, and currency exposure analysis. This software handles business reports that require data continually on a monthly, quarterly, semiannual, or annual basis.

XTABS is a crosstabulation package designed to analyze and manipulate sets of coded data like responses to surveys or questionnaires. The system will accommodate both discrete and continuous data.

SNAP allows you to plan and control a project by breaking it into its constituent activities and specifying the sequence in which activities will be done. You can describe the project in terms of these activities, their durations and resource requirements, and their logical relationships. The network is then analyzed to identify the critical phases of the project. The software allows you to examine alternate strategies until a workable plan is reached. As work progresses, the project can be monitored and controlled.

Actuarial Library utility programs allow you to evaluate any closed-form actuarial expression and provide for varying time-dependent interest rates, select mortality, joint life calculations, interpolations, and discrete or continuous operating modes. The Library also contains a package that facilitates computations for graduation techniques: interpolation, moving-weighted-average, Whittaker-Henderson, and fit and smoothness checks.

The Econometric Analysis System facilitates the quantitative analysis of time series, including simple regression and autoregressive and/or distributed lag models. The ability to interactively modify equations by adding or subtracting variables or varying assumptions lets you gradually build up a model.

QUICKDRAW is a production-oriented business graphics package used with the Hewlett-Packard Model 7221 plotter. This package allows you to develop line plots, bar charts, pie charts, and high-low-close plots in any size, shape and color. You can also control the text for footnotes, titles, legends, and other labels.

Statistical Analysis covers statistical methods such as the design and analysis of experiments, econometric analysis, modeling, and data reduction. Methods include descriptive, parametric and nonparametric statistics, statistical tests, model parameter estimation according to common regression and correlation methods, probability functions and distributions, random number generation, analysis of variance, and multivariate classification methods.

SIFT provides a wide range of time series analysis and forecasting techniques you can use with your own private database or with the public time series databases accessed through MAGIC. With a few simple commands, you can quickly obtain desired forecasts or perform analysis techniques including moving averages, exponential smoothing, curve fitting, decomposition, harmonic smoothing, trend-cycle analysis, and generalized adaptive filtering.

STARS allows you to create and store multiple sets of input assumptions for a model. It is intended for APL systems analysts who are writing customized models.

FASTNET is a project planning and management system based on network analysis and critical path techniques. With FASTNET you can perform critical path analysis, aggregation and scheduling of resources, and simple cost analysis. The extensive reporting and graphic features allow you to draw annotated network diagrams based on calculations or activity data.

APS (A Planning System) allows you to plan and control strategies within your organization, including sales forecasting, risk analysis, budget and financial plan control, and so forth. With APS you can evaluate alternative business strategies investments and cash flows, and much more.

Mailbox allows you to send and receive electronic mail with subsidiaries or branches in more than 600 locations in 46 countries served by the I.P. Sharp communications network. You can use their simple text editor to send messages to an individual or to a group together with "carbon copies" to others. You can mark your messages as urgent, registered, confidential, or personal. A complete directory of Mailbox members will tell you who belongs to the network.

COMMENTS:

I.P. Sharp's Application Software time-sharing database is quite different from other services described in this book. This service brings sophisticated numerical analytical tools and sophisticated modeling processes into the hands of personal computer users. The menu-driven programs allow almost any specialist and manager to utilize the power and versatility of the programs, and on-line help is available at a keystroke.

A-12 I.P. Sharp Public Data Bases

DATABASE NAME: I.P. Sharp Public Data Bases

VENDOR/PROVIDER NAME: I.P. Sharp Associates Limited

ADDRESS: 2 First Canadian Place, Suite 1900, Exchange Tower

CITY, STATE, ZIP: Toronto, Ontario, Canada M5X 1E3

TELEPHONE: 416-364-5361

CARRIERS/TOLL–FREE LINES: IPSANET, Tymnet, Telenet,
Telepac, Datex-P, Datapac,
PSS, Transpac, and Telex

COMPATIBILITY: Most any business level personal computer
and modem

GENERAL DESCRIPTION:

Established in 1969, the SHARP APS time-sharing service maintains the world's largest collection of on-line numeric databases. The service provides over 100 different databases containing 50 million times series of public data including data on economics, securities, banking, finance, energy, aviation, and insurance. Information from these databases as well as private data may be manipulated by their on-line applications software.

I.P. Sharp offers customers an extensive library of on-line applications software (see Appendix A–11 for details). The software programs allow you to retrieve data from the public databases and manipulate them for modeling, reports, and graphic presentations. The applications include the following:

Database retrieval and reporting.

Color business graphics.

Electronic mail.

Consolidation of budgets and plans.

Crosstabulation.

Project analysis, planning and evaluation (critical path).

Actuarial analysis.

Econometric analysis.

Forecasting.

Statistical analysis.

Lease evaluation.

Financial analysis.

Capital budget analysis.

Most of the public databases contain historical numeric data in time series form. A *time series* is a set of observations evenly spaced over time. The five major subject areas are aviation, economics, energy, finance, and actuarial. Some databases cover one country and others include many countries for an in-depth international picture. Daily data is entered daily, monthly is entered monthly, and so on.

Other than its normal time-sharing charges, I.P. Sharp makes no extra charges for the use of the data, for the number of data items read, or for a subscription fee.

Aviation Databases. The aviation databases include information on the U.S. aviation industry as well as European traffic and financial statistics, Canadian operating statistics, and international data on aircraft movements and airports. The OAG2 database contains detailed flight schedules of all airlines in the world.

Economic Databases. This area of the I.P. Sharp service gives detailed pictures of internal and international economies. You'll find socioeconomic data for Australia, Canada, Great Britain, West Germany and the United States. The databases include national accounts for more than 150 countries; internal economic data for the OECD nations; world debt figures for over 100 countries and regions; short- and long-term economic forecasts in textual form for 35 countries; macro-economic time series that predict statistics for the next five years (U.S.); textual reports on sociopolitical prognosis, domestic market forecasts, and external-account projections; values and quantities of international trade for 28 countries and 3,075 commodities; total liabilities and assets for 200 countries; and the 1981 Canadian Census.

Energy Databases. These databases focus on world-wide production, distribution and pricing of petroleum products. You'll receive a detailed picture of U.S. refining, stocks, imports and exports, and consumption of crude oil and petroleum products. You'll be able to find inventories of natural gas liquids and liquified petroleum gasses, coal and natural gas production, and energy consumption. You'll also find information about world-wide supply and demand and about production, consumption, trade, refining, and stocks. The *Petroleum Intelligence Weekly* database covers weekly crude oil production, key crude prices, and spot product prices. Other energy data includes Canadian retail gasoline volume and pricing, the DeWitt petrochemical newsletters and price forecasts, and U.S. electrical utilities.

Financial Databases. If you're interested in national

and international statistics for banks, governments, and corporations, the financial databases may provide the pricing and rate information you need. You'll find daily data on stocks, bonds, commodities, and interest rates for Europe, the United States, Canada, Australia, and the Far East. In addition, you'll find international data on money market rates and on currency exchange rates in 14 countries. Banking data covers the financial reports from the U.S. Federal Reserve Board, U.S. banks, Bank of Canada weekly banking and monetary statistics, and Canadian chartered banks.

Actuarial Databases. This section of the I.P. Sharp system contains over 200 tables of mortality on assured lives, annuitants, and general populations. There are also projection tables of projection scales, salary scales, withdrawal rates, disability rates, and remarriage rates.

COMMENTS:

I.P. Sharp makes available a unique collection of numeric databases on a number of subjects critical to corporations. You can retrieve and format information from these databases using the on-line applications software MAGIC and INFO-MAGIC (see the applications software discussion in Appendix A–11). Magic uses English-like words to help you retrieve, analyze, report, and plot data from these public databases. With the use of SUPERPLOT and Magic, data can then be displayed graphically.

The *Public Data Bases Catalogue* is quite well organized and explains in detail what each database contains. Each database description includes the following categories:

Category.

Creation Date.

Description.

Frequency/History.

Updates.

Source(s).

Access.

Online Documentation.

Documentation.

Mail System Contacts.

Notes.

Divided into subject categories, the manual provides over a full page of descriptive information for each database. See Figure A12–1 for a partial listing of the numeric databases offered. Additional reference guides are available for in-depth information. All of the written materials provided by I.P. Sharp are well organized and written in complete, easy-to-understand terms.

FIGURE A12–1   I.P. Sharp Public Databases   A Partial Listing

---

AVIATION
  Association of European Airlines.
  Aircraft Accidents.
  Commuter Online Origin-Destination.
  U.S. International Air Travel Statistics.
  Official Airline Guide.
  Air Charter.

ECONOMICS
  Australian Bureau of Statistics Data.
  Australian Export Statistics.
  Australian Economic Statistics.
  Business International Economic Forecasts.
  Business International Historical Data.
  1981 Canadian Census.
  Citibank Economic Data.
  Citibank Economic Forecast.
  United Nations Commodity Trade Statistics.
  West German Statistical Data.
  United Kingdom Central Statistical Office.
  United States Consumer Price Index.
  United States Producer Price Index.
  World Bank Debt Tables.

ENERGY
  Monthly Report of Heating Oil and Middle Distillates.
  Petroleum Argus Daily Market Report.
  DeWitt Petrochemical Newsletters.
  Electric Utilities Reports.
  Weekly Temperatures.
  Hughes Rotary Drilling Rig Report.
  Independent Chemical Information Services.
  United States Petroleum Imports.

FIGURE A12–1 *(concluded)*

International Petroleum Annual.
Canadian Retail Gasoline Volume.
Liquified Petroleum Gas Report.
Monthly Energy Review.
Lundberg Survey Share of Market.
United States Department of Energy.
Lundberg Survey Wholesale Prices.
Weekly Statistical Bulletin.

FINANCE
Australian Financial Markets.
Australian Stock Exchanges Indices.
Canadian Bonds.
Canadian Stock Options.
Canadian Department of Insurance Property and Casualty Insurance.
Commonwealth Bank Bond Index.
Commodities.
Currency Exchange Rates.
Disclosure II.
Canadian Department of Insurance.
Federal Reserve Board Weekly.
Financial Times Actuaries Share Indices.
Financial Times Share Information.
Hong Kong Stock Exchange.
Canadian Chartered Banks Monthly Statement of Assets and Liabilities.
Money Market Rates.
North American Stock Market.
Singapore Corporate Statistics.
Singapore Stock Exchange.
Sydney Stock Exchange Share Prices.
Toronto Stock Exchange 300 Index and Stock Statistics.
United States Banks.
United States Bonds.
United States Stock Options.
United States Quarterly Financial Report.
United States Stock Market.
Bank of Canada Weekly Financial Statistics.

OTHER
Actuarial Data Base.
National Emergency Equipment Locator System.

A-13 BRS/BRKTHRU

DATABASE NAME: BRS/BRKTHRU

VENDOR/PROVIDER NAME: BRS

ADDRESS: 1200 Route 7

CITY, STATE, ZIP: Latham, NY 12110

TELEPHONE: 800-345-4BRS; 518-783-7251 collect

CARRIERS/TOLL-FREE LINES: Telenet and Uninet

COMPATIBILITY: Most any business level personal computer
and modem

GENERAL DESCRIPTION:

BRS offers a number of different services including BRS/
AFTER DARK, BRS/INSTRUCTOR and BRS/BRKTHRU. The
newer BRKTHRU service is an easy to learn, menu-driven
system offering a full range of information databases. Of all
the services I logged onto, BRKTHRU was the easiest to learn
and the easiest to use.

Once you've logged onto the service, BRKTHRU offers
you four options:

1 Looking for information? . . . .

  Search Service

2 Want to hear the latest? . . . .

  Newsletter Service

98 Want to change your security password?

99 Sign off

To conduct a search, you enter <1> and press the carriage return. Then BRKTHRU presents you with eight database options:

1. Business and finance.
2. Medicine and pharmacology.
3. Physical and applied sciences.
4. Life sciences.
5. Education.
6. Social sciences and humanities.
7. Reference and multidisciplinary.
8. Enter any database label.

When you enter the desired area of interest, BRKTHRU lists the databases included in that category and the abbreviated label. When you enter the label you wish, the system will ask you if you want instructions and if you want to see a description of the database contents. Once you're familiar with the system instructions and the database contents, you can save some time by skipping the lengthier prompts; for example, you can enter <8> and the database four-character label.

Entering search terms is easy, too. You can use Boolean logic operators such as AND and OR as well as proximity operators. In fact, the system will automatically add ADJ (adjacent) between two words; for example, I entered <IN VITRO AND INFERTIL$> to find in vitro fertilization and infertility. When I asked for the system to print a search summary (a list of searches I'd performed), it printed <IN ADJ VITRO AND INFERTIL$>. Note that I could truncate the word infertile/infertility/etc. with the dollar sign ($).

The search menu offers a number of options: S = search, D = display documents, R = review your search history, PG = purge search statements, CD = choose new database, MM = return to main menu, and 0 = sign off. Each time you enter a search statement, you'll see the number of hits and then return to this menu. If you decide to display the records found you press <D> for display. Then the following series of menus appear:

ENTER NUMBER OF SEARCH ANSWER TO DISPLAY means to select the search statement number you wish to display. Then BRKTHRU asks if you want the short, medium or long form of the record(s) displayed:

ENTER S   FOR SHORT FORMAT

ENTER M   FOR MEDIUM FORMAT

ENTER L   FOR LONG FORMAT

If you wish you can view only brief bibliographic information using the "Short Format." Each record is numbered so you can record which ones you might wish to see in full. The medium format provides a synopsis. And, in a full-text database, the long format provides the entire article.

The next menu option asks you for which articles you wish to have displayed:

ENTER NUMBERS OF DOCUMENTS TO DISPLAY
IN FOLLOWING FORM:

1,2,3 ETC.   OR 1–10   OR ALL

If you enter <ALL>, all records will be displayed. If you only wish to see specific records, you can enter those record numbers. If you discover a flaw in your search strategy, you can stop the retrieval at the end of any screen of text. The records scroll up one screen at a time (24 or 16 lines) and pause for a carriage return. If you're retrieving long files, you can select a continuous scrolling mode when you log onto the system. However, in this mode, you cannot quit a search during the display process as you can in a screen-by-screen display mode.

Once you're familiar with the system, you can stack the commands on a single command line; for example, <D;4;S;1–10> means DISPLAY SEARCH #4 IN THE SHORT FORM FOR RECORDS 1–10. So, BRKTHRU offers both the ease of a menu-driven system and the speed of a command driven system. You will have to be familiar with the search strategies and proximity operators in order to narrow your search to reasonable limits. For example, you can use <WITH> to find two words in the same sentence and <SAME> to find two words in the same paragraph. You can limit your search to any given field such as title, author, and year: for example <CANCER AND LUNG AND 1984.YR.> will find 1984.

Although BRKTHRU offers discounted evening and weekend rates, it is more expensive than its BRS/After Dark cousin. For example, MEDLINE is $44 per hour (day) or $28 per hour (P.M.); ABI/INFORM is $70.00 or $26.50; *Harvard Business Review*/Online is $75.00 or $25.50; Management Contents is $75 or $25.50; PATDATA is $65 or $21.50; and CHEMICAL ABSTRACTS is $73 or $33. In addition, BRKTHRU charges 3 to 5 cents per record for displaying (downloading). Compared with BRS/After Dark, the evening rates are 50 to 75 percent higher. However, BRKTHRU offers a wider range of databases and charges no minimum monthly fee. You'll only pay a one-time $75 membership fee.

BRKTHRU provides a wide variety of databases. The Life Sciences databases include BIOSIS Previews, Pollution Abstracts, Drug Information Fulltext, International Pharmaceutical Abstracts, Health Planning and Administration, and MEDLINE. The Physical/Applied Sciences include such databases as CA SEARCH, Hazardline, COMPENDEX, and RO-BOTICS. The Business/Finance databases include ABI/IN-FORM, *Harvard Business Review*/Online, Management Contents, IRS Publications, PATDATA, Predicasts Annual Reports Abstracts, PTS/PROMT and PTS/F&S Indexes. The Social Sciences/Humanities databases include Family Resources, National Institute of Mental Health, Mental Measurements Yearbook, PsycINFO, Sociological Abstracts and REHAB-DATA. The Education databases include ERIC (Educational Resources Information Center), Exceptional Child Education, National College Databank, Resources in Computer Education, and Vocational Education Curriculum Materials. You also gain access to the Academic American Encyclopedia, American Men and Women of Science, Books In Print, Dissertation Abstracts Online, National Technical Information Service (NTIS), and Ulrich's International Periodicals Directory and Irregular Serials and Annuals.

BRS offers a number of other services such as toll-free customer service, discounted rates for educational purposes, a monthly BRS BULLETIN, SDIs, and off-line printing.

If you're looking for a broad range of information which is easily accessed, BRS/BRKTHRU may be just what you're looking for.

APPENDIX B _____
Modem Roundup

Buying a modem can be as simple as purchasing the defacto standard Hayes or as complex as evaluating the features and benefits of hundreds of products. The modem that will best serve your needs depends on what you want it to do. Chapter 9, How to Buy Telecommunications Hardware, and Chapter 8, How to Buy Telecommunications Software, described the various features and benefits of these hardware and software systems. So you may already have a good idea of what you're looking for in a communications system.

This appendix will acquaint you with many of the modems available. The product specifications and descriptions will help you decide if that product is worth investigating further. The description includes the manufacturer's name and address so you may request additional information. To help you locate them, the modems covered in this appendix are ordered alphabetically by manufacturer. Appendix C, Telecommunications Software Roundup, will provide additional information you may need. [Note: Some modems come with communications software either packaged in the form of a floppy disk or stored in the modem's internal memory (ROM).]

MODEM NAME: Intellimodem XT
              Internal Modem Card for IBM PC/PC XT/PC AT
              or compatible computer (half card size)

MANUFACTURER: BIZCOMP

ADDRESS: 532 Mercury Drive

CITY, STATE, ZIP: Sunnyvale, CA 94086

TELEPHONE: 408-733-7800

PRICE: $549

SPECIFICATIONS:

   Compatibility: Bell 103/212A Series

   Low Speed: 110 and 300 bps; asynchronous; 7 or 8 data bits; 1 or 2 stop bits; odd, even, space, mark or no parity

   High Speed: 1200 bps; asynchronous; 7 or 8 bits; 1 stop bit; odd, even, space, mark, or no parity

Dialing: Rotary-pulse or DTMF tone dialing

Command Buffer: 40 characters

Audio Monitor: High fidelity metal diaphragm monitor with volume control knob

Rear Panel: Modular RJ11C telephone line jack, modular RJ11C telephone set jack, status LED, volume control knob

Operation: Full or half duplex

Modes: Auto-dial, auto-answer, manual originate, manual answer, auto-repeat dial, automatic speed conversion

Receive Sensitivity: – 50 dBm

Transmit Level: – 10 dBm

Special Features: Mini card using only one slot
Automatic audio leveler eliminating volume changes during tone dialing
Self-test performed with each power up
Fully Hayes compatible

Software Features: IntelliSoft software supplied on diskette
Screen-labeled function key control
HELP screens throughout operation
Unlimited on-line telephone directories containing 50 telephone numbers
Automatic log on; X–Modem error checking file transfer protocol
Toggle printer on/off
Toggle recording to disk on/off
Access to DOS file commands while on-line
Error handling and messages to user

MODEM NAME: Intellimodem ST
Internal card for the IBM PC and compatibles (full length card)

MANUFACTURER: BIZCOMP

ADDRESS: 532 Mercury Drive

CITY, STATE, ZIP: Sunnyvale, CA 94086

TELEPHONE: 408-733-7800

PRICE: $499

FIGURE B-1   BIZCOMP Internal Modems

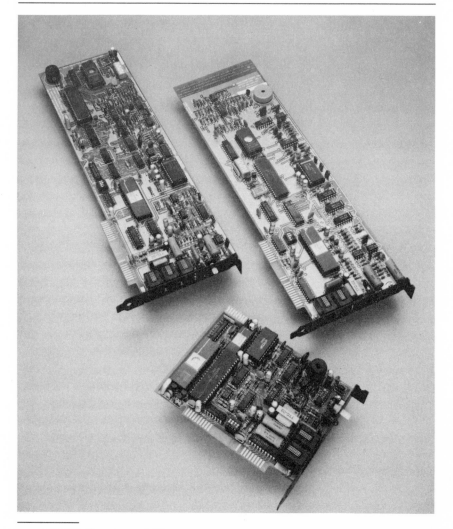

SOURCE: Courtesy of Bizcomp.

SPECIFICATIONS:

Compatibility: Bell 103/212A Series

Low Speed: 110 and 300 bps; asynchronous; 7 or 8 data bits; 1 or 2 stop bits; odd, even, or no parity

High Speed: 1200 bps; asynchronous; 7 or 8 bits; 1 or 2 stop bits; odd, even, or no parity

Dialing: Rotary-pulse or DTMF tone dialing

Command Buffer: 40 characters

Audio Monitor: Low profile piezoelectric monitor

Rear Panel: Modular RJ11C telephone line jack, modular RJ11C telephone set jack, status LED

Operation: Full or half duplex

Modes: Auto-dial, auto-answer, manual originate, manual answer; auto-redial; automatic speed conversion

Receive Sensitivity: – 50 dBm

Transmit Level: – 10 dBm

Special Features: Full length card using only one slot
Fully Hayes compatible
Audio monitor

Software Features: IntelliSoft software supplied on diskette
Screen-labeled function key control
HELP screens throughout operation
Unlimited on-line telephone directories containing 50 telephone numbers
Automatic log on; X–Modem error checking file transfer protocol
Toggle printer on/off
Toggle recording to disk on/off
Access to DOS file commands while on-line
Error handling and messages to user

MODEM NAME: Intellimodem XL
Internal card for the IBM PC and compatibles (full length card)

MANUFACTURER: BIZCOMP

ADDRESS: 532 Mercury Drive

CITY, STATE, ZIP: Sunnyvale, CA 94086

TELEPHONE: 408-733-7800

PRICE: $549

SPECIFICATIONS:

Compatibility: Bell 103/212A Series

Low Speed: 110 and 300 bps; asynchronous; 7 or 8 data

bits; 1 or 2 stop bits; odd, even, space, mark, or no parity

High Speed: 1200 bps; asynchronous; 7 or 8 bits; 1 or 2 stop bits; odd, even, space, mark, or no parity

Dialing: Rotary-pulse or DTMF tone dialing

Command Buffer: 40 characters

Audio Monitor: High fidelity metal diaphragm monitor with volume control knob

Rear Panel: Modular RJ11C telephone line jack, modular RJ11C telephone set jack, status LED, volume control knob

Operation: Full or half duplex

Modes: Autodial, auto-answer, manual originate, manual answer, auto-redial, and automatic speed conversion

Receive Sensitivity: – 10 dBm

Transmit Level: – 10 dBm

Special Features: Full length card using only one slot
Fully Hayes compatible
Dual mode command set featuring full Hayes compatibility plus Bizcomp PC: IntelliModem capability
Shared voice and data on the same line; switching between without hanging up
High fidelity audio monitor with volume control

Software Features: IntelliSoft Plus software supplied on diskette
Screen-labeled function key control
Displays all progress on the screen
Toggles between voice and data
HELP screens throughout operation
Unlimited on-line telephone directories containing 50 telephone numbers
Automatic log on; X–Modem error checking file transfer protocol
Toggle printer on/off
Toggle recording to disk on/off

Access to DOS file commands while
on-line

Error handling and messages to user

MODEM NAME: **Intellimodem EXT**

Stand-alone external modem

MANUFACTURER: BIZCOMP

ADDRESS: 532 Mercury Drive

CITY, STATE, ZIP: Sunnyvale, CA 94086

TELEPHONE: 408-733-7800

PRICE: $499

SPECIFICATIONS:

Compatibility: Bell 103/212A Series

Low Speed: 110 and 300 bps; asynchronous; 7 or 8 data
bits; 1 or 2 stop bits; odd, even, space, mark,
or no parity

High Speed: 1200 bps; asynchronous; 7 or 8 bits; 1 stop bit;
odd, even, space, mark, or no parity

Dialing: Rotary-pulse or DTMF tone dialing

Command Buffer: 40 characters

Audio Monitor: High fidelity 2-inch speaker with adjustable
volume control

Audio Leveler: Fast-attach, 30 dB dynamic range

Line Quality Display: Dynamic six–level multicolor LED bar
graph

Voice Toggling: Fully automatic Voice Insert with telephone

Call Progress Detection: Busy, dial tone, remote ringing,
modem, dead line, voice

Status Indicators: Eight front panel green LEDs (Send Data,
Receive Data, High Speed, Auto
Answer, Carrier Detect, Off Hook,
Terminal Ready, Modem Ready)

Controls: On/Off; volume, nine externally accessible DIP
switches

Operation: Full or half duplex

Interface: Serial 25–pin rear mounted female RS–232C

Connectors: RJ–11 line, RJ–11 telephone, power

Size: 7.5 inch L × 4.5 inch W × 1.5 inch H

FIGURE B–2   Tel-A-Modem 212 from Code-A-Phone

SOURCE: Courtesy of Code-A-Phone.

Power: Wall mounted transformer

Modes: Auto-dial, auto-answer, manual originate, manual answer, auto-redial

Receive Sensitivity: – 50 dBm

Transmit Level: – 10 dBm

Special Features: Fully Hayes compatible
Simple, fully automatic toggling between voice and data without hanging up

MODEM NAME: Tel-A-Modem
Two-line desk telephone with an intelligent modem to transmit voice and data simultaneously

MANUFACTURER: Code-A-Phone

ADDRESS: P.O. Box 5656

CITY, STATE, ZIP: Portland, OR 97228

TELEPHONE: 800-547-4683; 503-655-8940

PRICE: $695

SPECIFICATIONS:

Compatibility: Bell System 103 or 212A originate or answer

Low Speed Data Format: Asynchronous, 7 or 8 data bits, 1 or 2 stop bits, odd, even, or no parity

High Speed Data Format: Asynchronous, limited to 10 bits: 1 start bit, 8 data bits, no parity, 1 stop bit; 1 start bit, 7 data bits, odd or even parity, 1 stop bit; 1 start bit, 7 data bits, no parity, 2 stop bits

Dialing Capability: Touch-Tone or dial pulse dialing

Command Set: Unique to Tel-A-Modem (Not Hayes command set)

Audio Monitor: 2-inch speaker with volume control

Indicator Lights: Five lights on front panel: auto-answer carrier detect, command mode, receiving data, transmitting data

Rear Panel: On/Off switch, power jack, RS–232C connector, two modular phone jack connectors

Bottom: Two line ring volume controls, speaker monitor volume control

Operation: Full duplex

Interface: RS–232C serial

Receive Sensitivity: – 45 dBm

Transmit Level: – 10 dBm

Power: Wall transformer

Size: 5 inch × 5.5 inch × 9.5 inch

Telephone Hardware Specifications:

Number of lines: Two for simultaneous voice/data

Indicator Lights: Line 1 and 2—idle, busy, on hold

Telephone Keypad: Standard 12 button

Auto-dial Capability: Redial last number dialed 10-number directory storage

Software Compatibility: May be a problem since does not use standard Hayes command set.

FIGURE B–3   Codex 2131 from Codex Corporation

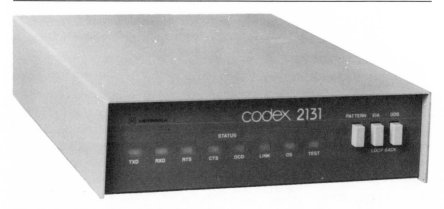

The Codex 2131 Digital Service Unit has an Integral Channel Service Unit. It is the functional equivalent of the Bell DSU 500A or Bell DSU 500B and CSU 550, however, the Codex 2131 offers the added features of switch selectable synchronous data rates of 2400, 4800 and 9600 bps.

SOURCE: Courtesy of Codex Corporation.

MODEM NAME: **Codex 2131 DSU/CSU Digital Termination Unit**

MANUFACTURER: Codex Corp. (Motorola, Inc.)

ADDRESS: 20 Cabot Boulevard

CITY, STATE, ZIP: Mansfield, MA 02048

TELEPHONE: 617-364-2000

SPECIFICATIONS:

Data Rates: 2400, 4800, 9600 bps switch selectable

Operating Modes: Four wire termination of Dataphone Digital Service (DDS) in point to point or multipoint applications

Standard Features: System status option, circuit assurance option, DDS slave timing, permanent RTS option, frame ground optionally connected to signal ground

Standard Test Features: Six front panel circuit status indicators, pseudo random test pattern generation and detection from front panel

Size: 2.75 inch × 9.75 inch × 12.75 inch

Interface: RS–232C serial

Data Format: Serial, binary synchronous in full duplex, half duplex, or simplex operation

Front Panel Indicators: Eight status information and three switches to permit diagnostics from front panel: data on transmit data pin, data on receive data pin, request to send, clear to send, data carrier detect, connected and receiving data from DDS network, receiving Out of Service pattern from DDS network, test mode, etc.

MODEM NAME: Datec PAL 212 Modem

MANUFACTURER: Datec, Inc.

ADDRESS: 200 Eastowne Drive

CITY, STATE, ZIP: Chapel Hill, NC 27514

TELEPHONE: 800-334-7722; 919-929-2135

SPECIFICATIONS:

Data Rate: 0–300 bps and 1200 bps

Compatibility: Bell 103/113 and Bell 212A

Data Format: Binary, serial, asynchronous

Automatic Dialer: Touch-Tone and rotary dial pulse

Command Buffer: 60 character

Transmission Standard: Low Speed—Frequency Shift Keying
High Speed—Differential Phase Shift

Operating Mode: Full or half-duplex; auto-originate/answer

Interface: RS–232C serial

Internal Option Switches: Test/ignore data terminal ready, data carrier detect follows carrier/forced TRUE, quiet mode/status messages sent, auto-answer/manual answer only

Dimensions: 7 inch × 1.75 inch × 6.66 inch extruded aluminum enclosure

Diagnostic Testing: Local (analog) loopback, via front panel control

Special Features:

Auto-answer/auto-dial

FIGURE B-4   Datec PAL 212 from Datec

SOURCE: Courtesy of Datec Incorporated.

Automatic speed/parity detection

Monitor speaker with volume control

Front panel

Command compatible with Hayes Smartmodem

MODEM NAME: **7212 Originate/Auto Answer Modem**

MANUFACTURER: Develcon Electronics Inc.

ADDRESS: 744 Nina Way

CITY, STATE, ZIP: Warminster, PA 18974

TELEPHONE: 800-528-8423; 215-443-5450

SPECIFICATIONS:

Compatibility: Bell 212A, Bell 103, and Bell 113

Operating Speeds: Full duplex, low speed asynchronous 300 bps

Full duplex, High speed asynchronous or bit synchronous 1200 bps

Indicators: Make busy, terminal ready, modem ready, send data, receive data, high speed, modem check, test

External Switches/Front Panel: Analog loop, self-test, remote digital loopback, digital loopback, high speed, voice/data

Interface: RS–232C serial

Physical Dimensions: 10 inch × 8 inch × 2.5 inch; 3 lbs.

Standard Features:

Full duplex synchronous or asynchronous operation
Built-in voice/data switch
Automatic auto/answer mode
Comprehensive local and remote diagnostics
Speed mode control and indication
Local and remote loopback testing
Busy mode selection
Lightning protection

MODEM NAME: 2 × 212 Two-channel Statistical Multiplexer and Modem

MANUFACTURER: Develcon Electronics Inc.

ADDRESS: 744 Nina Way

CITY, STATE, ZIP: Warminster, PA 18974

TELEPHONE: 800-528-8423; 215-443-5450

SPECIFICATIONS:

Compatibility: Bell 212A

Operating Speeds: Full duplex asynchronous 300 bps
Full duplex asynchronous 1200 bps

Indicators: Modem—Make busy, terminal ready, modem ready, send data, receive data, high speed, modem check, test mode
Multiplexer—Power, status, test

External Switches: Analog loop test, self-test, remote digital loop test, high speed, bypass, normal, loopback

Internal Options: Automatic answer, disconnect format, remote call/hangup, busy during analog test, remote digital loop command response, echo, linefeed, manual speed control, command message display

Interface: RS–232C serial

Physical Dimensions: 9 inch × 8.5 inch × 2.5 inch; Weight 3 lbs.

Standard Features:

Error detection and automatic re-transmission

Full duplex, asynchronous operation at 300 or 1200 bps

Two EIA RS–232C interfaces

Auto-dial/answer

Speed mode control and indication

Local and remote loopback testing

Touch-Tone and rotary dialing

Automatic last number redial

User-programmable hang-up code

Stores up to 10 numbers—speed dialing

Dynamic buffering up to 3,000 characters per port

Selectable parity

Lightning protection and battery back-up system

MODEM NAME: 6212 Originate/Auto Answer Modem

MANUFACTURER: Develcon Electronics Inc.

ADDRESS: 744 Nina Way

CITY, STATE, ZIP: Warminster, PA 18974

TELEPHONE: 800-528-8423; 215-443-5450

SPECIFICATIONS:

Compatibility: Bell 212A

Operating Speed: Full duplex, asynchronous 1200 bps

Indicators: LED initial power then SD/RD (flashing)

External Switches: Front Panel—Analog loopback, voice originate answer

Back Panel—parity, CD/DTR, Mode (terminal/CPU), character length

Interface: RS–232C serial

Physical Dimensions: 9 inch × 8.5 inch × 2.5 inch; Weight 3 lbs.

Standard Features:

Full duplex, asynchronous at 1200 bps

Autodial/answer

Local loopback testing

Touch-Tone and rotary dialing

Automatic last number redial

User-programmable hang-up code

Stores up to 10 numbers—speed dialing

Selectable parity

Lightning protection

MODEM NAME: 201B Data Modem

MANUFACTURER: Develcon Electronics Inc.

ADDRESS: 744 Nina Way

CITY, STATE, ZIP: Warminster, PA 18974

TELEPHONE: 800-528-8423; 215-443-5450

SPECIFICATIONS:

Data Rate: 2400 bps

Modulation: Differential coherent phase shift keyed (PSK)

Test Functions: Self-test, 511 character generator built-in, analog loopback, digital loopback

Anti-streaming Delays: 3, 3, 13, 54 seconds (strap operation)

Line Equalizer: Short haul, long haul U.S., long haul CCITT

Clear to Send Delay: 8.5 ms and 150 ms (user selectable)

Digital Interface: EIA RS–232C and CCITT.V.24

Package: Stand-alone low profile or rack-mounted printed circuit board

Dimensions: 9.76 inch × 2.44 inch × 10.81 inch; Weight 5 lbs

Indicators: Power, error, carrier detect, receive data, transmit data

Test Features: Analog loopback, digital loopback, self-test, test pattern

Features:

Private line 4–wire full duplex capability at 2400 bps

Local and remote test capability

Anti-streaming

FIGURE B-5   SAM 212A: Long-Haul Modem from
Gandalf Technologies, Inc.

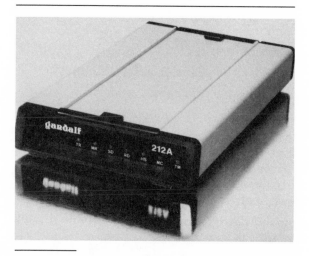

SOURCE: Courtesy of Gandalf Technologies, Inc.

No line conditioning required

8.5 millisecond turnaround time

Front panel rotary switch for convenient function
selection

LED indicators

RS-232C and CCITT V.24 interface

MODEM NAME: SAM 212A

MANUFACTURER: Gandalf Technologies Inc.

ADDRESS: 350 E. Dundee Road Suite 301

CITY, STATE, ZIP: Wheeling, IL 60090

TELEPHONE: 312-459-6630

PRICE: $618

SPECIFICATIONS:

Compatibility: Bell 212A, Bell 103/113 series

Data Rate: 1200 bps asynchronous and synchronous
0-300 bps binary, serial asynchronous

Terminal Interface: EIA RS-232C

Physical Size: 10 inch × 5.5 inch × 1.5 inch

Features:

Diagnostics facilitate isolation of modem faults and line impairments

Supports 7, 8, and 9 bit codes

Integral auto dialer for auto log-on

52 number recall, up to 32 digits each for auto-redial

Touch-Tone or Pulse dial automatically selected

Auto-answer mode automatically adapts to incoming speed

Menu of standard options to enable customization of parameters: speed control, transmitter timing, character length, auto-answer, answer mode indication, interface connects, loss of carrier disconnect and others

Self-test, analog and digital loopbacks, and remote digital loopback diagnostics

MODEM NAME: SAM 201

MANUFACTURER: Gandalf Technologies Inc.

ADDRESS: 350 E. Dundee Road Suite 301

CITY, STATE, ZIP: Wheeling, IL 60090

TELEPHONE: 312-459-6630

SPECIFICATIONS:

Data Rate: 2400 bps with switch selectable operation to 1200 bps

Operating Modes: Switched Network (DDD)—simples or half duplex

Two–wire private line—simples or half duplex

Four–wire private line—simplex, half duplex, full duplex

Modulation: Differential phase shifting keying (DPSK)

Interface: EIA RS–232C

Line Interface: Built-in auto-answer and manual dial DAA for use on the switched network.

Carrier Frequency: 1800 Hz carrier; 2025 Hz answer back tone

Indicators: Power on, test mode, DTR, modem ready, CTS, carrier detect, send data, receive data, error

Switches: Analog loopback, digital loopback, self-test, and voice/data

Dimensions: Stand-alone 14.25 inch × 11.125 inch × 2.375 inch; 7.4 lbs.

Features:

Operates at 2400 bps on either unconditioned 3002–type lines, two– or four– wire voice band private lines or on the switched network (DDD)

Switch selectable for 1200 bps operation

Compatible with 201C and the CCITT V.26 option B or A in synchronous mode

Built-in auto-answer and manual dial DAA for use on the DDD network

Stand-alone and rackmount models available

MODEM NAME: SAM 224

MANUFACTURER: Gandalf Technologies Inc.

ADDRESS: 350 E. Dundee Road Suite 301

CITY, STATE, ZIP: Wheeling, IL 60090

TELEPHONE: 312-459-6630

SPECIFICATIONS:

Compatibility: 2400 bps sync/async—CCITT V.22bis
Modes 1 & 2

1200 bps sync/async—CCITT V.22bis
Modes 3 & 4

0–300 bps async—Bell 103

Data Rate: 1200/2400 asynchronous and synchronous
0–300 bps asynchronous

Terminal Interface: EIA RS–232C serial and CCITT V.24/V.28

Modulation: 2400 bps—QAM; 1200 bps—DPSK; 300 bps—FSK

Diagnostics: Local digital loopback, remote digital loopback, local analog loopback, test pattern generator with error detector

Physical Size: Standalone 14.25 inch × 11.125 inch × 2.37 inch

Weight: 7.41 lbs

Features:

Autodialer allowing direct pulse and Touch-Tone dialing from the terminal keyboard

Answer mode automatically matches speed of incoming signal

Available in stand-alone or rack-mount

Operates over leased line or switched network

MODEM NAME: **Smartmodem 1200**

MANUFACTURER: Hayes Microcomputer Products, Inc.

ADDRESS: 5923 Peachtree Industrial Blvd.

CITY, STATE, ZIP: Norcross, GA 30092

TELEPHONE: 404-449-8791

SPECIFICATIONS:

Compatibility: Bell 103 and 212A

Data Rate: 300 bps and 1200 bps

Operation: Full or half duplex

Terminal Interface: RS–232C serial

Dialing: Pulse and Touch-Tone

Indicators: High speed, carrier detect, send data, receive data, auto-answer, TR and MR

Switches: Full or half duplex, enable auto-answer, and result code type

Special Features:

Auto-dial and auto-answer

Speaker for monitoring call status

Auto-redial

Standardized command language for compatibility with a broad range of communication software products

MODEM NAME: **Smartmodem 1200B Board Modem for the IBM PC**

MANUFACTURER: Hayes Microcomputer Products, Inc.

ADDRESS: 5923 Peachtree Industrial Blvd.

CITY, STATE, ZIP: Norcross, GA 30092

FIGURE B-6 Hayes Stack Smartmodem 1200

SOURCE: Courtesy of Hayes Microcomputer
Products, Inc.

TELEPHONE: 404-449-8791

SPECIFICATIONS:

Compatibility: Bell 103 and 212A

Data Rate: 300 bps and 1200 bps

Operation: Full or half duplex

Terminal Interface: Slips into long slot of IBM PC

Dialing: Pulse and Touch-Tone

Indicators: None (speaker used to monitor call progress)

Switches: Three switches instead of the eight on the Model
1200

Special Features:

Auto-dial and auto-answer

Speaker mounted on board for monitoring call status

Auto-redial

Standardized command language for compatibility with a
broad range of communication software products

Modem processor reset without power down

Added telephone jack to eliminate purchase of "Y" adapter

MODEM NAME: FDX 2400 Dial Modem

MANUFACTURER: Paradyne Corporation

ADDRESS: 8550 Ulmerton Rd.

CITY, STATE, ZIP: Largo, FL 33540

TELEPHONE: 813-530-2000

SPECIFICATIONS:

Data Rates: Synchronous: 2400, 1200, 600 bps
Asynchronous: 2400, 1200, 600, 0–300 bps

Compatibility: AT&T 212A, 103, 113
CCITT V.22A/B and V.22 bits

Application: Full-duplex, half-duplex, synchronous on-line synchronous and asynchronous terminal interface

Asynchronous Character Length: 8, 9, 10, or 11 bits

Data Transfer Rates (terminal to modem): 300, 600, 1200, 4800, 9600 bps, with buffer and flow control

Equalization: Automatic adaptive plus compromise in transmitter and receiver circuits

Scrambler: Self-synchronizing scrambler/descrambler

Data Terminal Interfaces: Asynchronous—RS–232C, V.24/V.28
Synchronous—RS–232C, V.24/V.28

Dimensions: 2.4 inch × 6.8 inch × 12.1 inch; Weight 3.75 lbs

Diagnostics: Local analog loopback/self-test, remote digital loopback/test, end-to-end test, remote access maintenance mode with configuration control

Indicators: Power on/off, test mode error, data terminal ready, transmit data, receive data, data set ready, carrier detect, clear to send, request to send, ring signal detection

Controls: 10–key multifunction keypad equipped with integral system status indicators—data mode, voice mode, originate mode, answer mode, auto-answer/call abort, future, remote digital loopback, local VF loopback, test pattern, and dial access (auto/man)

Special Features:

Dialer Capabilities (selective):

Integral, pulse, tone, autoselect, tandem/alternate

Terminal or front panel single-key execution, telephone handset

Telephone directory/scratch pad—10 entries of 40 characters each with pause, repeat, tandem/alternate linking

Complete protection against power failure

Voice and data operation

Unique HELP file to provide command file and directory/storage registers and permit the user to enter, change, and verify configuration parameters

Tandem dialing—sense OLD tone/NEW tone

Tone recognition—dial, ring, answer, trunk busy, ringback, voice (integral speaker)

Answer Capabilities:

Control modes—front panel, auto, terminal, handset, delayed, forced, Hayes mode

Ring Detection—terminal, front panel, speaker, handset

Call disconnect—terminal control, modem control, loss of carrier, forced disconnect

Reverse mode—establish call to modem configured for "Originate" mode of operation

Terminal Capabilities:

Telephone directory/scratch pad

Call progress monitoring

HELP files

Extended or Hayes mode selection

Terminal speed independent of modem signaling rate

Terse or verbose modes of operation

FIGURE B-7 Popcom Model X100 from Prentice

SOURCE: Courtesy of Prentice Corporation.

MODEM NAME: POPCOM MODEL X100

MANUFACTURER: Prentice Corporation

ADDRESS: 266 Caspian Dr.

CITY, STATE, ZIP: Sunnyvale, CA 94088

TELEPHONE: 408-734-9810

PRICE: $475

SPECIFICATIONS:

Compatibility: AT&T 103, 113, and 212A

Data Rate: 0–300 bps and 1200 bps

Operation: Full duplex

Dialing Capability: Automatic—Touch-Tone or rotary dialing

Command Line Buffer: 40 characters

Audio Monitor: Speaker with manual volume control and automatic command control

Interface: EIA RS–232C serial, asynchronous

Special Features:

Voice and data transmission during the same call

Automatic or manual dialing and answering

Reports to PC call-progress tones—dial tone, busy signal, remote ringing, talk, disconnect

Built-in speaker

MODEM NAME: VA212LC

MANUFACTURER: Racal-Vadic

ADDRESS: 1525 McCarthy Blvd.

CITY, STATE, ZIP: Milpitas, CA 95035

TELEPHONE: 408-946-7610

SPECIFICATIONS:

Compatibility: Bell 212A/103

Data Rate: 300 and 1200 bps asynchronous

Indicators: Five LEDs—transmit data, receive data, carrier detect, voice/data status, high/low speed

Dimensions: 9 inch × 6 inch × 1.5 inch; Weight 2.4 lbs.

Special Features:

Manual originate/auto-answer operation

Voice mode—disables auto-answer capabilities

Automatic self-test

Automatic identification of calling modem data rate

Automatically handles 9 and 10 bit character codes

MODEM NAME: VA212 Auto Dial

MANUFACTURER: Racal-Vadic

ADDRESS: 1525 McCarthy Blvd.

CITY, STATE, ZIP: Milpitas, CA 95035

TELEPHONE: 408-946-7610

SPECIFICATIONS:

Compatibilty: Bell 212A/103

Operations: Manual/automatic, originate/answer, full-duplex

Data Rate: 300 and 1200 bps asynchronous or synchronous with autobaud and automatic parity detection

Dialer Type: Tone, pulse, or automatic selection of either

Indicators: Liquid crystal display that can display the following messages—idle, on line, address:, number:, terminal, no tone, dialing, ringing, busy, failed, linking, voice, self-test, busy out, lo speed, hi speed, orig, answer, and so forth

Controls: Front-panel keyboard with 16 keys

Self-Tests: Automatic operational status monitoring, analog loopback, analog loopback data, remote digital loopback, remote digital loopback data, end-to-end, local digital loopback

Dimensions: 8 inch × 13.3 inch × 1.5 inch; Weight 3.4 lbs.

Special Features:

Terminal or modem operation

Integral automatic dialer; one-button redial

15–telephone–number memory

User programmable options

Software reset key returns to idle state

Battery back-up system for telephone directory storage

Tandem dialing for PBX compatibility carrier detect, voice/data status, high/low speed

MODEM NAME: VA4400 Series

MANUFACTURER: Racal-Vadic

ADDRESS: 1525 McCarthy Blvd.

CITY, STATE, ZIP: Milpitas, CA 95035

TELEPHONE: 408-946-7610

SPECIFICATIONS:

Speed/Compatibility: 2400 bps / CCITT V.22 bis
1200 bps/ VA3400 or Bell 212A
0–300 bps/ Bell 103/113

Data: Binary, Serial, synchronous, or asynchronous except for 0–300 bps which is asynchronous only

Interface: EIA RS–232C serial

Control Functions: Manual originate/answer auto-answer

Diagnostic Displays: Transmit data, receive data, request to send/speed indication, clear to send, data set ready, data terminal ready, ring indicator, carrier detect, status indicator

Diagnostics: Analog loopback/busy out, digital loopback
(local), transmit reversals, automatic self-test,
respond to remote test, initiate response to
remote test

Special Features:

First modem to operate full duplex at 2400, 1200 and
0–300 bps

Automatic adaptive equalization allows modem to change
its filtering and adapt to different line conditions

Automatic identification of originate/answer modem

MODEM NAME: 2400PA Full-Duplex Modem

MANUFACTURER: Racal-Vadic

ADDRESS: 1525 McCarthy Blvd.

CITY, STATE, ZIP: Milpitas, CA 95035

TELEPHONE: 408-946-7610

SPECIFICATIONS:

Data Rate: 2400, 1200, 300 bps

Compatibility: CCITT V.22 bis, Bell 212A and 103

Data Format: Binary, serial synchronous or asynchronous

FIGURE B–8A   Auto Dial VA212 from Racal-Vadic

SOURCE: Courtesy of Racal-Vadic.

FIGURE B-8B VA212LC from Racal-Vadic

SOURCE: Courtesy of Racal-Vadic.

Character Length: 8, 9, 10, or 11 bits

Terminal Interface: EIA RS-232C serial

Built-In Diagnostic Tests: Automatic self-test, analog loopback self-test, analog loopback data, end-to-end, local digital loopback, remote digital loopback, remote digital loopback data

Dimensions: 8 inch × 13.3 inch × 3.8 inch; Weight 5.6 lbs.

Autodialer Features:

Tone, pulse, or automatic selection of tone or pulse

Tandem dialing for use with PBX systems

Call progress detection—presence of dial tone, busy, ringback, answer tone, and carrier

Telephone and log-on directory—up to 15 telephone numbers, identification names, and log-on sequences of 60 characters in permanent non-volatile memory (built-in memory editor)

Linking—stored telephone numbers can switch to alternate number if primary connection fails

MODEM NAME: **Visionary 1200**

MANUFACTURER: Visionary Electronics Incorporated

ADDRESS: 141 Parker Avenue

CITY, STATE, ZIP: San Francisco, CA 94118

TELEPHONE: 415-751-8811

SPECIFICATIONS:

Data Rate: 1200 or 300 bps

Compatibility: Bell 212A and 103 series; originate or answer modes

Data Format: Serial; binary; asynchronous 7 or 8 data bits; 1 or 2 stop bits; odd, even, or no parity; half or full duplex

Interface: 2 EIA RS–232C ports

Buffer: 2K expandable to 48K

Intelligence: 8085 microprocessor with up to 16K byte control program

Dialing Mode: Touch-Tone or rotary pulse dialing

Display: LCD 3.5 digit clock

Indicators: LED status indicators—off-hook, carrier detect, transmit data, receive data, auto-answer, message waiting, and memory full

Dimensions: 9.5 inch × 11.35 inch × 2.5 inch

Special Features:

Real-time clock and calendar

Programmable auto-answer, auto-dial, auto-send, and reception, storage and retrieval of telephone numbers, custom commands, and text files

Sophisticated internal software

Send and receive messages directly from memory independent of computer

Automatically retrieve messages on on-line mail services; automatically stored in modem memory

Dial up and log onto on-line system with one keystroke

Store up to 24 pages (48K) of messages, phone list files, or user-defined commands

Battery backed-up 48K memory

APPENDIX C
Software Roundup and Reviews

Buying communications software can be one of the most difficult tasks in setting up a communications system. The software that will best serve your needs depends on what you want it to do. Chapter 8, How to Buy Telecommunications Software, and Chapter 9, How to Buy Telecommunications Hardware, described the various features and benefits of these software and hardware systems. So you may already have a good idea of what you're looking for in a communications system.

This appendix will acquaint you with many of the software packages available. The product specifications, descriptions, and review comments will help you decide if that product is worth investigating further. The product review includes the manufacturer's name and address so you may request additional information. To help you locate the reviews in this appendix, they are ordered alphabetically by software name. Appendix B, Modem Roundup, provides additional information. [Note: Some modems come with communications software either packaged in the form of a floppy disk or stored in the modem's internal memory (ROM). No internally stored software is reviewed in this appendix.]

SOFTWARE: ASCII PRO/ASCII EXPRESS PRO

MANUFACTURER: United Software Industries

ADDRESS: 1880 Century Park East, Suite 311

CITY, STATE, ZIP: Los Angeles, CA 90067

TELEPHONE: 213-556-2211

SPECIFICATIONS:

> Operating Systems: Apple IIe, Franklin 1000 and 1200, IBM PC and compatibles; CP/M 80 and CP/M 86
>
> Hardware Requirements: One disk drive; preferably two drives
>
> Transfer Protocols: XON/XOFF; XMODEM; block send, line at a time, character at a time
>
> Unattended Remote Mode: Yes; password protection
>
> Data Rates: 50–9600 bps (up to 38,400 bps for IBM PC)

Capture Method: Buffer and disk

Modems Support: All popular modems

Text Editor: Quite good

Macro Capability: Turnkey; chaining to other macros

Auto-dial Library: Up to 26 individual numbers and
       associated macro library files

On-Screen Help: Extensive

Supports DEC VT–100 Terminal Emulation: IBM PC Version
                only

Menu-Driven/Command Mode: Both

User-Definable Function Keys: Yes

Return to Operating System without Hangup: Yes

Documentation: Very good

Price: IBM PC Version—$189.95
   Apple Version—$129.95

COMMENTS:

This is one of the most sophisticated and complete telecommunications packages available for Apple, CP/M–based
machines, and IBM PCs. Novices and new users can use the
menu-driven mode to get started. More experienced users can
use the command mode for faster operation. On-line help
files provide instant access to information about operating
the system. An on-line command summary is available at a
keystroke. Although many of the commands are nmemonic,
others may be confusing: for example, G = Get file from
host, J = View text file, S = Send file, and T = Capture to
disk. This will take some memorization.

Up to 26 separate telephone numbers and log-on sequences may be stored. With the macro capabilities you can
design and store command files for accessing and downloading information from information services. The disk comes
with a number of sample macros for CompuServe, MCI Mail,
The Source, and so forth. The full-text editor allows you to
write macro files for automatic log-on sequences and to prepare text for electronic mail transfer. The text editor isn't
quite a word processor, but it is very capable. The optional

capture buffer allows you to increase or decrease the viewing speed on the screen. Anything viewed on the screen can be saved to the buffer and/or to disk. The remote mode allows password-protected, unattended operation by another computer for uploading and downloading files.

The manual is well organized and contains a telecommunications primer, a tutorial for getting started, and a tutorial for basic operation. The two-color printing and numerous screen prints are very helpful. The table of contents is very detailed; unfortunately, the manual lacks an index.

SOFTWARE: ASCOM

MANUFACTURER: Dynamic Microprocessor Associates

ADDRESS: 545 Fifth Avenue

CITY, STATE, ZIP: New York, NY 10017

TELEPHONE: 212-687-7115

SPECIFICATIONS:

    Operating Systems: MS–DOS, PC–DOS, CP/M–80, CP/M–86

    Hardware Requirements: One disk drive; preferably two drives

    Transfer Protocols: XON/XOFF; XMODEM; line at a time, BLOCK, BLOCK V

    Unattended Remote Mode: Yes; no password protection

    Data Rates: 50 to 19,200 bps

    Capture Method: Buffer and disk

    Modems Support: All popular modems

    Text Editor: None

    Macro Capability: Turnkey; chaining to other macros

    Auto-dial Library: None

    On-Screen Help: Extensive

    Menu-Driven/Command Mode: Both

    Return to Operating System without Hangup: Default—No; May be changed to Default—Yes.

    Documentation: Very good

    Price: $195

COMMENTS:

ASCOM is a full-featured telecommunications package that allows communication with on-line services and between personal computers. By offering both a menu-driven and command mode, the software is efficient for both novice and experienced users. On-line help is available at a keystroke. The mnemonic commands are easy to understand and use: for example, BAUD (BAU) = select baud rate to use, CONV = enter conversational mode, SAVE (SA) = save ASCOM parameter settings, and STAT (ST) = display current ASCOM status.

The auto-answer, auto-dial and auto-redial features facilitate logging onto other systems. The remote mode allows your computer to be operated unattended by a remote system. No provision for password protection is provided.

Batch Mode procedures provide for automatic log-on and search, dialing multiple remote computers, and requesting remote computers to send data without operator intervention. The Batch File procedures provide for automatic log-on and search. You write the batch file with your own text editor or word processor. Communication parameters for each service may be saved for future use.

ASCOM gives you access to a number of DOS commands, including delete, directory, rename, and run (for running another program while you're still connected on line).

ASCOM supports a number of popular file transfer protocols. The XON/XOFF procedure allows you to communicate with almost any computer. You can even specify that single lines be transferred instead of blocks. The popular XMODEM error-checking protocol is available as well as two proprietary protocols called BLOCK and BLOCK V. The BLOCK protocols can only be used with a computer using ASCOM. BLOCK V can resume an interrupted transfer at the point where transmission ceased. This is a handy feature.

The manual is well written, but it lacks an index. The two tables of contents (one for the users' guide at the front and the other for the reference manual at the back) are complete, but you must check both in order to find all the information you may want on a particular subject. Many screen prints help the user progress through menu operations. I could not find a description of how to use or program function keys.

This program is quite capable and should be examined by any serious telecommunications user.

SOFTWARE: BLAST

MANUFACTURER: Communications Research Group, Inc.

ADDRESS: 8939 Jefferson Hwy.

CITY, STATE, ZIP: Baton Rouge, LA 70809

TELEPHONE: 504-923-0888

SPECIFICATIONS:

> Operating Systems: MS–DOS, UNIX, APPLE DOS, CP/M and CP/M 86; capable of linking over 70 different micros, minis, and mainframes.
>
> Hardware Requirements: One disk drive; preferably two drives
>
> Transfer Protocols: XON/XOFF; BLAST (BLock ASynchronous Transmission)
>
> Unattended Mode: Yes
>
> Data Rates: Up to 19.2K bps
>
> Capture Method: Buffer and disk
>
> Modems Support: All popular modems
>
> Text Editor: None
>
> Macro Capability: Batch file macro programming language
>
> Auto-dial Library: Yes—through batch files
>
> On-Screen Help: Menus
>
> Menu Driven/Command Mode: Both—primarily command driven
>
> User-Definable Function Keys: None
>
> Documentation: Hacker level
>
> Price: Micro Version—$250

COMMENTS:

BLAST is a state-of-the-art communications package designed to take advantage of high-speed modem transfer capabilities and to offset satellite transmission delays (See Figure C–1) Its primary function is to link micros to micros, micros to minis, and micros to mainframes. However, the batch file capabilities allow it to be used to automatically retrieve infor-

FIGURE C–1 BLAST from Communications
Research Group

SOURCE: Courtesy of Communications Research
Group.

mation from on-line services. Unfortunately, the manual is
written at a macro programming language level and the novice user will have difficulty learning how to use these features.

BLAST has a series of menus and a default parameter file
that allows you to customize log-on parameters. Used in conjunction with the batch command files, BLAST is an effective
tool for accessing on-line services.

BLAST's greatest strength is in communicating with another BLAST system. In this mode it offers the following features: (1) very high resistance to noise by using small transmit blocks and bit-oriented protocol; (2) record access or the
ability to extract data from a remote file without transmitting
the entire file; (3) completely implemented use of full-duplex
capability so that transmission of different files can occur simultaneously in both directions; (4) status reporting while
transmission is in progress; (5) ability to initiate file transfer
in either direction; and (6) unattended operation. BLAST
consistently achieves a 50 percent greater throughput rate

than the XMODEM file transfer protocol. For electronic mail applications, BLAST offers substantial telecommunications expense savings.

SOFTWARE: Crosstalk XVI

MANUFACTURER: Microstuf, Inc.

ADDRESS: 1000 Holcomb Wood Parkway

CITY, STATE, ZIP: Roswell, GA 30076

TELEPHONE: 404-998-3998

SPECIFICATIONS:

Operating Systems: MS–DOS, PC–DOS, CP/M, CP/M–86, MP/M

Hardware Requirements: One disk drive; preferably two drives; 96K RAM

Terminal Emulation: DEC VT–100; IBM 3101; Televideo 910/920

Transfer Protocols: XON/XOFF; Proprietary Crosstalk protocol

Unattended Mode: Yes; password protection

Data Rates: Up to 9600 bps

Capture Method: Buffer and disk

Modems Support: All popular modems

Text Editor: None

Macro Capability: Turnkey; command files and script files

Auto-dial Library: Yes

On-Screen Help: Extensive

Menu-Driven/Command Mode: Command Mode with on-screen quick reference and help

User-Definable Function Keys: Yes

Return to Operating System without Hangup: Yes

Documentation: Very good

Price: $195

COMMENTS:

Crosstalk XVI was especially designed for 16–bit computer processors. With its menus and extensive on-line help, Crosstalk is as easy to use as a menu-driven system. However, it has the speed and directness of a command-drive program. The mnemonic commands appear on the screen and on-line help is only a couple of keystrokes away. The NEWUSER file allows you to quickly enter a customized phone list together with the communication parameters required. The STD.XTK file allows you to boot Crosstalk directly into the mode and communication parameters you wish to default to: for example, auto-answer mode at 1200–N–8–1 and logged onto drive B. Or, you could have Crosstalk log directly onto a service, enter your password and conduct a search. If the number is busy, Crosstalk will redial until a connection is made.

By pressing the HOME key you may view your communication parameters menu. By simply pressing ESCAPE (to enter the command mode) and entering the first two letters of the parameter, you'll be presented with your options. For example, if you enter BA (BAUD) you'll see which data rates are available. You can then enter your choice. At the bottom of the main menu screen, you'll see the dialing directory you've created: for example, MCI, SOURCE, and DJN/R. To dial and log onto that service, you enter the number beside your choice and press RETURN. You can also enter telephone numbers from the keyboard.

File transfers may be handled through XON/OFF line by line, by XMODEM protocol and by a proprietary Crosstalk protocol which is more efficient and accurate. During transfer, a status screen alerts you to any problems and posts what percentage of the file has been transferred. Another computer using Crosstalk can use remote mode to transfer files, view disk directories, and run programs without operator intervention.

You can custom design search strategies and store them on your disk. At a preset time Crosstalk can execute these command files in an unattended mode.

The manual is well written and illustrated. Novices will find it very helpful. Experienced users will appreciate its organization for quick reference. The manual does lack an index, and finding the manufacturer's telephone number is next to impossible.

Crosstalk is probably the most popular telecommunications software being used today. Its word-of-mouth reputation has propelled it to the top of the selling charts. Crosstalk's popularity is due to its simplicity, versatility, and power.

SOFTWARE: In-Search

MANUFACTURER: Menlo Corporation

ADDRESS: 4633 Old Ironsides Dr., Suite 400

CITY, STATE, ZIP: Santa Clara, CA 95054

TELEPHONE: 408-986-0200 (Customer Service 800-221-4237)

SPECIFICATIONS:

Operating Systems: PC DOS 2.0 (or equivalent) or later revision

Hardware Requirements: Two disk drives or hard disk system IBM PC or compatible—192K bytes of memory

Transfer Protocols: Custom designed for downloading Dialog on-line service files to buffer or disk

Unattended Mode: No; supports auto-log-on and predesigned search execution

Data Rates: 300 or 1200 bps

Capture Method: Buffer and disk

Modems Support: Most popular modems

Text Editor: For entering search strategies only

Macro Capability: Menu-driven methods for selecting Dialog databases and entering search strategy

Auto-dial Library: Communication services and Dialog log-on; will automatically redial and switch to alternate communication service if busy

On-Screen Help: Extensive; custom designed for Dialog on-line service assistance and In-Search software assistance only

Menu-Driven/Command Mode: Menu driven (may override In-Search menus to some extent, but may not enter directly into Dialog command system)

User-Definable Function Keys: No; custom designed function key layout with plastic reference keyboard overlay

Return to Operating System without Hangup: No

Documentation: Very good; includes computerized tutorial

Price: $399 (Demo Disk $5)

COMMENTS:

Menlo Corporation describes In-Search as "access software." In-Search is custom-designed to lead the novice through all the steps necessary to search the Dialog on-line information service. In-Search helps you decide which of Dialog's 200 databases to search, lets you enter your search strategy off-line, and automatically logs on and performs the search. In-Search automates your selection of records to download, the print format, and the downloading process. You can store the records in a memory buffer or capture them on disk.

All the information you need to use In-Search and Dialog is contained on the disk and is easily accessed with HELP keys. The well-designed graphic screens never leave you in doubt about what your next step is. An on-disk tutorial and the manual provide even more support. The manual is not only easy to reference for answering specific questions, but it also gently leads you into the search process. Before you know it, you've learned Boolean logic, downloading, and printing routines. It's almost painless.

When you begin using In-Search, the first screen you'll see looks like an index card file. (See Figure C–2.) With the cursor control keys you can "page" through this card file to find the subject category you wish to search. Since one subject may appear in more than one of Dialog's databases, you'll view information on each appropriate database. The reference card will contain the subject, the Dialog database number, a description of the database, the types of publications indexed, the years for which information is available, the current number of records in the database, and how often it is updated. At the bottom of the card appears the hourly charge and cost per record. If a subject includes more than one database, the databases are organized alphabetically within the subject. If the card doesn't give you enough information, sim-

FIGURE C–2 In-Search from Menlo Corporation—The Card Catalog

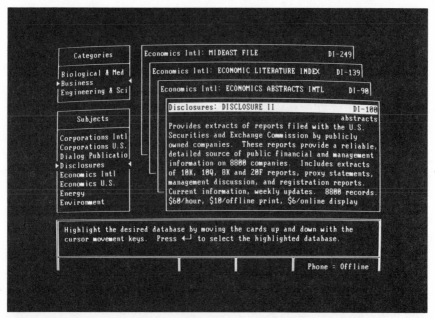

Menlo Corporation's In-Search software uses a "card catalog" presentation of over 200 online databases. A user identifies the most appropriate database for the search by scrolling through general categories, subjects, and detailed descriptions of individual databases.

SOURCE: Courtesy of Menlo Corporation.

ply press the FUNCTION 6 key "Data Sheet" to receive even more details about the database, including the file description (purpose), the subject coverage (major subject headings), the sources (types of publications), dates covered, update frequency, file size, file formats, and vendor contact information. In order to keep this information current, Menlo Corporation provides update disks every 2 or 3 months.

Once you've selected the most appropriate database, you proceed to a worksheet type of screen called a "search chart." (See Figure C–3.) This screen contains four columns and 14 rows in which you can enter your search strategy steps offline. Once you log onto the system, Dialog provides the number of references found for each search step and enters that number into the far right column labeled "Refs Found." You

FIGURE C–3 In-Search—Entering the Search Phrases

Set #	MEDLINE (1980-) DI-154 Search Keywords and Phrases	Index Selected	Refs Found
S1	caffeine		1427
S2	sleep		5866
S3	s1 and s2		28
S4	caffeine or coffee		1684
S5	sleep		5866
S6	insomnia		583
S7	sleeplessness		14
S8	s4 and s6		8
S9	s4 and s7		0
S10			
S11			
S12			
S13			
S14			

Enter keywords and phrases to search the selected database. To retrieve references press the command key, F9, and then the ↵ key. For help press the help key, F1.

Phone = Online

Menlo Corporation's In-Search software allows the user to organize a search strategy using key words and phrases. The program thoroughly searches the selected database and locates the references containing those words. References can then be saved, printed, edited, or read on-screen.

SOURCE: Courtesy of Menlo Corporation.

can enter up to 98 search requests of up to 50 characters each. You can further refine your search by requesting a list of the search fields available for that database: for example, abstract, author, journal name, and so forth. If you're looking for an article written by Ronald Reagan rather than an article about Ronald Reagan, you can select the "author" field to search. In-Search will also let you "expand" your search to find different forms in which information may be displayed: for example, "President Reagan" or "R. Reagan." Your search strategy can be saved on disk and repeated as necessary. The editing commands for this text file are similar to the WordStar word processing commands.

When you press FUNCTION 5 PHONE, In-Search automatically logs onto Dialog, enters your password, locates the database you've chosen, and conducts the search. If necessary, you can modify the search while you're on-line. If you decide to download the information, In-Search will prompt you for the records you wish to select, the file format available from that particular database and whether you want to download to the buffer, printer, and/or disk. The manual makes numerous suggestions about how you can save time (and money) with the In-Search features and good search procedures.

The status line at the bottom of the screen keeps you informed of your printer status, your modem connect status, your disk capture status, and whether insert (text) is on or off. The predefined function keys make accessing program capabilities quite easy. A plastic function-key overlay guides you step-by-step. (See Figure C–4.)

This program is a must for the occasional Dialog user. Not

FIGURE C–4   In-Search—Function Key On-Disk Help Menu

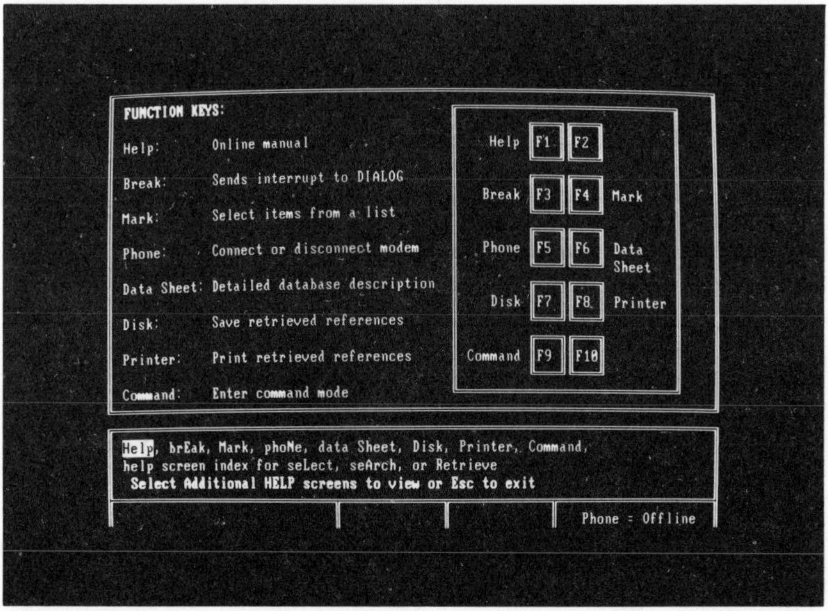

With Menlo Corporation's In-Search software, many search procedures can be completed with a single stroke of a function key. An extensive on-screen help program makes the program easy to learn and use effectively.

SOURCE: Courtesy of Menlo Corporation.

only can you save attending one of Dialog's classes (which cost over $100 and a day of your time) but you can also utilize your on-line time more efficiently. The intermediate and experienced user can also benefit by preparing searches before logging onto the service. Since In-Search gives you access to the full power of the Dialog system, even professional searchers will not be thwarted. By selecting the best database and designing your search strategy before connecting to the service, you'll save more in on-line charges than the program will cost.

SOFTWARE: Lync

MANUFACTURER: Norton-Lambert Corp.

ADDRESS: P.O. Box 4085

CITY, STATE, ZIP: Santa Barbara, CA 93140

TELEPHONE: 805-687-8896

SPECIFICATIONS:

Operating Systems: IBM PC and compatibles; MS–DOS, CP/M, MP/M, CCP/M, APPLE, TURBODOS, Z–DOS

Hardware Requirements: One disk drive; 64K memory

Transfer Protocols: XON/XOFF; XMODEM; block send, line at a time, LYNC Closed-Loop (proprietary)

Unattended Mode: Yes; password protection

Remote Mode: Yes

Data Rates: 75 to 9600

Capture Method: Buffer and disk

Modems Support: All popular modems

Text Editor: None

Macro Capability: Turnkey; command and batch files

Auto-dial Library: Yes; must enter identifying name

On-Screen Help: Yes

Menu-Driven/Command Mode: Command Mode only

User-Definable Function Keys: None

Return to Operating System without Hangup: Yes

Documentation: Good; on-disk tutorial

Price: $195

COMMENTS:

Lync provides many of the sophisticated features found with Crosstalk XVI and ASCOM. However, since Lync is a command-driven system without screen prompts or menus, you'll have to memorize numerous mnemonic commands. To enter the command mode, you simply type ESCAPE and then the command you wish; for example, you type LOG MCI to automatically dial and log onto MCI Mail. On-disk help is available by typing HELP or HELP <command>. Some of the commands can be confusing since they can be used in different modes; SAVE/T, SAVE/B, SAVE M8, and SAME/M offer four different transfer protocols. The manual explains when and how you should use each method. This may add an extra burden for many novices.

Lync may be operated in three modes: TERMinal, REMOTE, and Lync. The TERM mode is used for accessing online services. Lync is used to communicate with another computer having Lync software. The Lync mode offers a number of control features, including wild card file transfers, error detection and automatic correction protocol, accessing DOS commands on the remote computer, and the ability to run software on the remote computer (provided the software doesn't contain graphics: for example, not dBASE III and WordStar).

Lync allows you to automatically log onto services and to execute a preprogrammed search strategy. A number of preconfigured LOG files come on the disk; for example, MCI, EasyLink, CompuServe, and Dow Jones News/Retrieval. To dial a service, you enter the name of the log-on file: for example, MCI, EASY, or DOW. You can also use the DIAL command to enter any telephone number you wish. At any time you can change your communications parameters by entering the command mode and typing the new value. Operated in the unattended mode, Lync will call a service at a preset time and execute a series of preprogrammed instructions. If the number is busy, Lync will redial until a connection is made. All parameters can be saved, reloaded, or altered on-line.

Lync allows you to perform the following while you're on-line: return to the operating system, toggle printer on/off, view disk files and directories (locally and on distant computer), display help files, and run other programs.

With Lync you have complete modem control: voice to

data in one phone call; auto-dial, auto-redial, auto-answer, hang up; operation in non-autodial mode; unlimited phone directory; and autodial telephone directory. Lync automatically adjusts parity and data bits to match the computer you're calling.

The well-written manual has tutorials and an excellent index. You won't find the hand-holding in this manual that you do in In-Search or Crosstalk XVI, but, it does contain all the relevant information.

Although the versatility of the remote mode is quite exciting, I feel that for ease of use, Crosstalk XVI provides many of the same features Lync does.

SOFTWARE: ProKey

MANUFACTURER: Rose Soft, Inc.

ADDRESS: 4710 University Way N.E.

CITY, STATE, ZIP: Seattle, WA 98105

TELEPHONE: 206-524-2350

SPECIFICATIONS:

Type of Software: Keyboard/Software enhancer

System Requirements: IBM PC and compatibles; IBM 3270PC with one disk drive minimum

Operating Systems: All versions of MS–DOS or PC–DOS

Memory Requirements: 64K (96K for large programs like WordStar); ProKey uses approximately 12K of memory

Software Compatibility: Smartcom II, PFS Products, Crosstalk and many others

Documentation: Good

Price: $129.95

COMMENTS:

ProKey is not a telecommunications software package. Despite this, it can enhance the performance of your telecommunications software as well as other software you may use, such as word processors and database managers. One of its primary advantages is standardizing the function keys and control codes used by each software application. Anyone who's used more than one computer application has run into this difficulty. Just think how nice it would be if the text-editing commands for your telecommunications software and for your word processor were the same. Since a single keystroke will invoke a sequence of commands stored in your ProKey macro file, you can simplify many multiple-step command sequences; for example, you can create a macro (command file) that will automatically install your communication parameters. ProKey can make almost any software package easier to use.

If you're discontented with your keyboard layout, ProKey can redefine almost any key on the keyboard. You can move the RETURN key or move the BACKSPACE key anywhere you wish. If you'd like to try the DVORAK keyboard layout, ProKey will do that for you automatically. Also, people with handicaps can redefine multiple key functions that may be impossible for them to execute with one hand.

You can also store text in macros: for example, search statements, names and addresses, and boilerplate text. Anything you can type can be a ProKey macro.

ProKey key definitions may be created while you're operating the software. By simply pressing ALTERNATE + (pressing the ALT key and the plus sign), you can begin entering your macro definition. Once you've completed the definition, you press ALTERNATE – (press the ALT key and the minus sign). From that point on, the new key definition will be stored for future use.

A keyboard enhancer improves your efficiency and helps you standardize software application command structures. Used in conjunction with telecommunication packages, ProKey macros can actually enhance their capabilities. With ProKey you can design your own function keys for those packages that do not offer function key definitions.

The manual seems to have all the information you'd want to know about ProKey. It contains numerous examples and suggestions that stimulate you to think about how ProKey can make your life easier. However, it could stand better organization.

It's hard to believe I ever got along without ProKey.

SOFTWARE: PC/InterComm

MANUFACTURER: Mark of the Unicorn, Inc.

ADDRESS: 222 Third Street

CITY, STATE, ZIP: Cambridge, MA 02142

TELEPHONE: 617-576-2760, Ext. 22

SPECIFICATIONS:

Operating Systems: PC–DOS, CP/M

Hardware Requirements: IBM PC and compatibles; 128K memory; one or more disk drives

Transfer Protocols: XON/XOFF; XMODEM

Unattended Mode: No

Data Rates: 50–19,200 bps

Capture Method: Buffer and disk; screen save; file save

Modems Support: All popular modems

Text Editor: None

Macro Capability: Function key definitions only—maximum of 23 characters per function key; 40 keys (ALT–, CTRL–, SHIFT–)

Auto-dial Library: None (use modem dialing instructions)

On-Screen Help: Yes

Terminal Emulation: DEC VT–100

Menu-Driven/Command Mode: Both

User-Definable Function Keys: Yes

Documentation: Fair; no tutorials or examples

Price: IBM PC Version—$99

COMMENTS:

PC/InterComm offers many of the features available with other communication packages as well as a few unique ones. However, I found it a bit cumbersome to use, and the manual was difficult to follow.

FUNCTION 9 is the "key" to everything. When you press this key, the main menu appears, offering you a number of options. You can select your option by using the arrow keys to move the highlighted marker or by entering the number of the item you wish to use. Unfortunately, this menu is designed chronologically instead of functionally; that is, the setup options appear first, then the options you'd use for daily activities. Option #1 is "port options;" Option #2 "interface options," and so forth. Number 5, "file functions," is the area you'd be using most frequently and therefore logically should be the default option (#1). The manual explains that you can access a few program functions by entering a command; for example, ALT–T for transmitting a file, ALT–S save the text stored in the buffer to disk, and ALT–X save the screen to the disk.

The setup menus are quite helpful and easy to use. Once you've customized your parameters for a particular system, you can save them to disk. I couldn't find a way to display the auto-log-on file names so you'll have to remember what they are: for example, MCI for MCI Mail, DOW for Dow Jones News/Retrieval, and so on.

Although PC/InterComm doesn't support macro command files, you can achieve some of these conveniences by programming the function keys. Each function key holds up to 23 characters. You can use shift, alternate and control with the function keys to expand your options to 40 keys. (Note: The $35 PC–TALK III program can handle up to 126 characters.) The "Answerback Message" may hold up to 23 characters: your name, for example.

Printer support consists of using the Shift-Print Screen or Control-Print Screen for a screen dump or continuous printing operations.

Incoming data can be collected and saved in a buffer or into a disk file. Since the buffer is limited in size, you may lose data if you download to the buffer only. Data in the buffer can be viewed and saved to the disk. You can save the contents of a single screen to disk. Data stored on the disk cannot be viewed until you exit to DOS and use the TYPE <filename> command.

To help you log on, the manual takes you through the setup procedures and then refers you to your modem manual for dialing instructions. My Signalman Mark XII (Hayes compatible) will dial a number when I enter: ATDT<phone#>. Though somewhat crude, this procedure seemed to work well. An auto-dial directory would certainly improve this program. Even the $35 PC-Talk III program offers this feature.

With no tutorial or examples, the manual frequently leaves you in the dark. The manual is organized by menu items. Each menu is dissected into its component parts. This makes the manual easy to reference, but the overall process is difficult to piece together.

This program has many basic features common to telecommunications packages. However, without auto-log-on, macro command file, and an auto-dial directory, I feel that PC–TALK III for $35 is really a better buy. And PC–TALK III is easier to learn and use.

SOFTWARE: PC–Talk III

MANUFACTURER: The Headlands Press, Inc.

ADDRESS: P.O. Box 862

CITY, STATE, ZIP: Tiburon, CA 94920

TELEPHONE: 415-435-9775

SPECIFICATIONS:

Operating Systems: IBM–PC and compatibles

Hardware Requirements: One disk drive; preferably two drives

Transfer Protocols: XMODEM; XON/XOFF binary, and pacing (line at a time)

Unattended Mode: No

Data Rates: 75–9600 bps

Capture Method: Disk

Modems Support: All popular modems

Text Editor: None

Macro Capability: Function key definitions only—maximum of 126 characters per function key; 40 keys (ALT-, CTRL-, SHIFT-)

Auto-dial Library: Yes

On-Screen Help: Extensive

Menu-Driven/Command Mode: Both

User-Definable Function Keys: Yes

Return to Operating System without Hangup: Yes

Documentation: Very good (provided on your disk)

Price: Freeware—You pay nothing for trying the program; if you decide to use it, send $35

COMMENTS:

Some people may believe that a $35 telecommunications package can't be much. It's true that you can't get something for nothing; however, since this program isn't advertised or marketed through normal (and expensive) channels, the manufacturer can sell it for far less. PC–Talk III is the program of choice for thousands of computer hobbyists who access local bulletin boards. It's easy to use, effective, and inexpensive.

Within minutes you should be able to begin communications. At the main menu all you do is press ALT–D and the dialing directory appears. You can record up to 60 different telephone numbers with identifying names and communications parameters. The directions for building the phone directory appear on the screen. To dial a number in the directory, you simply enter the identifying number beside the entry. You can also manually dial a number not listed in the directory.

If the number is busy, you enter ALT–Q to auto-redial until connection is made. Once you've established connection, you may upload or download text files to and from your disk with only a couple of keystrokes. If you want to upload a letter to MCI Mail, you'd enter ALT–T (transmit). PC–Talk prompts you for a file name and off it goes. If you need to send the file line-by-line (with a pause at the end of each line), you simply enter the file name with a pause command and the number of seconds the system should wait between lines: for example, < filename = p2 > to pause 2 seconds at the end of each line transmission. If you wish to use the XMODEM error checking protocol, you enter < filename = x > at the prompt. You can also perform a screen dump to disk by pressing ALT–S. PC–Talk doesn't offer buffer storage. You can view (ALT–V) the downloaded file after the transmission is complete.

Printing is accomplished with the SHIFT–PRINT SCREEN and CONTROL–PRINT SCREEN keys. Since your printer may not be able to keep up with the data transmission rate, you may wish to print after the download is complete. If you wish to know your elapsed time on line, press ALT–Z.

If you use alternate telephone numbers—Telenet, Tymnet, and Uninet—each number will be a separate entry in the directory. If you need to access the same service using different communication parameters, you'll need separate entries for each; for example, CompuServe at 300 bps and CompuServe at 1200 bps. You can change your parameters on-line by pressing ALT–P and selecting your new set of values: for example, going from 300–E–7–1 to 1200–N–8–1. Installing your default parameters is as easy as pressing ALT–F and stepping through the menu selections.

The only feature PC–Talk lacks is the ability to execute macro command files for automatic retrieval applications. This deficit can be overcome to some extent since each function key may be programmed to hold up to 126 characters. With the use of CTRL–, ALT–, and SHIFT–, the 10 function keys can represent 40 different macros. So you can enter your name, account numbers, passwords, and even search strategies into these keys. (Some of the newer public domain modifications even offer macro capabilities. You're still obligated to pay the $35 for these modified versions. You can obtain them from computer clubs and download them from many public bulletin boards.) Programming the function keys is quite simple. You just press ALT–K to view the function key directory and follow the on-screen instructions.

The PC–Talk manual comes on the disk for you to print— 70 double-spaced pages. The manual is very complete and easy to read. In addition, PC–Talk offers on-line help in the form of a command summary (press HOME), and prompted and menu-driven operations that lead you easily through numerous operations. I used PC–Talk for over six months and never printed the manual. That's how easy the program is to use.

You're encouraged to copy PC–Talk and give it to your friends. (That's different!) The manufacturer even tells you how and reminds you to copy the documentation too. In addition, the manufacturer encourages you to modify the listable, BASIC program in any way you desire. Headlands has incorporated many user modifications into the program. That's one of the reasons it's so well done.

If you don't plan to use macro command files, unattended or remote modes, you can't beat PC–Talk's ease of use, utility, and price.

SOFTWARE: PFS:ACCESS

MANUFACTURER: Software Publishing Corp.

ADDRESS: 1901 Landings Drive

CITY, STATE, ZIP: Mountain View, CA 94043

TELEPHONE: 415-962-8910

SPECIFICATIONS:

Hardware Requirements: IBM PC and compatibles, IBM PCjr, MS–DOS computers and Apple IIe; 128K memory; one disk drive

Transfer Protocols: XON/XOFF; not designed to support personal computer data links

Unattended Mode: Auto-log on; auto search (limited number of stored phone numbers and searches)

Data Rates: 300 and 1200 bps

Capture Method: Buffer and disk

Modems Support: All popular modems

Text Editor: None; Built-in data encryption routine

Macro Capability: Memorizes previous dial-up, log on and search procedures for repeating

Auto-dial Library: Eight services only

On-Screen Help: Extensive

Menu-Driven/Command Mode: Both

User-Definable Function Keys: No

Return to Operating System without Hangup: No

Documentation: Very good

Price: IBM PC Version—$95; Apple IIe Version—$70

COMMENTS:

PFS:ACCESS offers many attractive features for the on-line searcher. And, it's easy to learn and simple to use. By following the menus and using a few predefined function keys, you can upload and download information, save information to disk, turn the printer on and off, and view data stored in the memory buffer. However, this program only supports personal computer to on-line service communication, not personal computer to personal computer communication. For some companies, this limitation poses no difficulty at all.

The ACCESS Main Menu lists eight services, a set up menu for your modem and an exit (to DOS). ACCESS has predefined five popular service log-on files: CompuServe, Dow Jones News/Retrieval, EasyLink, MCI Mail, and The Source. Three other choices (#6, 7, and 8) are available for you to define your own log-on files. If you don't use the services listed, you can erase them and replace them with those you do use. ACCESS makes it very easy to write an auto-log-on command file. All you do is manually log on once and enter the correct sign on (and if you want search) information. After you've proceeded as far as you want to automate, press FUNCTION 4 to stop the "recorder." From then on, when you select that service from the main menu, ACCESS repeats the log-on for that service. Since you have only eight service choices (or automatic log-on sequences) you cannot store as wide a variety of command files as you can with other communications programs. However, you don't have to learn anything about constructing command files to design ACCESS auto-log-on procedures. I used ACCESS to search BRS/BRKTHRU and the auto-log-on feature worked perfectly.

While you're connected to the service, you can review information stored in the 32K buffer, information you've already viewed on the screen. All you have to do is use the cursor control keys (arrow keys, HOME, END, PGUP, and PGDN) to view text stored in the buffer. If you place the cursor at the beginning of previously viewed text, the PRINTER ON and DISK SAVE commands will begin their operations from that point forward. This feature is very handy and easy to use.

FUNCTION 2 toggles the printer on and off. And FUNCTION 6 toggles the disk saving procedure on and off. Used together with the buffer viewing capabilities, these keys make saving and printing a real pleasure. ACCESS has difficulty keeping up with 1200 bps downloading with the disk-saving feature turned on. And, if you log off of the service, the disk-saving procedure is discontinued. (ACCESS only provides for 300 and 1200 bps data transfer rates.) You can tell how much of the file ACCESS has saved to disk because the line being acted on is highlighted. If you get too far ahead of this marker, you could lose information out of the top of the 32K memory buffer. In practice this didn't happen even when downloading very large files. The time-consuming disk-saving routine will certainly cost you extra money due to extended connect time. I also downloaded several files to the system disk when I forgot to indicate the drive name in front of the file name: B:BRS, for example. You cannot change the default drive to B drive. When I downloaded to a 160 character per second printer, ACCESS had no problem keeping up.

The status line at the bottom of the screen keeps you informed of what's going on and what to do next. If you've turned the printer on, you'll see a highlighted message to use FUNCTION 2 to toggle the printer off. The nature of the status line changes according to what you're doing.

ACCESS seems to be pretty foolproof. It warns you if you're going to overwrite an existing file, and it even allows you to replace a full disk with a formatted one to continue downloading.

The only problem I had was knowing where in the buffer to locate my cursor to continue the download on the new disk. The only weakness of this system is that if at any time you return to the main menu, you erase all text in the buffer. Should you do this accidentally, you might erase the buffer before you've had an opportunity to record valuable information. When you log off, you must return to the main menu (and erase the information stored in the buffer).

ACCESS doesn't provide a method for viewing the disk directory or data stored on the disk, so you'll have to use the DOS TYPE command or your word processor to view the files.

Although I couldn't get ACCESS to automatically log onto a club bulletin board system, it did upload and download files to the system. ACCESS also would allow me to encrypt my uploaded file to electronic mail, for example.

PFS:ACCESS is a very fine, relatively inexpensive communications package. However, if you need a large number of auto-log-on and search files, if you need computer-to-computer communication, if you need efficient downloading to disk, or if you want true unattended operating capabilities, you'll need to buy a more expensive package like Crosstalk XVI and ASCOM. ACCESS's advantage is that it takes very little time to learn how to use it, and it seems to be foolproof. On-screen prompting and menus help you know what to do next. The manual is good, although it could be better organized. Its index could be improved. I tried looking up several things and found some of the references inaccurate. The screen prints and the numerous large-print subtitles will help you find the information you need.

SOFTWARE: Telmerge

MANUFACTURER: MicroPro International Corp.

ADDRESS: 33 San Pablo Avenue

CITY, STATE, ZIP: San Rafael, CA 94903

TELEPHONE: 415-499-4022

SPECIFICATIONS:

Operating Systems: IBM PC and compatibles or 3270 PC
Works only with WordStar 3.3 or later;
64K with PC–DOS 1.1 or later; 128K
for PC–DOS 2.0 or later

Hardware Requirements: Two drives

Transfer Protocols: ASCII transfer

Unattended Mode: No

Data Rates: 110 to 9,600 bps

Capture Method: Printer and disk

Modems Support: Hayes compatible 300/1200 bps

Text Editor: Use WordStar 3.3 or later

Macro Capability: Limited

Auto-dial Library: Eight predefined services; one user
definable; auto-redial

On-Screen Help: Function key definitions; brief status line

Terminal Emulation: DEC VT–100 and IBM 3270

Menu-Driven/Command Mode: Menu and predefined
function keys

User-Definable Function Keys: No

Return to Operating System without Hangup: No

Documentation: Fair

Price: $145

COMMENTS:

Telmerge is MicroPro's companion program for its very popular WordStar program. I tried running Telmerge without installing it to my WordStar disk and it wouldn't run alone.

So unless you have WordStar Version 3.3 or later, Telmerge isn't for you.

Telmerge comes preprogrammed for logging onto eight popular on-line services: ITT Telex and TIMETRAN, Easy-Link by Western Union, OnTyme Messaging Service, MCI Mail, RCA Telex and TELEXTRA, CompuServe Information Service, Official Airline Guide, and The Source. A ninth menu choice is STD for User-Defined Service. You can change services on the Main Menu; however, you'll feel like you're having to learn a macro programming language to do so.

Each of these services has eight predefined function keys (FN 3–10) which are specific to that service. FUNCTION 1 and FUNCTION 2 can be programmed for your own customized use. For example, in the STD log-on file F3 = DIR, F4 = SEND, F5 = USERID, F6 = PASSWD, F7 = LOG, F8 = HDCOPY, F9 = BREAK, and F10 = HANGUP. By editing the STD file in nondocument mode, you can customize it for a particular service: for example, entering your password, user ID number and so forth.

F7 LOG toggles the disk saving feature on and off. You can only receive data using the ASCII transfer mode with no error checking. When you press F7, Telmerge automatically sets up a disk file called STD.LOG (or another name you designate). A different download file is created for each service. If you want your download file to be on a different drive, you can specify that drive in the file name in the STD file: for example, < B:SEARCH.LOG >. If you download a second file to your log file, the first file will be saved and a new file created. This is somewhat limiting if you wish to download a number of different files that you wish to keep separate.

F4 SEND allows you to designate a file to transmit. You can only transmit data using the ASCII transfer mode with no error checking. When you press F4, Telmerge will ask you to designate the file name you wish to transmit. During upload Telmerge converts the WordStar file to standard ASCII code and strips control codes (printing codes such as underline and bold) from the file. This is especially helpful for Word-Star users who must otherwise have a program to convert their nonstandard ASCII code before uploading to an elec-tronic mail service or to a non-WordStar user. Most electronic mail services will crash if they receive control codes in the text file, so in this regard, Telmerge offers character filtering not found on other popular packages.

F8 toggles the printer on and off. F9 sends a BREAK signal to the service. And F10 issues a HANGUP command to your modem.

The program seems to be functional and easy to use. I did have a couple of problems. With WordStar, MailMerge, and CorrectStar all on my IBM 360K diskette, there isn't enough room to install Telmerge. Since I run WordStar in a RAM disk, I could install it (temporarily) into my RAM disk. If I didn't have this feature, I'd have to remove one of the programs from a system disk and install Telmerge on that disk. Therefore, I'd end up having to trade out program disks to do data transfers or one of the other functions. Also, I use Pro-Key to make WordStar much more efficient. I've redefined a number of function keys with ProKey. When I invoked Telmerge, these function key definitions interfered with the Telmerge function key definitions. Therefore, I had to exit from ProKey before loading in Telmerge.

The error protection and recovery is pretty poor. For example, if you terminate a file transfer, you may not be able to get back to the on-line system's menu. If your modem isn't turned on, Telmerge won't tell you that. The status line at the top of the screen tells you if you're dumping to your printer or to your disk; but since my internal clock displays in the upper right hand corner of the screen, I couldn't read the log status (on or off).

The manual is rather poor. Although all of the functions and auto-log-on commands are explained in a type of glossary, few examples and no screen prints are available to lead you through rather complex procedures. The manual does explain the standard setup for each service. It's obvious from the selection of services on the main menu that Telmerge was intended as an electronic mail tool and not an on-line database search tool.

If your primary need is electronic mail, Telmerge may be a good companion program to WordStar. However, if you plan to access on-line database services, Telmerge leaves a lot to be desired.

ADDRESS: 5923 Peachtree Industrial Blvd.

CITY, STATE, ZIP: Norcross, GA 30092

TELEPHONE: 404-449-8791

SPECIFICATIONS:

Operating Systems: IBM PC and compatibles; TI Professional, Wang PC, HP 150, and DEC Rainbow 100

Hardware Requirements: One disk drive; preferably two drives

128K of available RAM

Transfer Protocols: XON/XOFF; XMODEM; proprietary error checking protocol

Unattended Mode: Yes; password protection

Data Rates: 110–9,600 bps

Capture Method: Disk

Modems Support: Hayes Smartmodem and compatibles

Text Editor: Good

Macro Capability: Yes

Auto-dial Library: Up to 25 remote systems with auto-log-on command files; preprogrammed for 15

On-Screen Help: Extensive

Terminal Emulation: DEC VT–52, VT–100, and VT–102

Menu-Driven/Command Mode: Menu driven

User Definable Function Keys: No

Return to Operating System without Hangup: No; however, many DOS–like functions are available within Smartcom itself

Documentation: Good

Price: $149

COMMENTS:

Smartcom II may be purchased separately or may be included with a Hayes modem purchase. This menu-driven software is relatively easy to learn and to use. Many of the auto-log-on files are already written except for adding local access numbers and personal identification. The software allows you to store communication parameters for up to 25 remote systems. Other useful features include macro security, which protects passwords, account numbers, and other personal information.

The newest version of Smartcom includes XMODEM file transfer protocol and DEC terminal emulation. You can store up to 26 command sequences in a Batch Command Set directory. These sequences will log on and send and receive files at preset times in an unattended mode. You can even chain several batch sets to sequentially access several computers so you can leave or retrieve messages. These features allow you to take advantage of lower on-line rates after hours and to compensate for time zone differences.

When Smartcom II comes up on your screen, you are presented with a menu of choices: for example, Begin Communication, Edit Set, Select File Command, Change Configuration, Change Printer Status, Display Disk Directory, and End Communication/Program. Several menu choices will have asterisks instead of choice numbers beside them; for example, Receive File and Send File. Since you've not logged onto a service, these options are not available.

The Change Configuration choice allows you to designate your printer port, printer baud rate, and dialing parameters. The Parameters screen informs you of your transmission parameters, telephone parameters, function key definitions, and protocol parameters. At the bottom of the Parameters screen you're told that "Standard Values May Not Be Changed Press F1 To Continue." So, don't plan to change parameters.

At this point you should press <B> to select Drive B since the Smartcom system disk is nearly full. When you enter Selection #1 Begin Communication, you'll see the Communications Directory which lists all of the preprogrammed services as well as any numbers you've entered into the directory. The standard communication values contained in the Communications Directory choice "Z" may be used to design a customized log-on parameter file for another service, person, or bulletin board.

The "Select File—Create" menu choices allow you to use

Smartcom's text editor to create a memo or letter for transmission. The Select File command also prompts you for many DOS–like commands: rename, erase, display, and print. With these commands you can print and display text files, erase files, and rename them at will.

Saving incoming files to disk is easier than sending files. When you're communicating, several function key definitions appear at the bottom of the screen: F1 Menu, F3 Print, F4 Disk, F5 Macro, and F6 Break. Anytime you wish to return to the main menu, simply press F1. F3 toggles the printer on and off, and F4 toggles the disk saving on and off. To send a file, you must return to the main menu (F1) and select Send File. Smartcom will then prompt you for the file name you wish to send. You can display the disk directory at the bottom of the screen for reference.

Smartcom is a very workable program that is easy to use. The manual could be better organized and would benefit greatly from an index. Many print screens and illustrations help you understand the explanations. Smartcom lacks the speed and versatility of programs which can be both menu-driven and command-driven, like Crosstalk XVI. In many ways, though, it's easier to learn and use.

SOFTWARE: TRANSEND PC ComPlete

MANUFACTURER: Transend Corp.

ADDRESS: 2190 Paragon Drive

CITY, STATE, ZIP: San Jose, CA 95131

TELEPHONE: 408-946-7400

SPECIFICATIONS:

Operating Systems: IBM PC and compatibles; 256K RAM required

Hardware Requirements: Two drives

Transfer Protocols: XMODEM; XON/XOFF; proprietary error checking

Unattended Mode: Yes; password protection

Data Rates: 300 to 19,200 bps

Capture Method: A disk-based buffer that is always on

Modems Support: All popular modems

Text Editor: Good

Macro Capability: Turnkey; chaining to other macros

Auto-dial Library: Yes; multiple addressing capability for automatic distribution to many locations

On-Screen Help: Extensive

Terminal Emulation: Supports DEC VT–100

Menu-Driven/Command Mode: Extensive menus and predefined function key use

User-Definable Function Keys: No

Return to Operating System
  without Hangup: No; however, many DOS–like functions are available within PC ComPlete

Documentation: Manual—Fair;
                 On-disk menus and prompts—excellent

Price: $229

COMMENTS:

When I read about PC ComPlete, I thought, now finally here's the telecommunications package for me. Unfortunately I was a bit disappointed. Probably most of that disappointment was due to the quality of the manual, which is printed in a reduced type-size and which has tutorials that are almost totally irrelevant to everyday tasks. I finally gave up on the manual and decided that trying to figure out how to use the program would be easier. And it was.

PC ComPlete is a totally menu-driven system that utilizes function keys better than almost any program I've seen. At the top, the status screen pictures the function keys in the arrangement they appear on the IBM keyboard. The definition for each active key is displayed to the side. With this help, plus a status line telling you what your options are, you'll seldom get lost. The only problem is that you'll have to study the manual to learn the differences between definitions that seem to overlap: for example, "Be a Terminal" and "Send & Receive Mail."

You can toggle the help screen on and off with FUNC-TION 1 Full Screen. Sometimes this is necessary in order to see the screen of text downloaded from the on-line service. Although I'd probably learn which function keys to use during repetitive operations, their constant definition changes (depending on which screen you are viewing), add complexity to the operation.

The main menu consists of four columns filled with rectangular boxes. In each column, the top two boxes (or baskets, as they refer to them) are predefined: IN, OUT, ADDRESS BOOK, SENT, SERVICES, (RESERVED), YOUR PC, and WASTE. Sixteen of the "baskets" are empty. The manual tells you to think of these baskets as file folders which can be filled with information. You can copy information from one basket to another: for instance, from your "file folder" to your WASTE basket. And in some cases, PC ComPlete will transfer information automatically: from the OUT basket to the SENT basket. The graphics for looking into these baskets are some of the best you'll see on the IBM. When you select a basket, the rectangle appears to zoom out like a window and take you to a different function. The ADDRESS BOOK basket enlarges to let you enter the name and identifying information for PC ComPlete users and Electronic Mail systems.

The SERVICES basket will let you enter information about on-line information services and computer bulletin boards. And, YOUR PC will let you set up the default communication parameter for your computer. During the installation and set-up procedures, I noticed that PC ComPlete installs the macro (dialing and log-on) files onto the data disk. Therefore, you cannot use just any formatted disk for a data disk. In addition, the default for downloading is A drive and should be changed to B drive since A drive (the system disk) is almost full. All the other defaults appear to be set appropriately.

If from the main menu, you select an empty basket, you'll enter the very nice PC ComPlete text editor, which allows you to write memos and letters to send via electronic mail. You can even automatically address these baskets using the information in the ADDRESS BOOK. When you call a particular electronic mail service, PC ComPlete will automatically download your mail into your IN basket and upload the files going to that service. All of this can be done at a preset time to accommodate time zone differences and to take advantage of lower, off-hour rates. These files are not available to send to the SERVICES (on-line databases and bulletin boards)—an unfortunate limitation.

As with PFS:ACCESS, you can create an auto-log-on file by recording one manual log-on session. After that, PC Com-Plete will remember the log-on steps to repeat: for example, entering your name, customer ID, and password. During the auto-log-on session, the keyboard is locked out so you cannot modify the sequence. If you want to change the auto-log-on file, you'll have to learn how the commands work. Macro command files may contain up to 10,000 characters and can be designed to automatically log on and perform a search at a preset time. The manual discusses these macro commands, but, most novices won't want to get this involved. PC Com-Plete allows you to view and to edit the macro file.

Uploading and downloading of files for SERVICES can only be done in the XMODEM transfer protocol. This isn't always appropriate, since users may want to compose mes-sages off-line and upload an ASCII file to a bulletin board. You can view the first few lines of the file to transmit by us-ing the INSERT key; however, the text appears in a window so briefly (one second) that you cannot begin to read it.

PC ComPlete automatically opens a disk file that records the entire in and out transactions during a communications session. So, if you're uploading a large file, you must have enough space available on your disk to record that file again. You cannot remove and replace the data disk during on-line sessions. If you plan to print any of the data recorded on the disk, you'll have to use a word processor to edit the data prior to printing, because every prompt and keystroke from both computers is recorded on the disk. You can toggle the printer on and off during transmission to record specific informa-tion.

Transend puts most of its strength into electronic mail ap-plications. Although PC ComPlete can be used to search elec-tronic databases, this is not its strongest suit. If the manual were improved, many novices would find PC ComPlete a very workable system. At present, though, I believe they might find it confusing and somewhat difficult to learn.

GLOSSARY

ACK   An error-checking control code sent from a receiving computer to the transmitting computer to indicate that data has been received correctly. Short for ACKnowledge. See also NAK.

Acoustic Coupler   See modem, acoustic.

ASCII   American National Standard Code for Information Interchange; the standard binary character code used for data communications and personal computer processing. See also binary code.

Auto-Answer   Automatic answering capability; without operator intervention, the modem and the software must be able to recognize an incoming call, answer the phone, and perform handshaking routines to establish communication with the calling computer.

Auto-Dial   Automatic phone dialing capability; without operator intervention, the modem and the software must be able to open a channel to the phone and dial a number entered from the keyboard or retrieved from a stored telephone directory.

Auto-Log-On   The ability of telecommunications software to without user intervention provide log-on information to a database service: for example, account number, personal ID, password, and so forth.

Auto-Redial   Automatic redialing capability; the modem and the software can hang up from a dialing process and redial the number at specified intervals. Some software will allow you to dial alternate numbers, such as Telenet, then Tymnet, and then Uninet.

Autosearch   The telecommunications software ability that allows you to preprogram a search strategy to be executed without user intervention.

Batch Command File   The telecommunications software ability that allows you to preprogram a search strategy that can be automatically executed. Batch files allow the computer to at preset times sequentially log onto several different services, perform preprogrammed searches, and upload and/or download files.

Baud The rate at which data is transmitted over telecommunications lines. 300 baud is equal to 300 bits per second or approximately 30 characters per second. At higher data rates, bits per second (bps) is the more accurate term.

BBS (Bulletin Board System) A hobbyist on-line computer that can be called by personal computer/modem users for leaving and retrieving messages and uploading and downloading files. Many BBSs are supported by computer clubs and stores.

Binary Code A code that uses two distinct characters (bits); for example, the ASCII binary code uses ones and zeroes to indicate a yes/no or true/false condition. Just as dots and dashes represent Morse code components, the ones and zeroes indicate the ASCII code components.

Bit A binary one or zero; the smallest piece of data in data transmission; seven or eight bits compose a byte which is roughly equal to one character. See also stop bit, start bit, and parity bit.

Bits per Second (bps) A measure of data transmission rate; 300 bps (baud), 1200 bps, and 2400 bps are the most popular data transmission rates. Since it takes approximately 10 bits to represent one character, 300 bps is roughly equal to 30 characters per second.

Block A discrete quantity of information on which error-checking procedures may be performed to insure accurate data transmission.

Boolean Logic Operator A symbolic logic notation that permits the expression of conditional search statements: for example, AND, OR, and NOT. These operators are incorporated into search statements to focus the search to the exact information required.

Boot Short for bootstrap: a program-starting program. A cold boot is performed by turning the computer on. A warm boot is done by resetting the computer in a way that erases all information from RAM (temporary memory). During the boot process the computer "looks" at the disk drive to see if a program is there for reading (loading) into the computer.

BPS See bits per second.

Break A signal sent to the on-line computer that tells it to stop what it's doing: for example, to stop displaying a file. See also break key.

Break Key A key on the computer keyboard designated by the telecommunications software as the key which will send a BREAK signal. See also break.

Buffer Memory used to store information to be displayed, printed, and/ or stored on disk. Data can be downloaded into a buffer much more rapidly than it can be printed or written on a disk. By downloading data into the buffer, you can save on-line time. Some software captures to a buffer which can be displayed on the screen after logging off of the service.

Bulletin Board System (BBS) See BBS.

Byte   Seven or eight bits of data composing one character or symbol; a computer word. See also bit.

Carrier   An electromagnetic wave of constant amplitude, frequency, and phase which can be modulated (varied in amplitude, frequency, or phase). Modulation impresses data and information on the carrier wave. Used in data transmission over airways and telephone lines.

Carrier Detect   The ability of a modem to sense that a carrier is present on the telephone line. A requirement for auto-dial and auto-answer capabilities.

Centronics Parallel Port   See port, parallel.

Character   A symbol, letter, number, or punctuation mark; roughly equivalent to a byte. See also byte and bit.

Characters per Second (cps)   A measure of printer speed.

Checksum   An error-checking calculation performed on a block of data to determine if the transmission was accurate. See also parity bit and XMODEM.

Christensen Protocol   See XMODEM.

Command Driven   An on-line service or telecommunications software package that responds to direct commands typed by the user. See also menu driven.

Compatible   A much maligned term meaning that equipment and/or software will work with one another; for example, Hayes compatible means that a modem uses the Hayes protocol and command set or that a piece of software will work with a Hayes (or Hayes compatible) modem.

Compression   The reduction of the number of bits required to represent information in data transmission or storage. Also called compaction.

Connect Time   The amount of time a modem is connected to and communicating with an on-line service. A measure that frequently determines the amount you pay for using that service.

Controlled Vocabulary   A limited set of keywords that may be used to search a database. See also thesaurus.

Cover-to-Cover   A database that includes all articles and significant editorials from publications included. See also selective coverage.

CPU   Central Processing Unit; the computer processor that acts on the data; the part of the computer controlling the interpretation and execution of program instructions.

CPU–Based Charges   An on-line fee schedule that charges for the amount of time the search demands of the CPU. Frequently used by time-sharing services.

Data   Digitally represented information; basic elements of information that can be processed or transmitted over telecommunication lines.

Data Bank   Another term for on-line database. See on-line database.

Database An organized collection of information: for example, a telephone directory or index card file. Computerized databases have a number of things in common. Each major category (file) is composed of records: for example, article bibliographies. And each record is composed of fields: for example, title, author, publication, and so forth. On-line databases may be accessed over common telephone lines for searching and downloading information.

Database Provider The company that compiles and enters data into the computerized database file. See also database vendor.

Database Vendor The company that puts the database on line for searching. The vendor provides the sophisticated computer systems for database storage and on-line retrieval.

Data Communications The transmission, reception, and validation of data; data transfer between two computers.

Data Compression See compression.

Data Encryption The coding of data for security reasons.

Data Set Synonymous with modem. See modem.

Data Transfer Rate The average number of bits per second transferred; see also baud and bits per second.

Data Word Format The number of bits required to form a character or symbol of information: for example, seven data bits, one start bit, one stop bit, and one parity bit.

Default The automatically assumed settings for software or a piece of equipment. The default settings may be changed by repositioning switches and/or changing program parameters; for example, resetting the default data transmission rate from 1200 bps to 2400 bps; changing the printer from single space to double space; and changing a telecommunications program default from originate mode to answer mode.

Directory The table of contents for a floppy disk; tells you the name of the files and their size in bytes.

Documentation The instructions telling the user how to use a piece of equipment or a software package. Documentation may be in the form of a printed manual and/or may be stored on the disk and made available in the form of on-screen prompting and help files.

Document Retrieval Downloading information from the on-line database: for example, printing bibliographic citations retrieved in a search.

Document Retrieval Service A third-party service that for a fee will provide printed copies (reprints) of articles.

DOS (Disk Operating System) A program that manages the way a disk-based computer works: for example, accessing information stored on the disk, manipulating files on the disk, and storing information on the disk.

Download Retrieving information from an on-line computer. Downloaded information may be viewed on the screen, printed on a printer and/or stored on magnetic media such as a floppy disk. See also upload.

Electronic Mail A computerized telecommunications network that allows you to send electronic data (mail) to a central computer. From the central computer the "mail" is forwarded to one or more recipients either electronically or on paper.

Emulation The ability of a personal computer and software package to mimic a data terminal such as the DEC VT–100. The on-line service perceives the incoming information as coming from a computer terminal and not from a personal computer.

Error Checking The ability of telecommunications software to monitor transmissions for accuracy. See also XMODEM.

External Modem See modem.

Flow Control The ability of the telecommunications software to regulate the rate at which data is transmitted. See also XON/XOFF and pacing.

Free Text Search The ability to search the entire text of the database instead of searching limited fields such as the article titles or using a limited keyword thesaurus.

Full Text Database A database that contains entire articles instead of just abstracts or bibliographic information.

Gateway An on-line computer service that provides a path to on-line services and has the advantage of providing you with one log-on procedure, one subscription fee, no monthly minimums, and someday perhaps user-friendly software that simplifies your search.

Gateway Software A telecommunications software package designed to simplify the searching procedures for usually one specific on-line service: for example, In-Search for Dialog and Winning on Wall Street for Dow Jones News Retrieval.

Handshake Protocol A predefined exchange of signals or control characters between two modems and computers that set up the conditions for data transmission. Also called handshaking.

Hardware Computer equipment: for example, a personal computer, printer, modem, and external buffer.

Hit The number of citations found to meet the criteria of a search strategy.

Information Broker A third party service that for a fee will perform on-line searches for you.

Integrated Software Telecommunications software compatible with and used with other applications software; for example, Telmerge is integrated with WordStar and Mite is integrated with Framework.

Interface A shared communication boundary; for example, a modem interface (serial port) and a printer interface (parallel or serial port). See also port, serial and port, parallel.

Keyboard Utility   A program that allows you to custom define your keyboard.

LED (Light Emitting Diode)   A low-energy lamp used to signal operating activity: for example, the indicators on a modem for high speed, carrier detect, and send/receive.

Log Off   To sign off of an on-line service.

Log On   To sign on an on-line service; includes providing user ID, password, account number, and so forth.

Macro   A single command which calls forth a series of instructions: for example, a function key that prints your password or an entire log-on sequence.

Menu   A list of multiple choice options. Selecting an item from the menu tells the software which operation to perform next.

Menu Driven   A program that the user operates by selecting menu choices. See also menu and command driven.

Microprocessor   See CPU.

Modem (MODulator/DEModulator)   An electronic device that transforms a digital computer signal into an analog form (continuous wave form or noise) suitable for transmission over common telephone lines. The modem converts a two-level (binary) signal into a two-frequency sequence of signals (pulse audio tones). At the other end of the transmission, the receiving modem changes the pulse audio tones back into digital code to communicate with that computer. See also modem, acoustic and modem, direct-connect.

Modem, Acoustic   A modem that converts digital data into tones that are detected by the telephone handset mouthpiece and transmitted over telephone wires. At the other end an acoustic modem translates the audio tones into a binary signal for a computer or terminal. See also modem.

Modem, Direct-Connect   A modem directly wired into the telephone line. The modem converts the computer's digital signals into a two-frequency sequence of analog signals for transmission. At the other end of the telephone line it converts the two-frequency signals into digital signals for a terminal or computer. See also modem.

Modem, External/Stand-alone   A modem that is housed in a separate case and has its own power supply.

Modem, Internal   A modem board or card that plugs directly into a slot inside the computer.

Modem, Smart/Intelligent   A modem that contains a microprocessor that allows it to auto-dial, auto-answer, define data formats, disconnect automatically, and redial. See also modem.

Modem–7   See XMODEM.

NAK A control-code message sent by the receiving computer to indicate that the previously sent data block contained a transmission error. The transmitting computer will respond by retransmitting the block. Short for No AcKnowledgement. See also ACK.

Noise Extraneous sounds and/or electromagnetic interference which disrupt data communications.

Off-Line Disconnected from the computer or not communicating with the computer; for example, an off-line printer.

Off-Line Print A service provided by the on-line service whereby they print the citations requested by your search and then mail the printout to you.

On-Line Connected to and communicating to the computer.

On-Line Database See database, database vendor, database provider, and gateway.

Operating System See DOS.

Pacing A data flow control method that regulates the rate of transmission from the transmitting computer; for example, PC–TALK III allows you to designate a pause between each line of text uploaded.

Parallel Port See port, parallel.

Parameter A variable that delimits a process; for example, telecommunication parameters include data rate, number of stop bits, number of data bits, odd or even parity bits, and so forth. See also protocol.

Parity Bit An extra bit (binary one or zero) added to a computer word (byte) which indicates if there are an odd or even number of ones in the word. This information can be used by error-checking protocols to determine if the data transmission was accurate.

Peripheral A piece of equipment attached to but not part of the computer: for example, a modem, a printer, a joy stick, a mouse, and an external buffer.

Port An electrical plug or socket that permits access to the computer; an interface between the computer and peripheral equipment. Peripheral devices such as printers and modems plug into ports. See also port, serial and port, parallel.

Port, Parallel An interface that allows one byte (character) or eight bits of data to travel simultaneously through eight wires to and from a peripheral. Printers usually plug into the parallel port. The most common parallel port used in the personal computer industry is the Centronics. See also port and port, serial.

Port, Serial An interface that allows bits to travel in single file (one after the other) through a single wire to and from a peripheral. Modems and sometimes printers plug into serial ports. The most common serial port used in the personal computer industry is the RS–232C. See also port and port, parallel.

Printer An electromechanical peripheral device that allows a computer to output printed information (hard copy).

Printer, Letter Quality A printer capable of producing typewriter quality print: for example, daisywheel, ball, ink jet, and laser printers.

Printer, Matrix A printer that forms characters by printing a series of dots. By using double-strike modes, matrix printers can also produce almost letter-quality or correspondence quality print. Matrix printers can also print graphics.

Protocol The rules that govern the format, timing, sequence, and error control of transmitted data. See also parameters.

Proximity Logic The ability to qualify a search statement by designating that one term be found within a certain position relative to a second term: for example, within the same sentence or within the same paragraph.

RAM (Random Access Memory) In a computer, the temporary internal memory used to store program instructions, data being operated on, and processed data. Since RAM is volatile, it is erased when the computer is turned off, when power is temporarily interrupted or when the computer is booted. See also ROM.

Random Access Memory See RAM.

Read-Only Memory See ROM.

Remote Mode A telecommunications software capability which allows a personal computer to be controlled or operated by a remote computer. This is especially useful for people who want to operate their computer from home or while on a business trip.

Response Time The time that elapses between an inquiry to an on-line computer and its answer (response).

Retrocapture The ability of some telecommunication software packages to store downloaded information into a buffer, which may be viewed, printed and/or stored to disk even after logging off of the service.

ROM (Read-Only Memory) In a computer, the permanent memory stored in computer chips: for example, the bootstrap program. Modems may also have a ROM chip containing telecommunication program instructions.

RS–232C Serial Port See port, serial.

SDI See selective dissemination of information.

Search (Search Statement) One or more commands that tell the on-line computer how to find desired information.

Searcher An expert at searching on-line databases.

Search Strategy The logic used to formulate a search statement. See also Boolean logic operator and proximity logic.

Selective Coverage A database that contains only selected articles from listed publications. See also cover-to-cover.

Selective Dissemination of Information (SDI) The ability to store a search strategy with the on-line service so the service can repeat the search each time the database(s) is updated. The search results may be printed off-line or downloaded to the user the next time the system is logged on.

Serial Port See port, serial.

SIC Code A standardized numeric code used to identify business categories. Each digit of the code successively narrows down the business category. Used in formulating search strategies.

Smart Modem See modem, smart/intelligent.

Smorgasbord Database Service An on-line service that provides a very large variety of databases: for example, SDC Orbit and Dialog.

Software The instructions that tell the computer what to do and how to do it. See also telecommunications software.

Start Bit The first element (binary one or zero) in each character (byte) that prepares the receiving device to recognize the incoming information. See also bit.

Start-Stop Transmission A group of data elements (bits) that are preceded by a start and followed by a stop signal (bit).

Status Line A portion of the display that informs the user of the status of the telecommunications process: for example, line busy, connect at 1200, printer on, disk save on, and so forth.

Status Screen A display that informs the user of the current program parameters or defaults: answer mode, 1200 bps, 8 bit word length, Touch-Tone dialing, and so forth. See also parameters.

Stop Bit The last transmitted element (bit) in each character (byte) which permits the receiving device to come to an idle condition before accepting another character.

Telecommunications Software An applications program (set of instructions) that tells the computer and the modem how to transmit and receive data via the modem. Telecommunications software varies in sophistication from the most simple commands that allow connection and transmission to the very complex programs that provide extensive hand-holding and on-disk help procedures. Telecommunications software allows you to command the modem (providing it's capable) to auto-dial, auto-answer, auto-redial, automatically log on, automatically search the database, automatically log off, and operate in remote mode, to mention only a few features available.

Text Editor Software that allows you to create messages for transmission and/or to edit downloaded files; a simple word processor.

Thesaurus A limited vocabulary the on-line system can recognize and search for. Usually the thesaurus is stored on-line for reference.

Throughput The average number of characters per second actually transmitted by the system. See also bits per second.

Time-sharing A multiuser mainframe computer that can be accessed over common telephone lines and used for computer processing. Businesses use time-sharing computers for a number of applications their own computers can't do satisfactorily: for example, to relieve peak overloads, to utilize sophisticated proprietary software such as modeling, and to handle confidential data such as payroll.

Toggle A toggle turns a device or feature on and off; that is, to the opposite state. For example, Function 5 might be used to toggle (switch) the printer on and off.

Transparent Mode A program that is "transparent" to the user. It runs in the background so the user isn't overtly aware of its presence: for example, a keyboard utility.

Truncate In a search statement, to abbreviate or shorten a word with a symbol so as to present it in a more generic form. The dropped characters are represented with a wild card symbol such as a dollar sign or exclamation point: for example, INFERTIL$ for INFERTILITY and INFERTILE.

Unattended Mode The ability of computer software and hardware to operate without user intervention: for example, at a preset time to log on, perform a search, download citations, and log off.

Upload To transmit data to another computer. See also download.

Videotex (View Data) An interactive data communications system that allows cable television viewers to search for information.

Wild Card Character A character that can be substituted for one or more characters: for example, for truncation purposes. See also truncate.

Word Length The number of bits in a computer word (byte or symbol); usually seven or eight data bits. See also bit and byte.

Workstation A personal computer or terminal.

XMODEM A commonly used error-checking protocol used for uploading and downloading data files. May be called MODEM-7 and Christensen protocol.

X–OFF/X–ON A transmitter off/transmitter on flow-control protocol used extensively for uploading and downloading ASCII text files. No error-checking is performed.

INDEX

Financial Times, 17
Flow control, 265
Foreign database; *see* Database
Framework, 89
Free-text search, 47, 265
Freeware; *see* Software
Friction feed, 103–4
Full duplex, 84
Full-text database; *see* Database
Function key; *see* Keyboard

G

Gateway, 5–6, 14, 265
Gateway software; *see* Software
General information database; *see*
  Database
GRANTS, 23
Guaranteed minimum, 51

H

Handshake protocol, 79–80, 97,
  265
Hardware, 265
  standardizing, 99–100, 110
  telecommunications; *see*
    Modem; Personal computer;
    and Printer
Harvard Business Review, 23
Hayes, 108–9
Hazardline, 127
Head librarian; *see* Staffing
  requirements
HELP, 49, 81, 113
Hit, 52, 71, 115, 265
Huttonline, 21

I

I. P. Sharp, 21
I. P. Sharp Application Software,
  184–88
I. P. Sharp Public Data Bases,
  188–93
IBM 3101, 90
In-Search, 76, 88, 98, 113, 235–40
INFORM, 23
Information
  broker, 15, 265
  carrier; *see* Telecommunication,
    service
  consultant, 60, 66–67

Information—*Cont.*
  needs analysis; *see* Needs
    analysis
  services, 38
    proactive, 33, 38, 57, 60,
      65–66
    reactive, 33, 57–59, 66
Information Science Abstract, 23
Initialisms, 122
Integrated Services Digital
  Network (ISDN), 131
Integrated software; *see* Software
Intellimodem EXT, 204–5
Intellimodem ST, 200–2
Intellimodem XL, 202–4
Intellimodem XT, 199–200
Interactive Data Corporation (IDC),
  21
Interactive video, 131
Interface; 101, 265–66; *see also*
  Port
Internal modem; *see* Modem
International Petrochem Report, 17
ITT's Dialcom, 28–29

J–K

Japanese Economic Information, 26
Jargon, 121
K (kilobyte), 105
Kermit, 83
Key word, 5, 111, 121–22
Keyboard, 100–101
  function keys, 82, 100
  numeric keypad, 100
Keyboard programming, 84–85
Keyboard utility; *see* Software
Knowledge Index, 23–24, 54,
  157–60

L

Language, 47
Latin America Commodities, 17
LED (Light Emitting Diode), 108,
  266
LEXIS, 13, 21, 27–28, 45, 127,
  130, 139–44
LEXPAT, 18, 27–28
Legal database; *see* Database
Legal Times, 17
Library of Congress, 124

3 5282 00108 5607